DAWN
OF THE GODS

Frontispiece Plate I. Women dancing to the lyre; pottery from Palaikastro, after 1400 B.C.

DAWN OF THE GODS

Jacquetta Hawkes

With photographs by Dimitrios Harissiadis
and other illustrations

1968
CHATTO & WINDUS
LONDON

Published by
Chatto and Windus Ltd
42 William IV Street
London WC2

★

Clarke, Irwin & Co. Ltd
Toronto

SBN 7011 1332 4

Designed and produced by
George Rainbird Ltd
Marble Arch House
44 Edgware Road
London W2

The text was set in 12/14 point Bembo by
Oliver Burridge Filmsetting Ltd, Crawley.
The text and colour plates were printed in Italy by
Amilcare Pizzi S.p.A., Milan.
The book was bound in Italy by
Legatoria Editoriale Giovanni Olivotto S.p.A.,
Vicenza

To my generous friends
Lena and Christos Tegopoulos

Preface

I have written this book in the form of a continuous historical narrative, covering not only Minoan and Mycenaean times, but also a little of what went before and after them. This is very much more difficult to master than a scheme based on such categories as arts and crafts, religion and so on, but I hope that in spite of certain awkwardnesses of construction it will gain in readability and meaning. If I have introduced some ideas that are of special interest to myself – such as my insistence on the contrasting feminine and masculine personalities of Minoan and Mycenaean culture – I hope that no one will be provoked. Perhaps at least these mild idiosyncrasies will save this book, in spite of its fine illustrations, from being assigned to the coffee table.

For my part I feel nothing but admiration for good photographs (the more the better), and I am quite sure that "lookers" can learn more than "readers" about the vision of life of these Bronze Age peoples. I am immensely indebted to Mr Harissiadis for succeeding in taking nearly all the objects I had specified, and in doing so with such skill and feeling. I recognize that the modern love of lavishly illustrated books is causing great inconvenience to museum staffs, and I know that Mr Harissiadis would want to join with me in thanking the directors and staffs of the museums he visited. Dr George Dontas at the National Archaeological Museum in Athens, Dr Stelios Alexiou at Heraklion, Dr E. P. Deïlaki at Argos and Nauplion, and Dr Nicolas Yalouris at Chora and Olympia were unfailingly courteous and helpful. We owe a particular debt of gratitude to Dr Nicolas Yalouris, whose unstinting assistance and advice at all stages of the work have been of the utmost value. For special permission to reproduce certain items I wish to thank Professor Carl Blegen, Dr John Boardman, Professor J. Caskey, Mr C. Davaras, Dr E. P. Deïlaki, Mrs Dorothea Lang, Dr Doro Levi, Dr Spyridon Marinatos, Professor G. E. Mylonas, Dr Nicolas Platon, and Mr John Sakellarakis.

I should like to thank Mr Christos Tegopoulos for most generously putting a car and driver at my disposal when I was visiting museums and sites – and equally his wife who suddenly decided to come with me and proved an ideal companion and trouble-shooter. Our travels and visits, especially at Olympia, were made easier by Dr Nicolas Yalouris. I am also much indebted to Dr Peter Warren of Cambridge, who undertook to vet my entire text. He was properly critical of my facts and tolerant towards my theories, so that I was able to adopt about 99 per cent of his suggestions.

I am grateful to a number of kind archaeological correspondents, but I will not give their names for fear that they should think I was trying to incriminate them.

Contents

Colour Plates

Introduction

Greece, Crete and all those islands that rise in such clear perfection from the Aegean Sea offer a world of allurements. Very few people who enter it, even as the most harassed of tourists, fail to respond, or, if they can, to return. This world, with its blending of natural with man-made beauties, of past with present, has them in thrall. When I was last at Mycenae, standing on the Bronze Age ramparts, a woman led her jostling goats among the rocks of Mount Elias and sang a loud song that seemed as radiant as the air yet had an archaic sadness. History seemed palpable; a marvellous afflatus.

Many people have brought home such experiences. Many more go to Greece to find them. So it has happened that just when the dominance of Classical education is at an end, when few of us read Latin and fewer still Greek, there is a vast increase in the numbers who are able to see something of the Hellenic world itself. It is a further irony that they are able to see it with a breadth of vision that was denied to even the greatest Classical scholars of the past.

At the beginning of this century Sir Arthur Evans wrote: "Less than a generation back the origin of Greek civilization, and with it the sources of all great culture that has ever been, were wrapped in an impenetrable mist." Our recognition of great culture may no longer be so exclusive, but it is certainly true that until the eighteen-seventies the beginnings of Hellenic culture appeared isolated in time and space as though a seed had fallen suddenly from heaven to produce this miraculous flower.

It is, of course, archaeology which has provided the wide-angle lens enabling us to see the whole Greek horizon. This book will try to reveal, through its words and pictures, something of the history and quality of life of the fifteen hundred years or so that went before, and contributed to, the great age of Classical Greece. First it seems fitting to give a summary account of the discoveries and arguments that have made it possible to reconstruct an area of the past that had been "wrapped in an impenetrable mist".

Curiously enough the mist appeared more impenetrable by the mid-nineteenth century than it had before. The Greeks themselves had not only founded much of their cultural life on Homer, but had not doubted that the Iliad and Odyssey gave a true picture of their own history. When, with the Renaissance, a passion for Greek literature returned to Europe, the general truth of the human aspect of the epics was probably accepted.

Scholarship and a rationalistic approach produced scepticism. Most European scholars came to believe that the Iliad and Odyssey were either a collection of imaginary folk tales put together by minstrels, or the creation of a single great poetic genius. Supporters of these two opposing schools of thought debated against one another, but were equally scornful of those who could still be so naïve and unscientific as to believe that the epics preserved genuine historical traditions.

While the learned were becoming more "enlightened" and therefore more sceptical of Homeric history, one may assume that many ordinary readers of the classics continued to accept it as simply as the Greeks themselves had done. Among them was Heinrich Schliemann, who had been born to the family of a Mecklenburg pastor in 1822.

It was to be given to Schliemann to prove that there had indeed been splendid Bronze Age kingdoms in Greece, memories of which had been handed down to Homer. And after him it was to be given to Arthur Evans to carry the story still further back into the past by unearthing the wonderful Cretan civilization that had inspired the cultural life of the mainland kingdoms.

The recovery of lost civilizations must always count as among the greatest deeds possible to explorers of the past – that is obvious enough. Not only are gaps in the historical jigsaw filled in, helping the picture to emerge, but mankind may be suddenly enriched by the recovery of lost works of art and perhaps of a whole lost artistic tradition. Schliemann and Evans did this for us in revealing the two closely related civilizations that came to be known as the Mycenaean and the Minoan. They did more than that, however. Both were men of extraordinary energy, imaginative power and self-confidence, and so were able to impart to their discoveries a dramatic colour and shape that made them live.

Schliemann's story was the more extraordinary. His father had brought him up on tales of the ancient world, and at a tender age he became convinced that so great a city as Homer's Troy could not have disappeared and that he himself would find its remains. Many poor boys have determined first to make a fortune in order to carry out some quite other ambition. Very few have kept to their programme.

Schliemann did. Starting in the humblest way in a grocer's shop, he worked so prodigiously that he raised himself to a position where he could make one fortune in Russia and then another in the United States. He was a brilliant linguist, and during the eighteen-fifties taught himself modern and ancient Greek as a first step towards his Homeric future. Later he went to Paris to master such rudiments of archaeology as were then available, and at last in 1868–9 was ready to reconnoitre in Greece and Anatolian Turkey.

It is astonishing that no one before this dedicated amateur of archaeology had made any serious attempt to test the historicity of the Homeric tradition with the spade. By this time great discoveries had already been made in the Assyrian cities of Mesopotamia, and prehistorians were excavating in Europe. Yet the Classicists preferred to stick to their books and their studies; digging in the dirt was not for them.

The situation is even harder to understand when it is remembered that the sites of many of the deserted Homeric places were traditionally known – among them Mycenae itself in the Argolid, and Knossos in Crete. Troy was one of the places which had been forgotten, although Homer made it clear that it was not far from the Hellespont – the modern Dardanelles. Schliemann inspected the rival sites, and recognized the promise of the large mound known as Hissarlik which stood on the promontory between the Dardanelles and the Aegean. "I confess," he wrote, "I could hardly control my emotion when I saw before me the immense plain of Troy, whose image had hovered before me even in the dreams of my earliest childhood."

Troy is of no direct significance for this book. It is only necessary to recall how Schliemann started digging at Hissarlik in 1870, and drove his huge trenches through the mound until he uncovered a fine walled city which had perished in flames. Hidden in its walls he found a hoard of splendid golden ornaments. Almost inevitably he saw this as Priam's city, burnt after its capture by Agamemnon and his Greeks. It is now known that he had dug too deep and reached a far older horizon; the Homeric city lay higher up in the mound. The more important thing was that he had indeed found ancient Troy and so begun the rehabilitation of Homer as a source of history.

Inspired by his success, Schliemann was determined to follow the Homeric trail. It was therefore to be expected that, having satisfied his lifelong desire to find the remains of Troy, he would turn next to Mycenae, Agamemnon's capital and the accepted scene of the famous tragedy that followed his return from Troy. Here the conditions were very different from those offered by the formless mound of Hissarlik. The Lion Gate and much of the massive ramparts of the citadel were intact. The huge royal tombs with their corbelled domes that stood outside the walls were well known, and were attributed by popular tradition to characters in the Homeric story – Atreus, Clytemnestra and Aegisthus.

At Mycenae Schliemann had another ancient guide as well as Homer. Pausanias, a Greek traveller and sightseer, had visited the place in the second century A.D. and had been shown the alleged graves of Agamemnon and of those who had been murdered with him. Schliemann's careful reading of Pausanias had convinced him that, contrary to learned opinion, these graves lay not in the outer town but within the walls of the citadel itself. When, therefore, he opened his first full season of excavations in the summer of 1876, he began digging just inside the Lion Gate. His good judgment was quickly rewarded by the discovery of the Upper Grave Circle with its royal burials and their marvellous grave furniture – to be described in Chapter Four. Because the bodies had been laid at the bottom of pits cut deep into the rock, these are always known to archaeologists as the Shaft Graves.

When Schliemann saw the bearded gold mask (plate 23) and the gold breastplate resting on crumbled bones, he believed that this was the body of King Agamemnon himself. Other burials he identified as those of his murdered companions. In fact, as later researches were to show, these men and women of the royal house had ruled in Mycenae during the sixteenth century B.C., some three centuries before Agamemnon could have led his host to Troy. They had lived at the very beginning of the Mycenaean Age, whereas the Trojan War was fought towards its end. Once again Schliemann had been misled by an obsession with Homer that made him attribute every splendid thing he found to his heroes.

After his opening of the royal graves, Schliemann made more soundings inside the citadel at Mycenae and was lucky enough to come upon the big wine-mixing bowl known as "The Warrior Vase". Although he could not know it, these painted warriors dated from a time much closer to the Trojan War than did his "mask of Agamemnon" and the other royal treasures. This was true also of the king's hall he uncovered inside the tremendous walls of Tiryns (plate 34).

Once Schliemann had led the way into the Mycenaean Age, others more professional took over its exploration and ordering. Greek archaeologists and expeditions from many lands were soon able to prove not only that Mycenaean culture had prevailed over much of mainland Greece, but also that settlers and traders had carried its goods and its influence through the Aegean and the eastern Mediterranean. At the same time the slow, exacting task of piecing together a chronological framework was undertaken. The English archaeologist, Flinders Petrie, had already found Mycenaean pottery in *datable contexts in Egypt, and other such finds made links with the historic civilizations of the Orient. In this way it proved possible to establish a system tied in with the known Oriental chronologies and based upon the distinctive and rapidly changing Mycenaean pottery styles. Now the four to five centuries of the Mycenaean Late Bronze Age could be subdivided and historically understood.*

Scholars who stayed in their studies benefited from the work of the diggers. Students of Greek religion and mythology, for example, were soon able to see that all the places where myths and legends clustered had been important centres of Mycenaean life. In this way it had already become apparent how deeply Hellenic religion must be rooted in the Bronze Age past long before the finding and decipherment of Mycenaean texts.

By the end of the century much had been done; but one large problem still remained. Mycenaean culture, with the splendid works of art that had already come to light at Mycenae, Vaphio, and elsewhere, appeared strangely isolated. Was it of native growth, or, if not, from where did its creators come? Scholars were sharply divided. Some extremists believed it to owe everything to the high civilizations of the Orient; those at the other extreme saw this as a mirage oriental. *Moderates rightly argued that Oriental influences, which were plainly evident in Mycenaean art, did not prevent the native European element from remaining paramount. The debate involved another, lesser, puzzle. It was surprising that so developed a civilization as the Mycenaean appeared to be without any form of writing.*

It was at this point that the second brilliantly successful and dominating figure entered the arena of Aegean studies. If Arthur Evans seems less remarkable than Heinrich Schliemann, it is through no deficiency of character. Because by his day the archaeological approach was well established, he could not be a pioneer. Again, because his father was an English antiquary of distinction and the family was rich, he had no career struggle to provide him with a triumph.

There was much in Greek tradition to point to the early importance of Crete. Stories of divinities and heroes were set in the island: Zeus himself was allowed to have been born there. The legends of the Cretan king, Minos, ruler of the seas, who had exacted a tribute of Athenian girls and boys to be sacrificed to the Minotaur, suggested memories of a political power which had vanished by Classical times. Archaeology lent support to tradition. Seal-stones found in the island showed that the ancient Cretans had possessed their own distinctive script.

It was his pursuit of this script that first led Arthur Evans to Crete. It was obvious that Knossos, the traditional capital of Minos, was the best place to dig. Moreover, when Evans first went there he was able to pick up enticing antiquities, including fragments of painted stucco. Then he was brought an inscribed clay tablet from Knossos. That settled it. By 1900 he had bought the site and was ready to dig. He was about fifty years old.

The excavation began at a tremendous speed, for the ruins of the last phase of the great palace lay only just below the surface. Within a few weeks two acres had been uncovered and many treasures brought to light – including quantities of inscribed tablets. By the next year Evans was ready to announce to the world that he had discovered in Crete a literate palace civilization with a lovely and original art. A few years later again, he recommended that this civilization should be called Minoan, after the legendary Minos.

Evans continued to dig at Knossos for a quarter of a century. As he opened up the deeper levels, proving the earliest palace to have been built at the beginning of the second millennium B.C., it became more and more evident that here in Crete was the source of much of the Mycenaean culture of the mainland. Indeed Evans himself, dazzled by what he had found and influenced by the tradition that Minos had exacted tribute from Athens, was certain that from the time of the Shaft Graves onwards, Mycenaean civilization had been implanted by a Cretan settlement of mainland Greece.

For some time this view was meekly accepted. Then opposition developed among Mycenaean specialists – led by another Englishman, Professor A. J. B. Wace. He and his supporters were sure that many of the fine things found in Greece but said to be Minoan imports were in fact native Mycenaean. Professor Wace not only denied that the mainland kingdoms had ever been subject to Knossos, but went so far as to claim that during the last brilliant phase of the palace Knossos was subject to the mainland.

So there began another of the battles which are so frequent in archaeology, and which, in spite of the heat engendered, are probably more stimulating than harmful.

One of Professor Wace's sympathizers was the American Professor, Carl Blegen. The exact site of Nestor's Pylos, one of the great Homeric settings, had long been disputed. Determined to locate it, Blegen and Greek colleagues tramped the beautiful but rough Messenian countryside. The hill of Epano Englianos near Chora, with its commanding view southwards to the Bay of Navarino, seemed the most likely site. There were sherds and building fragments among the olive groves and tombs of the domed type designed for royal burials.

Professor Blegen began his trial trenches in the spring of 1939, and on the opening day turned up frescoes, stucco floors and inscribed clay tablets – the first to have been found in mainland Greece. Mycenaean civilization, then, had its written records, but as the tablets were very like those from Knossos, it seemed probable that they were written in some Minoan language.

Professor Blegen was confident that he had found the "Palace of Nestor", and the prospects looked bright. Then the Germans, the French, the English, the Italians, the Greeks, and at last the Americans – so many of the countries whose archaeologists had worked together in Crete and Greece – sent their armies against one another. The six hundred tablets from Epano Englianos were consigned to the vaults of the Bank of Greece.

Blegen could not return to his Pylos until 1952. This was the very year in which the last of the really revolutionary discoveries in Minoan–Mycenaean archaeology was to occur: the decipherment of the later type of tablets and the proof that they were written in an archaic form of Greek. The results of this discovery, so startling to all those who had held the language to be Minoan, appear at the end of Chapter Two. Here something must be said of the decipherment itself.

His extraordinary success in breaking the code of the tablets, and the tragedy of his death in a motor crash within a few years of that success, have made the name of Michael Ventris almost as well known as those of the greatest excavators.

Like Schliemann he had a marvellous gift for languages, and as with Schliemann his interests began early. He was studying Egyptian hieroglyphs at the age of seven, and when as a schoolboy he heard old Sir Arthur Evans lecturing on the still undeciphered Cretan tablets, he resolved that he should be the first to read them. This determination remained with him even when he chose archi-tecture as a profession.

Neither the language nor the script of the tablets was known, and the hoped-for "bilingual" inscription failed to come to light. In these circumstances decipherment was generally regarded as impossible. Yet, working only in his spare time, Michael Ventris succeeded. His intellectual gifts, combined with a photographic memory and some knowledge of war-time code-breaking, carried him through even against his own preconception that the language involved was Etruscan. Broadcasting in June, Ventris unexpectedly announced: "During the last few weeks I have come to the conclusion that the Knossos and Pylos tablets must, after all, be written in Greek – a difficult and archaic Greek seeing that it was five hundred years older than Homer . . . but Greek nevertheless."

This news caused a great stir among the experts; but there were many doubters. What did the young architect know of archaic Greek? Then a most fortunate thing occurred. Blegen, as has been seen, returned that year to continue the excavation of the "Palace of Nestor". He unearthed one tablet among many others which, by giving pictograms as well as written names for a number of different types of utensils, provided striking confirmation for the Ventris syllabary. Ti-ri-po, for example, appeared with a pictograph of a tripod.

The proof that the archives of the palace of Knossos were written in Greek was seen to provide a final justification for the views of Professor Wace and the "mainlanders". There could no longer be any doubt that Knossos had been subject to a Greek dynasty at the time of the last palace. The violent disagreement that has blown up over the actual date of this Greek ascendancy in Crete, provoked mainly by that astringent debater, Professor Leonard Palmer of Oxford, has made it unwise to write with certainty about the age and affinities of some of the late features of the palace of Knossos. These chronological uncertainties have been temporarily increased, until the evidence is digested, by Professor Marinatos's claim that Minoan Crete was devastated by a huge volcanic eruption in the island of Thera.

However, no book would ever be written if the author waited for finality in archaeological know-ledge and opinion. What is wonderful is how much has been established during the past century. A brief introduction of this kind has only been able to touch on what might now be called the trend-setting events. There has been no space to describe even such great undertakings as the Italian excavations at Phaistos or the French at Mallia, or the continuing discoveries of the Greeks at the fourth great Cretan palace at Kato Zakro. Nothing has been said of the finding, in 1951, of the Lower Grave Circle at Mycenae or of the partial unearthing of Mycenaean Athens. As for the patient work that is gradually serving to bridge the gap of the "Dark Age" separating Mycenaean from Hellenic Greece, it has had to be ignored in spite of its significance for the final chapter of this book.

Yet it can still be hoped that some impression has been given of the advance of our understanding since the day when Heinrich Schliemann was moved to tears by his first sight of windy Troy. In the following chapters I must try to use what has been won with so much work – and at the same time with so much zest and enjoyment – to tell the history of the Bronze Age Cretans and Greeks and evoke their creative genius. They merit our concern for they were, after all, the mother and father of Western civilization.

Chapter One

The Birth of Athena

In the dim inner sanctuary of the Parthenon, Phidias's towering statue of Athena was of gleaming ivory and gold. Half hidden in the shadow behind her golden shield lurked a bronze-green python.

Athena! The goddess and her city of Athens stand at the heart of our dream of western civilization. The Parthenon, the Acropolis, and the divine figure itself with helmet, shield and wise bird have been printed on our minds as symbols of that marvellous moment in human history – the flowering of Greek civilization. Athena has had proud descendants – Britannia among them – and her greatest temple has survived to inspire scores of imitations. In many cities past and present an *Athenaeum* has been built to house some ideal of intellectual light. Nor even now are her powers outdated, for, among all her other concerns, she presided over the advancement of technical skills.

A daughter of Zeus, one of the exalted ones of Olympus and of Homeric epic, the goddess whose temples and statues and festivals dominated the birthplace of democracy, we see Athena in the clear light of the Classical world. Yet there in the shadow of her shield hid the python, and her aegis too was snake-bordered.

While her name and her association with birds (even with the owl) reach far back into the prehistoric past, it is the snake which most forcefully expresses Athena's great antiquity. The python survives from days when the goddess was identified with the protective snake of house and palace, and when her interest was more with the earth and physical life than with the sky and the light of thought.

Although, like all deities, Athena had changed with the times, she had come into the world an incalculable age before Phidias made his chryselephantine masterpiece. By that date in the fifth century B.C. she had already been lodged on the Acropolis for nearly a thousand years, and her origins were far older still. Myth gave her a sudden birth: she sprang fully armed from the head of Zeus. Yet in truth the Lady of Athens perfectly embodies the long-drawn genesis, gestation and birth of Greek civilization. It is for this reason that she has insisted on becoming patron goddess of this book.

At the present day, when European civilization can be said to have conquered the world, but when, through its very success, it is in danger of losing its quality and ideals, it may be a good moment to look back at the origins of that Greek way of living and thinking that inspired Europe for so long. Because the early formative period was over before there were more than the scrappiest written records, it has to be studied mainly through its material remains. These may leave much unsaid, but at least they cannot lie. No one can look at these works of art and fine craftsmanship, reproduced with all the power of modern photography, without entering into a closer sympathy with their creators.

Moreover, although it is true that no literature was being written down during the formative age with which this book is concerned, an oral literature was on the tongues of all men. Tales of gods and human heroes passed from generation to generation, were compressed, added to, confused – but never lost the ancient elements embedded in them like fossils. So when in the eighth century B.C. the first great works of European literature, the Homeric epics, came to be composed and perhaps already written down, they incorporated genuine memories of the heroic past of the Bronze Age. So, too, although the memories were fainter and more completely metamorphosed, did some of the legendary tales recorded by Classical and later authors.

While, then, the history of Greek origins must be largely composed from the possessions, dwelling places, fortifications and graves of the Bronze Age peoples concerned, with no more than some palace accounts by way of written record, it is given a unique quality by this retrospective revelation in a great literature. The Homeric epics send beams back into the darkened past to gild the centuries of the Greek heroic age. And when these beams chance here and there to light up objects – a shield, a helmet, a gold cup – that are known also from actual relics taken from the earth, they generate a very special kind of historical excitement. It is as though one were to discover Hamlet's sword or Lear's surrendered crown.

Using these three forms of evidence, material remains, the palace accounts on their clay tablets, and the Homeric and later stories, this book will show how the great achievements of Classical Greece grew out of the events of its prehistoric past. The most crucial phase was in the days of the Mycenaean kings in the closing centuries of the Bronze Age. But the genesis was much earlier, and one must begin with genesis.

Stated with the greatest permissible simplicity, that genesis took place – as seems appropriate – when a predominantly feminine force united with a predominantly masculine one. The feminine half of the union was the Minoan civilization which had flowered in Crete as peoples and cultural ideas had reached the island from the eastern Mediterranean. The masculine force was provided by peoples coming into mainland Greece from a more northerly direction and overland. These peoples, who, as they spoke a Greek language, can be called Indo-Europeans, were not yet civilized. The coming together of two so sharply contrasting partners engendered the miracle child of Greek culture, in which masculine and feminine traits were perfectly balanced.

To say that peoples and their cultures represent masculine or feminine forces is, of course, to speak metaphorically. Yet it has substantial meaning. The spontaneous creation of cultures and civilizations through some subtle interplay between time, place and the seemingly infinite possibilities of the human psyche, is one of the most significant as well as delightful aspects of history. Each cultural "form" tends to develop one group of human potentialities at the expense of others. So one people may evolve a highly permissive outlook while another is repressive; one may pay most respect to warlike valour, another to the peaceful arts; one may be preoccupied with death and its service while another thinks more of the enjoyment of this life.

It is in this sense of selective development within the limitless range of creative possibilities open to humanity that the Minoans can be said to have given brilliant expression to the characteristics that we associate particularly with the feminine personality, while the cultural traditions which the early Greeks brought with them from the north were dominated by masculine traits. In Greece and the Aegean the two met, and there ensued some degree of racial mingling and almost complete cultural fusion.

Athena has been chosen to symbolize the fruits of this union. Like Classical Greek culture itself, she shows a fine balance of masculine with feminine traits. She was first of all a womanly protectress of cities, but came to be a warlike goddess of victories; she was concerned with man's most intellectual pursuits, but also with weaving and other female skills; her face was feminine but strong-featured; her dress combined the flowing gown of Greek women with helmet, spear and shield. Her wisdom came, as wisdom must, from this same balance between the creative poles of life.

It has just been said that the myth of her birth is untoward because in historical truth her advent was neither abrupt nor motherless. But the story can be given a more acceptable interpretation. Before Athena was delivered from his head, Zeus had swallowed the pregnant Metis. If this can be taken to mean that the masculine Greek culture swallowed the feminine Minoan one, but that the resulting offspring possessed the normal share of her digested mother's inheritance, then this is a fair rendering of what happened in the lands round the Aegean Sea between 2,500 and 3,500 years ago.

It is right to begin the story of the Greek parentage with the feminine half, for by the time the earliest barbarian forebears of the Greeks had begun to thrust down into mainland Greece the Cretans were already well advanced in creating their Minoan culture and making their island the first outpost of civilization in Europe.

The Minoans were to develop a way of life as peculiarly their own as any in the world, and yet their history can only be understood as a part of a tremendous stirring of the human spirit, a surge of achievement, that had advanced from the valleys of the Tigris and Euphrates and the Nile, spread through Anatolia, and lapped round all the eastern Mediterranean.

The long, slow-moving early episodes of the story of the civilizing of the lands and islands of the Aegean Sea are dominated by one theme: the advance of cultural progress from the Orient towards the west. At the present time knowledge of man's first steps from a hunting to a farming economy is in a state of flux as in one region after another it is found that they were taken much earlier than was formerly supposed. It still seems likely, however, that the tentative beginnings of this new way of life, with all its implications for an increased and more settled population, were in South-west Asia in the upland territories lying between the eastern end of the Mediterranean and the Zagros mountains.

If this was where the domestication of plants and animals began, the lie of the lands made it inevitable that farming would soon be extended into the huge Anatolian peninsula (Asia Minor). The southern plateau became one of the most progressive areas for the new economy. Indeed, by the seventh millennium B.C. Anatolia was already supporting settlements large enough to be called towns, as well as innumerable villages and the strongholds of powerful chieftains.

So the new way of life spread westward through Anatolia. It is not certain how large a migration of people and animals was involved. There were hunting tribes already living in the peninsula, and they must have played a part in developing the farming economy once the basic knowledge and skills had been brought to them.

While eastern Anatolia is directly linked with Syria and with the upper Euphrates–Tigris valley, the much isled and indented west coast belongs to an independent sphere. Forming the eastern bounds of one of the most intimate and delightful of inland seas, it has usually turned its back on the Orient and maintained links with the Aegean world. Here, round the Aegean, conditions were excellent for the small-scale farming of the Stone Age. In those days, long before man and his goats had been able to strip the hills of their native dress of oak, fir and cypress, water was far more plentiful and the climate near perfection. Vines and olives, always to be a source of jollity and wealth, probably grew wild, and there was an abundance of game – deer, long-horned goats, wild pig and cattle.

The Mediterranean basin itself was attractive to seafarers, and within it the Aegean, in spite of its sudden storms, might have been designed as a nursery sea for elementary navigation. Land-locked on three sides and with the long, narrow islands of Crete and Rhodes forming natural moles protecting the fourth, southern, side, its waters were usually calm, or at least navigable. Moreover, the scatter of

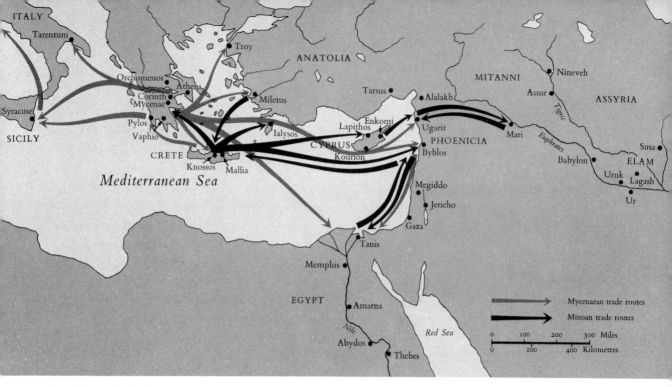

The Eastern Mediterranean.

islands large and small meant that navigators need seldom be out of sight of land.

It seems that the first farming colonists from Anatolia reached mainland Greece by boat, for their settlements are concentrated along the eastern seaboard. Whatever may have been the situation in Anatolia, it appears that these newcomers found Greece very sparsely populated. The introduction and early development of farming must therefore have been entirely in their hands as they arrived with their livestock and their seed grain to set up bridgeheads of cultivation in the strange country. They certainly did not all come at once. The passage of the Aegean being so easy, fresh groups must often have ventured across to a country where good land was to be had for the taking. Nor, it seems, did they completely lose touch with Anatolia. There was almost always to be a certain give and take between the two sides of the Aegean.

In time there were villages, sometimes very large villages, all the way from Thessaly to the Peloponnese. Although they knew nothing better than stone tools, these people were in many ways quite as well off as the modern Greek peasantry. They built themselves substantial rectangular houses of mudbrick, grew wheat and barley, and kept sheep and goats, cattle and pigs. In Thessaly at any rate, which at this time was the most prosperous part of Greece, the villagers depended almost exclusively on their own flocks and herds for meat. Perhaps they did not go hunting because their supplies of beef, mutton and pork were so plentiful that they had no need to; or perhaps they preferred to keep out of the way of the huge wild bulls and the lions that were to be encountered in the virgin country beyond the boundary of their fields and pasturelands.

These stone-using peasantries did not live without colour and a certain style. (When "functionalism" is being preached it is worth remembering that always and everywhere, if they have the smallest margin of leisure, men and women have devoted much of it to decorating themselves and their possessions and to creating "useless" works of art.) Very probably it was the village women who were fond of weaving, and who before the end of the sixth millennium B.C. were making excellent pottery. They had learnt how to produce a pale paste which enabled them to lay on bold and handsome designs in a vivid red paint. Looking at these bowls and platters, one can feel the confident enjoyment with which the potters must have worked.

They soon established their own decorative style. Anyone can recognize this first painted pottery of Greece with as much certainty as that of the famous Athenian ceramic artists of four thousand or so years later. Yet it is fascinating to discover that the fashion for decorating crockery with coloured paint was one that had spread from South-west Asia very much as the basic farming economy had done a long time before. If one could have seen them, the little groups of women who probably worked together outside their houses kneading, shaping, painting and firing their pots and pans would have appeared part of an utterly remote, unchanging, self-contained peasant society. Yet in fact what they were doing was by no means unrelated to the practice of other pot-painters not only in Anatolia but away in villages and townships in Iraq and Persia. Given the necessary time, neighbouring peoples communicated, ideas got around, in the Stone Age as they do today. The cultural stimulus pulsing from the Orient through Anatolia and along the Mediterranean shores was one that was to continue through the Bronze Age and play its part in the creation of Greek (as later of Christian) civilization.

One of the forms of intercourse which served to keep distant communities in touch with one another was the prosaic one of trade. It might have been expected that in these simple societies every village would have been self-supporting. So they could be if necessary, but if an exchange of goods would improve their living conditions then they were capable of arranging it. In most parts of Greece there was a shortage of the flint that was needed for knives and sickles and awls and other cutting or piercing implements – possibly including razor blades for the men. At various points along the Mediterranean basin volcanic heat had produced a black glassy substance called obsidian which, except for its brittleness, is superior to flint for the manufacture of keen edges or points. Obsidian had already been bartered among the hunting tribes, so it is not altogether surprising that it was being obtained over quite long distances by even the earliest of the farming communities in Greece.

The source of supply in Anatolia was from the volcanic ranges of the central peninsula. The Greek villages are assumed to have got their supplies from the island of Melos. Undoubtedly when the obsidian traders came with their glittering black lumps (for tools were worked up locally) they would have brought news and tales with them as well.

The patterns of settlement and trade make it clear that the sight of boats setting out across the waters of the Aegean on voyages more ambitious than those under-taken by the coastal fishermen would not have been extraordinary, although it may have been unusual. The truth of this is made obvious by the peopling of Crete.

Evidently this delectable island was beyond the reach of the hunting peoples, and in their day was uninhabited. There it lay in its untouched beauty and promise, its powerful limestone spine rising to the presiding peaks of the White Mountains, Mount Ida and Lasithi. At that time the upper slopes were covered with cypress and fir, and lower down grew a rich variety of trees – oak, myrtle, oleander, juniper and tamarisk among the most common – with almond, quince, pear, mulberry, offering their fruits. Among the animals that had enjoyed a domain untroubled by the wiles of men was the graceful Cretan ibex, probably a relic from the age when Crete was united with the Dodecanese.

It was very probably from the Dodecanese that boats set out to bring the first human beings to break into this innocent paradise. The settlers themselves may not have been natives of the south-western angle of Anatolia, but the route by Rhodes and Karpathos made a ready line of access into eastern Crete. It was a route that was to become of increasing importance as time went by, until in the Bronze Age it was one of the main sea thoroughfares linking the civilized people of the Aegean with those of the Levant.

The one hundred and sixty miles of the northern coast of Crete offered many good harbours, and it was not long before settlement had been pushed westward. Communities, some living in caves, were probably to be found on most of the fertile soil of sea plains and valleys. If a large part of this mountainous island was always to be uninhabitable, it did not matter at a time when there was plenty of good land to be had for the clearing. The bare summits themselves were to be peopled not by the human settlers but by their divinities. An uprooted people will not live long without identifying sacred places, and in much of Crete the high peaks dominate the surrounding country with a distant authority that might easily arouse awe. It may have been quite early that they, as well as their caves and gushing streams, began to be identified with deities, and it would be told how a goddess was born here and her consort there. Caves were favourite birthplaces for the gods.

Among places to be chosen for settlement by the first immigrants was the low hill, or Kephala, that thousands of years later was to become the site of the palace of the great rulers of Knossos. The original human occupation of this to-be-hallowed ground was very different. A party of some size but still, it seems, too much on the move to burden themselves with crockery, made an encampment there, building temporary huts and cutting storage pits into the rock. Yet even these pioneers were using obsidian and cultivating both wheat and barley. It seems that some epidemic sickness may have struck them, for seven young children were buried among the huts.

This camp on the Kephala was probably set up before 6000 B.C. If so, then sailings to Crete began almost as early as those directly across the Aegean to mainland Greece. Certainly the hill itself was occupied for a very long time before anyone thought of living in palaces. The pioneers either themselves found the means to return to the oriental practice of building in fired mudbrick, or were succeeded by further immigrants who brought the tradition with them. A village of close-packed houses with a conglomeration of little squarish rooms grew up and flourished until it came to cover as much as eleven acres. It would not have looked out of place in the contemporary Levant.

There were new arrivals and cultural changes, yet always the source seems to have been Anatolia or the east Mediterranean. Then the top of the mound that had accumulated from the collapse and rebuilding of mud houses and the piling of rubbish was levelled off, and the earliest palace built on it. It is hard to tell whether there was continuity between the last of the simple settlements on the Kephala hill and the foundation of the palace. As a comparable sequence of events took place on Phaistos, another Bronze Age palace on the southern side of the island, it seems that there must have been some continuity of sentiment and tradition at least – or why should these precise locations, without exceptional natural attractions, have been chosen for royal dwellings? As it was, whenever the sovereign left his apartments or throne room and walked in the central courtyard of his palace he passed over the spot where, some eight yards below his feet, the child casualties of the ancient pioneers lay buried.

Here at Knossos, where a modest Stone Age village supports the most famous of all Minoan sacred foundations, it may begin to be apparent why an account of the peopling of the Aegean by obscure and time-dimmed farming folk should have any relevance for the theme of the birth of Athena. It is relevant partly because this Stone Age peasantry must have provided the bulk of the racial stock on which Minoan civilization was to be founded, but far more because their culture, particularly as embodied in their religious tradition, already expressed that "feminine" side of the goddess's parentage.

All the peoples who became involved in the westward spread of farming inevitably shared in a very broad and loose cultural unity. Each area had its own strong distinguishing features, but also had some essential elements in common. Something of the same state of affairs still persists in the peasant life of the Mediterranean basin, where, in spite of national differences, such things as the cultivation of similar crops, including olives, almonds and vines, small terraced fields, tight-packed and whitewashed villages, ox-drawn ploughs and carts, give a strong impression of a Mediterranean culture.

Today the most significant division has been made by the presence of the conflicting Christian and Mohammedan faiths. Not only was there no such religious division in the Stone Age, but the whole idea of dogmatic and hostile religions would have been impossible. At that time, and indeed until the development of Judaism, there was a general recognition of the common source and meaning of religious experience, and men sought not to oppose but to identify and reconcile their deities and their worship. If it were not so, Athena as we know her could never have been begotten.

The Stone Age peasantry shared the same kind of unity as that now found in the Mediterranean. Nearly all raised cattle, sheep, goats and pigs, and cultivated varieties of wheat and barley. Most tended to congregate in compact villages or towns. It has already appeared how even specialized cultural ideas such as the painting of pottery could prove infectious and spread over enormous areas.

It might be expected, perhaps, that peoples sharing so many of the same worldly circumstances would also have similar religious beliefs and practices. Yet the extent to which this appears to have been true is still astonishing. All over South-west Asia early farming communities seem to have focused their worship upon fertility and the life-creating forces expressed through a maternal figure in human form. As the new way of life spread westward through the slow migrations of people and the infectious spread of cultural knowledge and skills, this form of religious preoccupation spread also. It was accepted among the stone-using farmers all the way from the Levant to Britain, and nowhere was it more dominant or more creative than in the Aegean. The concentration of the sense of the worshipful and sacred upon maternal power undoubtedly strengthened the feminine element in the individual psyche, and hence throughout society.

To interpret the religion of vanished peoples from the few material manifestations left behind in the earth is a hazardous and audacious undertaking. If the interpretation is sometimes allowed to become subjective, that need not mean that it is wrong, for the psyche which lives again in every human being as the generations rise and fall has not been totally transformed. It makes an unbroken chain between present and past. The bodily experiences open to the men and women of thousands of years ago were identical with those of today; the mental and emotional ones were not altogether different.

The material evidences of the religious life of these Stone Age farmers consist very largely of formalized statuettes of women (carved or modelled) which they kept in their houses or sometimes provided with sacred houses of their own. In making these images they called attention to the reproductive function, giving them huge breasts and buttocks, and often the mountainous bellies of advanced pregnancy. Moreover they usually set them in a squatting position, which at that time may have been the accepted position for childbirth. (It still is in many of the lands where the earliest of these figures were made.)

These eight-thousand-year-old symbols of fertility and motherhood were not the first of their kind to have been conceived and made. At twice that span of years, certain of the hunting tribes of Europe and Asia made statuettes of women apparently identical in intention, although less standardized and sometimes more powerful as works of art. With hunters the fertility of fields was not yet a concern, and the images must have been a projection of their desire for the reproduction of their own kind and of the animals they hunted.

Whether the tradition of making these images of maternity was maintained without break as men adapted themselves from the hunting to the farming way of life is uncertain. Such archetypal forms are universal, and may emerge as powerful elements of culture at different times and places without contact save through the flow of the human mind. What is certain, however, is that among the early cultivators of western Asia and Europe the tradition was so distinctive and so coherent both geographically and historically that it must imply a common religious belief. It was carried from the Orient towards the setting sun as an integral part of the new economy. When, in the Bronze Age, civilization grew from the rootstock of the prehistoric peasantry, this religion appeared in the light of history as the worship of goddesses of many names and attributes but all to be recognized as one – the Mother Goddess or Great Goddess whose realm spread almost as far as Bronze Age civilization itself.

Although the goddess of the cultivators was probably at home in South-west Asia, and kept considerable power there in historic times as Inana, Ishtar, Astarte and other divine ladies, she was to rule most powerfully and longest in the Mediterranean lands. In Asia Minor, where her images had been made over thousands of years, she rose above the surface of prehistory as the Cybele of the Phrygians and the Lydian Artemis, whose worship as a goddess of birth affronted St Paul at Ephesus. She was exceptionally powerful in the islands, notably in Cyprus where Aphrodite was to have her most famous temple, and in Malta where her name was never to be recorded, but where she was granted fine temples and was portrayed in images extraordinarily ample and voluptuous.

Meanwhile, in the lands and islands of the Aegean the goddess and her worship were introduced with the earliest farming, and the cult was only reinforced by later emigrants from Anatolia and through trade and other contacts with the eastern Mediterranean. Her images are found from the first in the mainland villages and in Crete. Before the end of the Stone Age many of the smaller Aegean islands had been settled, and the Cyclades in particular supported a population that throve on trade in the native obsidian and marble, and also probably on piracy. These islanders also used their marble to carve the finest stylized images of the goddess ever to be conceived. In some they still saw her as the abundant mother, suggesting the broad hips, full belly and squatting posture. But in others they were already seeing other aspects of the divine female – such as were to come into their own in the days of civilization. They showed her tall, slender, small-breasted, and with an abstract simplicity hardly to be understood again until the present time (pp. 29, 47).

On Naxos, Amorgos and Syros they were made, these marble evocations of the goddess, on Despotiko, Antiparos and Keros. They were made also in Crete. In the later centuries of the third millennium B.C. there was friendly intercourse between the larger island and the Cyclades, and visitors from one side or the other would have found little difference in the prevailing worship of the Great Mother.

At first the people of the Cyclades were in the ascendancy, and their high-prowed ships were well known in the eastern Mediterranean. Then Crete took the lead. This was the time when the future spirit or "form" of Minoan civilization was being determined. Ways of looking at life and nature and of rendering them in art, as well as ways of building and other practical affairs, already presaged what was to come. The Cretans were beginning to use copper, and they worked gold into frivolous ornaments for their persons. There were no true palaces as yet, but large houses with courtyards already had some dignity.

Crete was no longer a backward southern outlier of the Aegean. The advantages of her position on the routes to Egypt and the Levant were being realized. Ideas and occasional goods were imported from both Egypt and Syria, where true urban civilization was now flourishing. Then, about 2000 B.C., there was a sudden quickening of the pace. By now the Cretans had absorbed the influences from the high civilizations to the south and east of them, and were transmuting them into their own wholly original style. There was a dramatic increase in trade, wealth, skills and social organization. On the levelled summit of the ancient mound on the Kephala the first palace of Knossos was built, and a city grew up round it. The goddess who had presided over a population of farmers and artisans led by unpretentious local chieftains became the supreme divinity of an island nation that, under its sacred royal house, was to create one of the most subtle and brilliant civilizations ever to come from the mind of man.

It was just at this time when Minoan culture was taking wing that the first people speaking Greek, or a language in which Greek was rooted, began to arrive in Greece. Although it was to prove to be of exceptional significance, this influx was only part of far wider migrations that were to change languages and ways of life throughout Europe and much of Asia. Towards the end of the third millennium B.C. the Indo-European peoples began their expansion – which at first was explosive, causing disturbances all the way from Mesopotamia to Central Europe.

Correctly used, the term Indo-European applies not to race but to language. In this sense all the races of man can now be said to be Indo-European, for at the present day there is no very considerable area outside eastern Asia where some Indo-European tongue is not spoken as either a first or a second language. Yet it is hard to doubt that at the outset of this astonishing diffusion the early Indo-European tongues were spread from their homeland by movements of people who were racially akin.

This homeland appears to have been the expanse of grassy steppe to the north of the Black Sea, between the great barriers of the Carpathians and the Caucasus. Here the people on whose tongues the original language took shape were pastoralists who also practised agriculture. As often among pastoralists, their social structure was strongly patriarchal, and it can be assumed that they were tough and warlike. Their divinities, too, were patriarchal, and perhaps partly because they were steppe people who could readily lift up their eyes to mighty ranges, these divinities lived on mountain-tops and ruled the skies.

Their steppe heritage gave them one endowment unknown to the peasant societies of the Levant and Mediterranean: horses. They seem early to have learnt to domesticate them as draught animals, yoking them to wagons that lumbered along on solid wooden wheels. The early migrations of the Indo-European peoples are likely to have been the first of all expansions made possible by the use of horse-drawn wagons – just as the American drive to the West is likely to be the last.

The expansion began towards the end of the third millennium B.C. Those tribes that headed southward and were eventually to enter Greece may have moved down the west side of the Black Sea. If this is so, then some of them may have swung eastward into north-west Anatolia, destroying and resettling the city of Troy. An alternative is that these peoples came from further east and reached Greece by way of Anatolia.

It is not known whether at this time the northerners spoke what could be called Greek or some more generalized Indo-European language ancestral to it. Homer often referred to his Greek heroes as Achaeans, and for convenience, to distinguish these earliest Greek ancestors from later arrivals and from the Classical, or Hellenic, Greeks themselves, they will be called Achaeans here.

The Greece that awaited their conquest was in very much the same condition as

Abstract simplicity: stone-carved head of goddess from the Cyclades, second half of third millennium B.C.

the rest of the Aegean, only, because the sea roads were now the main thoroughfares of civilization, the mainland peoples were lagging behind the maritime
islanders of the Cyclades and Crete. However, the settled basis of their existence
was not very different. They, too, lived in permanent villages and small walled
towns, and in a few favoured spots such as Lerna on the Gulf of Argolis they built
substantial houses. They seem to have spoken the same language that prevailed in
Crete and south-west Anatolia, and there is no reason to doubt that the Mother
Goddess enjoyed the same pre-eminence. At Delphi itself, later to be seized by
Apollo and become the greatest of Greek sacred places, there was probably at this
time a shrine dedicated to the goddess of earth.

The advance of the northerners may have checked for a while as they settled in
Thessaly, finding good pasture for their beasts in the country dominated by the
snowy, cloudy summits of Mount Olympus.

On these Thessalian plains images of the Mother Goddess had been made and
venerated for over a hundred generations of peasant lives. Now the patriarchal
invaders came with their pantheon of Indo-European gods ruled by the father-
figure Zeus - who did not care for the dark, slow earth but ruled the sky with
lightning in his hand. The Father still liked to preside over lesser gods and men
from a mountain-top, and here in the new land Olympus was waiting for him.

Down below, among fields and pastures, the ancient goddess may have been
identified with his spouse or with other female divinities, but she could no longer
be supreme. It was one stage in the clash and mingling of northern Indo-European
and Mediterranean traditions. And in a land where the southern culture was not
very much more developed than that of the invaders, the Mediterranean tradition
must have been submerged.

With Thessaly occupied, the southward thrust continued, and seems to have been
bloody and destructive. Many of the old towns, Lerna among them, were sacked
as the warlike Achaeans penetrated into every part of mainland Greece. They spared
the islands, for although they had left the steppes for a maritime land, they had not
as yet taken to the sea. But when the invaders fanned out from the Isthmus of
Corinth to occupy the stony-fingered hand of the Peloponnese, it was certain that
sooner or later they would encounter the Cretans, now civilized and active seafarers. In this encounter the Mediterranean tradition would for a time prevail.

The Achaeans and the Cretans, representing the parentage of Athena, have now
been brought face to face. The date is about 1900 B.C. To understand her birth it is
necessary to skim over subsequent centuries that will be the subject of later chapters.

For several hundred years the two peoples and their contrasting cultural personalities did not affect one another at all deeply. There was some trade between them,
but even that was spasmodic. The Achaeans maintained their martial outlook,

fortifying their chieftains' strongholds such as those at Tiryns and Mycenae (plates 20, 21, 34). There was no true urban life, and even the rulers had not progressed far beyond barbarism. The Cretans, on the other hand, were becoming decade by decade more finely civilized in their ways. The great palaces of Knossos, Phaistos and Mallia rivalled those of the Orient in their refined amenities, and far outshone them in their art and sparkling style. The cities that grew up round them had streets of comfortable, two-floored houses. They rambled over mild slopes and had no forbidding walls. If protection was needed, it was given far away at sea, where Cretan ships were clearing the Aegean of pirates and keeping their own shores inviolate.

The ladies of the court could walk among the flowers, birds and butterflies of the gardens dressed with a sophisticated elegance. Their hair was coiled and curled; tightly-fitted jackets supported and temptingly displayed their bare breasts; from slender waists their skirts widened flounce below flounce to the ground.

The confidence and liveliness of these ladies was surely enhanced by the presence of the Great Goddess. The symbols of her cult were all round them in the palace, and her rites, refined by art into spectacles and games, played an important part in their lives. She was manifest in various forms, but the most significant was as the protective divinity of the palace whose shrine would be found near the royal apartments.

In a treasury at Knossos that probably held the furniture of a shrine, there were two female figurines (plate 13). Both were dressed as fashionably as the court ladies themselves, but one of them had snakes wound round her breasts and writhing along her arms, and the other held out a snake in either hand. A miniature shrine contained no images of the goddess herself, but instead three columns each with a bird perched upon it (p. 32). These, with the horns of consecration and the double axe, were the most familiar symbols of the divine presence.

At about the time when the images of the snake goddess were being set up in their Knossian shrine, a dramatic change was taking place in the relationship between the islanders and their neighbours on the mainland. By 1600 B.C. Crete was approaching the height of her power. She was exercising a strong influence on mainland Greece.

On their side the Achaeans enjoyed a sudden access in wealth and ambition, and opened themselves to Minoan culture. They imported Cretan goods, and they imitated them. The rulers, although they retained their masculine, warrior temper, fortifying their citadels and glorying in the possession of splendid weapons, turned themselves from barbarian chiefs into palace-dwelling princes. Greece was now divided into small kingdoms, each with its royal house. Of these, Mycenae came to be the wealthiest and commanded the greatest military strength. It is for this reason

that from the sixteenth century B.C., when they accepted so much of Minoan civilization, the Achaean Greeks are said to have entered the Mycenaean Age.

As part of this acceptance, the Mycenaeans took to themselves a part of Minoan religious practice. Zeus and the other gods they had brought with them kept an important place, but the Mediterranean goddess was made welcome, especially in her role as protectress of the royal house. Her symbols appeared at Mycenae and the other mainland centres in exactly the forms they had assumed in Crete, and tribute was poured out at her shrine.

Often the Achaeans referred to the household goddess simply as Lady of the place of her shrine – as Roman Catholics will now refer, for example, to Our Lady of Lourdes. She may sometimes already have been called Athena. The name itself is un-Greek and was perhaps in use among the Minoans. Certainly at least four of the symbols of the Minoan goddess – the snake, the bird, the pillar and the shield – were to be inherited by the Classical Athena.

Meanwhile she was to experience varying fortunes. In course of time, inevitably, the unwarlike Minoans had to surrender their dominant power to the Mycenaeans who had once learnt so much from them. Yet although Mycenaean culture had by now grown away from its Minoan origins, the goddess still kept her position on the mainland as guardian of the royal houses.

Then, through the inroads of still barbarian Greeks from the north, the Achaeans in turn lost their power. But now there was no one ready to take on the inheritance of civilization, and for a time city and palace life with their aristocratic wealth and culture disappeared from the Aegean.

Through these rougher times, however, the goddess still lived in men's minds, and her memory lingered on in the old sacred places. Probably the local people always maintained her shrines and brought offerings there. For when the light of civilization returned to them, the Greeks often built temples dedicated to Athena, Hera and other goddesses upon the exact site of the Mycenaean palaces where the household shrines had stood.

The direct descent of Athena from the ancient goddess is most plainly seen at Athens itself. If the Cretans had some influence on Attica during the height of their power, they may themselves have introduced their goddess – possibly even installed her on the Athenian Acropolis. More certainly she would have had a shrine there when the rock was fortified with Cyclopean walls and Mycenaean kings lived in a palace on the north side near the present Erechtheum. The barbarian onslaught which destroyed most other Mycenaean kingdoms was repulsed at Athens – greatly to the glory of the protecting goddess. Traditionally, therefore, the city enjoyed an unbroken continuity of life and faith through the obscure ages of Greek history. This did not, of course, mean that Athenian society did not change with the rest.

Epiphany of the Goddess: doves on sacred columns. Part of a miniature shrine. Clay. From the Old Palace of Knossos.

The royal house of Erechtheus disappears from history just as surely as the palace on the Acropolis fell into ruin.

When in the seventh century the embers of civilization were again being blown to a glow, a temple to Athena was built where the Mycenaean palace had stood. The base of one of the palace columns was incorporated below the foundations of the archaic temple. Later the lovely little temple of Athena Nike (of Victory) was perched on a Mycenaean bastion above the Propylaea, and Athens was given her splendid crown in the great house of Athena Parthenos (the Virgin). The private protectress of a Mycenaean royal house had evolved into the public guardian of a democratic city.

During this time the goddess had inherited much from the Achaean–Mycenaean side of her parentage. She had become more masculine. Indeed in the Homeric epics (which reflect the nature of the divinity in the eighth century when they were composed rather than of the Mycenaean age in which they are set) Athena shows a most warlike spirit. Today everyone knows that a Ministry of Defence is in fact the same thing as a Ministry of War. So it is easy to understand how the former protectress developed Amazonian qualities. Yet Athena never quite surrendered to the masculine principle. It is well known that she had to contend with Poseidon for the possession of Attica, and that she won by the gift to the people of her olive tree. Her triumph is celebrated in sculpture in the west pediment of the Parthenon. With the return of civilized values her more peaceable nature regained the ascendancy, and it was easy to recognize in Athena the old feminine guardian of life.

This was how Phidias saw her when he made his chryselephantine statue. He cannot have failed to know that she had a long history behind her. He would have been perplexed if he could have been shown the images of the snake goddess which in his day were lying buried in the rubble of Knossos. That flounced skirt might have struck him as frivolous, and the challenge of those bare breasts might have startled him. But he knew about the snake, and the bird and the pillar, and he would have heard the heretical tradition that, so far from leaping from her father's head, she had been quietly born in Crete. He would readily have understood that the Lady who watched over Knossos was one with his goddess, guardian of Athens and its intellectual adventure. The sculptor may perhaps have been thinking about such long-ago things when he placed the python behind Athena's shield.

Plate 2. "Like Chinese brush work". From the palace of Knossos, 16th century B.C.

Chapter Two

Island Civilization

When about four thousand years ago the people of Crete rather suddenly adopted the arts of civilized living, the history of civilization itself was still short and un-complicated. While its birth had been made possible by the development of a farming economy, these two events did not take place in precisely the same territory. In the upland regions where farming had first flourished, the small peasant communities failed to take the fateful next step to city life.

The principal reason for this failure may have been social. The villagers and inhabitants of the small market towns jogged along comfortably, leading the kind of life that might represent the ideal of modern anarchism. There seems to have been no challenge to stimulate them to live in much larger communities with greater specialization in the crafts and professions, and therefore no reason for the growth of strong central governments, priesthoods, the keeping of temple and palace records and all the other elaborations that arise from urban life or unified national states.

These advances were made, for the first time on earth (whether for the first time in the universe who shall say?) in the two huge river valleys of the Tigris-Euphrates and the Nile.

As the people living along the foothills fringing the Tigris and Euphrates and their tributaries had been among the earliest to develop the farming economy, it is natural enough that it was in this valley system that high civilization originated. Concerted effort and planning were needed to clear and drain, and in time to irrigate, the great stretches of dead flat valley bottom. But once brought under cultivation these flood plains were very fertile and could feed far greater numbers than the upland fields of the early agriculturalists.

In this way the formation of larger social units and more powerful and extended government was at once made possible and stimulated. Moreover, the rivers themselves helped to bring both prosperity and a kind of unity. They flowed too fast and violently to allow easy water transport, but they did make it possible for the raw materials that were lacking in the lower valley to be brought downstream. This traffic also provided communications over an enormous area from eastern Anatolia and Syria down to the Persian Gulf.

Plate 3. A goddess in her sacred cave? Pottery head from Psychro – probably the Diktean cave.

During the second half of the third millennium large cities had come into being along much of the valley, the wealthiest and most powerful being those created by the Sumerian people in the south. They had their crowded markets and close-packed streets where metal workers, jewellers, gem-cutters and other artisans practised their crafts, and each was dominated by the temple of the city god or goddess, and the palace of the ruler who was the god's earthly regent.

Each city state was the absolute possession of its presiding deity. The citizens held their land from him on sufferance; they paid their rent of grain, oils and other produce into the god's storerooms. Priests ran the government and filled the professions such as law and medicine. No more complete theocracy could have been devised.

The Sumerians and their successors held somewhat gloomy views of man's relationship with the divine world, believing that he had been created solely to toil for the gods. Perhaps because the Valley of the Two Rivers saw violent floods, frequent invasions, and ceaseless power struggles between the city states themselves, they expected life to be painful and uncertain.

While the Mother Goddess had been dominant among the prehistoric settlers, with civilization sky gods took command. Anu, a distantly exalted Lord of Heaven, was supreme, and his will might often be enforced by the more potent Enlil who had storms at his command. Next to them, however, came Nin-tu, "the Lady who gives birth", the Mother Goddess once again – in more civilized guise. Nin-tu took third place with Anu and Enlil in the Council of the Gods. She now had a consort Enki, Lord of Earth, who fertilized her womb with life-giving waters.

The Nile valley offered conditions that were at least as promising for the growth of civilization as those of Mesopotamia. The extent of cultivable soil was less, but every year it was enriched by the inundation. Also, for many hundreds of miles the Nile was easily navigable in both directions, the prevailing north wind making it easy for ships to sail upstream. With their river highway and their protecting desert walls, the Egyptians could be led to feel a sense of national unity. Before the end of the fourth millennium B.C., all Egypt from the Delta up to the First Cataract was under the rule of a single divine king. In five centuries the Pharaohs were powerful enough to be able to command such tremendous works as the building of the pyramids.

The ideas of civilization may have been brought to the Nile valley from Mesopotamia, but they matured very fast and soon assumed their own highly distinctive form. Egyptian civilization as a whole was as unlike Sumerian as hieroglyphic was unlike cuneiform writing.

For one thing, it remained more rural. Although population grew round the great temple establishments of the royal capitals, true urban economy failed to develop. This, linked with the survival of social grouping of a totemic kind, probably accounted for the Egyptian feeling for birds and animals manifested in their art and in their religious imagery.

Another difference lay in the fact that whereas the kings of the Asian city states were regents for their divinities, Pharaoh was himself a god with an exalted place in the Egyptian pantheon. The more confident and optimistic outlook of the Egyptians in the early days owed much to their faith that god was on the throne and all right with the world.

While the peoples of Mesopotamia expected disturbance, made much of a god of storms, and always feared a return to chaos, the Egyptians put their faith in an ideal of unchanging order. They were familiar with the invariable cycle of their seasons; the flood came at its appointed time; the sun followed its regular courses, crossing the untroubled blue above their narrow valley. The sun god Re was the greatest of their divinities, and Pharaoh was his son. The order they had established was good and must be maintained for ever.

The Egyptians loved everyday life. They lavished so much attention on death not from any morbid obsession but because it appeared as the enemy of the unchanging. They were determined to defeat it. Just as in Mesopotamia, the Mother Goddess, who had been worshipped by the Stone Age peasantry, had a secondary but still powerful position in the pantheon. She appears as a sky goddess, Nut, giving birth to the sun, but more clearly as Hathor, often represented as a cow, and recognized theologically as the mother of Pharaoh. Later she merged into the great Isis, who was often depicted with the cow horns of Hathor carried gracefully on her head. Isis with Osiris represented the resurrection or rebirth aspect of the Mother Goddess which came to mean more to the Egyptian people than the royal cult of Re.

By the third millennium B.C., then, high civilizations had been brought into being in these two river valleys of South-west Asia and of North Africa. They were as distinct from one another as all later civilizations were to be. Probably no single thing created by one people could ever be mistaken for its counterpart created by the other. The temper and values of the two cultures were also quite unlike. Yet certain prime assumptions were the same. Both Egyptians and Sumerians saw everything in the world about them as charged with divine power, and expressed this encounter with divinity in terms of the interrelated gods and goddesses of a pantheon that existed in time (creation stories) as well as space. Seeing the cosmic order of the gods as a hierarchy, both peoples believed that human society should be its earthly reflection, and for this reason gave unbounded power to holy kings and their priests.

Assumptions such as these, to be repeated on the other side of the world in the pre-Columban civilizations of America, must represent experiences of the psyche common to all mankind. At a certain stage in mental and cultural evolution, this is how the external world appears to human consciousness. The vision of the world that was granted to man in the early morning of civilization was to remain fundamentally unchanged until it was revolutionized by the Greeks. Yet it will be suggested that already, long before that time, the Cretans, with their feminine response to life, had done something to free the human spirit from enslavement to its gods.

By the middle of the third millennium the germ of civilization had been carried eastward from Mesopotamia to another great river valley, the Indus. It was to flourish there for about a thousand years before it collapsed in the face of Indo-European invasion. Simultaneously with this extension to the east, some elements, at least, of civilization were spreading westward. At first it was only in Crete that they were able to inspire an altogether original culture, offering man new experiences in the young venture of civilized living.

The lands round the eastern shore of the Mediterranean became the principal intermediaries through which the achievements of the river-valley civilizations made themselves felt in the west. Inevitably Palestine and Syria had been strongly influenced by these great neighbours lying on either side of them, and small city states grew up among the Canaanites to the south and the Amorites to the north. Partly because it was dominated and fought over by Egypt and Mesopotamia, this Levantine region never supported a great or stable land power – it was left to the religious genius of the Hebrews to bring it to the front of history.

Prosperity did, however, come to the coastal cities of Syria, ideally situated to handle trade between Asia, Egypt, Cyprus and the west. The Amorite city of Byblos early became important, and it is possible that Tyre and Sidon, too, had already begun to trade. Then, as will appear, Ugarit surpassed them all, becoming the first really great international port in the Bronze Age world. By sail and oar, ships carrying cedar wood from the slopes of Lebanon, Cypriote copper, wine, olive oil, ivory, purple-dyed Syrian cloth and other luxury goods were plying sea routes that linked all the lands of the eastern Mediterranean.

The intercourse between Egypt and Crete, which was to be of great historical significance, followed a complicated pattern. While undoubtedly some traffic reached Crete directly from Egypt, other Egyptian produce and cultural influences reached the island indirectly by way of the Levant.

One of the busiest Cretan ports was Mochlos in the wide Bay of Mirabello, now an island but probably in those days a promontory able to afford shelter on one side or the other according to the winds. Another was the nearby islet of Pseira, with good anchorage in a sheltered cove. Vasiliki, an inland town in the same region, prospered early and could already boast a small palace, probably belonging to a local ruling family enriched by overseas trade. It may have been built before there was anything to equal it at Knossos.

These centuries from about 3000 to 2000 B.C., when eastern Crete was in advance of the rest of the island, cover the first, Early Bronze Age, phase of Minoan culture. It was not until the "great leap forward" at the beginning of the second millennium that the Cretans far outstripped their neighbours in the Aegean, and succeeded in creating one of the most remarkable civilizations in world history.

Already, however, its nature must have been largely determined. One would like to be able to look into the minds of the people to discover mental qualities that could explain the highly distinctive personality of the budding Minoan culture. Such insights are denied, but it may still be worth taxing the imagination in an attempt to appreciate how life would have appeared to the islanders during this formative time. One can at least hope to gain some understanding of external conditions that were not without influence on what was to follow.

The Cretans would have been conscious of kinship with other Aegean peoples, and particularly with the inhabitants of the adjacent parts of Anatolia. They spoke related languages and may even have been able to understand one another if trading or other interests brought them together. The islanders probably also found that these neighbours had similar domestic arrangements and looked much like themselves - that is to say most of them were small, slender, dark-haired and neat-featured. They would have understood their religious life and their worship of the Mother Goddess.

On the other hand an island always has a potent effect on its inhabitants. Its frontiers are immutable, divinely determined rather than due to mere human vicissitudes. Strangers cannot easily cross them unnoticed or unopposed. This sense of being sea-protected, "the envy of less happier lands", gives island people a sharp awareness of their identity and of their difference from everyone else. Even today in the Isle of Wight, a modest patch of land fitting close to the English shore, people from the mainland are called "overners" and are regarded as inferior aliens. An island home, in short, greatly enhances that belief in belonging to a chosen race that is native in every human breast.

It is true that the Aegean was full of islands, but Crete's greater size and much greater isolation must even at this early period have allowed its people a certain self-confidence and awareness of themselves. How far were they aware of the two great civilized powers of Asia and Africa with whom, directly and indirectly, they were in faint contact? How much can they have understood of the possibilities of civilization?

The Cretans must, of course, have been aware of the directions in which Egypt and Mesopotamia lay. They were accustomed to their own merchant adventurers setting off from harbours such as Mochlos when the winds were favourable, hoist-ing their big square sails and setting their high prows towards the east. When they returned men, women and children rushed down to the anchorage and marvelled at the strange and sometimes fine goods that the sailors were unloading. No doubt the privileged ladies, living in some style in places such as the little palace at Vasiliki, waited eagerly for luxury objects, perhaps precious stones or gold to be worked into ornaments, or strings of faience beads. Ships' captains must have carried rough maps of the eastern Mediterranean in their heads, and would have been very ready to tell stories of what they had seen and describe the size and wealth of the Levantine ports. Perhaps they would have made people laugh by describing the Semites with their heavy beards and curling black hair, and trying to pronounce a few words of their outlandish language.

Ventures such as these would have been rare and have affected few people, and there is nothing to prove that in these early days any Cretans travelled as far as the Valley of the Two Rivers to see the wonder of the crowded cities and huge ziggurats, or to penetrate the courts and witness the pomp and riches of the kings. As for the Nile valley, the Delta was only four hundred miles away – and the Libyan coast much less. Perhaps there were a few people, either native Cretans or foreign wanderers and exiles who had been to Memphis, who knew the great river busy with shipping, the temples coming down to the waterside, and had stared up at the pyramids, then still white and gleaming, the hardly credible witness of what men could achieve when imagination commanded both wealth and power.

One can be fairly sure that the élite of the island would have had some kind of picture in their minds of marvellous lands far overseas, but they would not know what was real, what exaggerated, or when travellers' tales merged into myths and legends. Yet perhaps already they seemed real enough to exercise some attraction, to make the unbroken horizons of their glittering sea an invitation to sail rather than an enclosure to serve them in the likeness of a wall. Certainly, although not many of their ships went on long voyages, the idea of maritime enterprise, of the lure of the sea roads, was already beginning to inspire the islanders. In a few generations it would bring them greatness.

In some ways this earliest period of Minoan culture was less one of preparation for the greatness to come than one of waiting. It seems more like a fertile field ready for the seed to be cast into it than like a building site where foundations are being laboriously laid in preparation for the swift erection of the elegant house. It is true that some technical advances were being made. Copper was being used in increasing quantities for the manufacture of some necessary implements, although there was still a lack of tin to harden it into really serviceable bronze. Overseas trade may have led to the building of larger and more fully seaworthy vessels; the popu-

Left Cretan youth. Head of an acrobat, from a sword-hilt. Gold. From the palace of Mallia, *c.* 1600 B.C. *Right* Early skill in shaping stone. Black-and-white veined limestone. From the island of Mochlos, 2400–2000 B.C.

lation is likely to have been steadily increasing. Partly inspired by Egyptian models, craftsmen had learnt to cut out and polish beautifully formed vases, jugs and other vessels from finely coloured and patterned stone. The well-to-do for whom such craftsmen worked were able, as has already appeared, to live in residences of many rooms with smoothly plastered walls; the ladies of these houses could deck themselves with crystal beads, gold chains and armlets; could put sprays of papery gold leaves and flower-headed gold pins in their hair, and even sew golden stars, sequin-like, on to their dresses. Probably owing to the trade that made these elegancies possible, the men were acquiring a sense of individual ownership and property. They caused stone and ivory cutters to make them seals each with a design that would serve to stamp the bale or the oil or wine jar as their own. When they died these gentry were carried to decent family tombs, usually like round houses built above ground, and were laid to rest dressed in their finery and keeping possession of their seals.

Undoubtedly the beginnings of civility were already there, but they were modest and affected few people. If merchants or other travellers familiar with Egypt or Mesopotamia ever landed in Crete they would have recognized that the natives had certainly shown themselves capable of profiting from their contacts with the

Ritual play with bulls began early. Clay rhyton from Koumasa, *c.* 2200 B.C.

Orient, but they would hardly have guessed that this rustic island of small harbours and peasant villages was soon to outshine the rest of the Mediterranean.

This is true, yet it is also true that the essential nature that was to distinguish Minoan culture from all others could have been detected – and in spite of its debt to the Orient, it was not Oriental. Among the few things that have survived, this spirit shows itself most happily in those seals the purpose of which was so largely practical and prosaic. The seal makers not only incised pictures and patterns on the flat sealing surface, but also sometimes carved the handles in the round in the form of animals and birds.

The glyptic art of the seals themselves, already very deft in its cutting, includes lively scenes of everyday life. The islanders' preoccupation with the sea is reflected in pictures of ships, fish and fishermen; the wildlife of the mountainsides in brilliant studies of ibex and wild boar. Other subjects show both work and play – a potter, and a man seated under a tree playing draughts. Among the seal handles carved in stone, bone and ivory are figures of monkeys, a sheep, and a dove with her young clustered below her breast.

These seals and a few other little carvings of men and animals are no more than the tentative beginnings of Minoan art. They show borrowing of Egyptian and Oriental ideas, and if great claims are made for them it can only be because it is hard not to overvalue them as a presage of what was to come. Yet it is true that already they show two of the enduring characteristics of the Minoan spirit: a direct feeling for nature even in its humblest forms and free from any interposing symbolism, and an exhilarating vitality and sense of movement. Egyptian artists made closely observed and truthful studies of human and animal figures, yet with few exceptions they were posed, motionless, as though frozen in the Egyptian ideal of an unchanging eternity.

The Minoan vitality was to be as evident in abstract patterns as in figures, and this too is already apparent in the earliest seal-cutters' art. Some show whirling, spiralling quadrilateral designs that manifest all the movement of a child's windmill in a breeze. This particular structure as well as the energy with which it was charged were to appear in full vigour in the centuries ahead.

The draughts player can also be recognized as expressing something at least of an aspect of Minoan life that was to assume great importance in the days of high civilization. Some scholars have seen this life as perfectly expressive of the idea of *Homo ludens* – of man whose cultural achievements sprang in part from an urge for play – a serious play that may have ritual meaning. Board games concerned with contending forces can have such undertones, and the magnificent gaming board in gold, ivory and crystal found in the last palace at Knossos proves that kings or queens might play them.

The most potent and significant form of ritual play that was to be perfected among the Cretans was, of course, their bull-leaping (p. 121). Even this sacred game was, it seems, already beginning to take shape in these early days. A lively but uncouth vessel, a rhyton intended for pouring libations, is in the shape of a bull, with human figures, far too small in proportion to the beast, clinging to the head and horns. It dates from about 2200 B.C.

Finally, the presiding figure of the Goddess was already a powerful presence. As she had been worshipped through the millennia of the New Stone Age, her continued supremacy in the early Bronze Age was to be expected. In fact it is only surprising that her development seems to have been delayed during this period. There is no known representation of the Goddess that looks towards her future grace, or is artistically equal to the seal carvings. This was the time when images of the divinity were being brought into Crete from the Cyclades (p. 27), but they were not the best of their kind, and most of the native renderings were very poor indeed. Sometimes she was shown in the form of a rhyton, where she appears with a turban-like head-dress, large eyes, necklace and open robe. She clasps her breasts – which are big spouts jutting brutally through the robe. It is as though the primitive tradition of the Goddess were so deeply entrenched in this still predominantly rustic island that it held out for the time against the civilizing influence of the Orient. Yet the large eyes, elaborate necklace and clasped breasts link the prehistoric deity with some of her more courtly descendants.

The ever-changing yet eternal Goddess. (*a*) *left* Abstract simplicity. Parian marble. From the Cyclades, *c.* 2400 B.C. (*b*) *right* An elementary naturalism. Pottery. From a grave near Pylos, style of *c.* 1800 B.C.

Left First appearance of horns of consecration? From the island of Mochlos, 2200–2000 B.C.

(c) *left* Natural movement and feeling. Pottery. From Phaistos, c. 1500 B.C. (d) *right* Palace sophistication. Faience. From treasury of shrine in the palace of Knossos, 16th century B.C. (detail of figure in plate 13).

(e) Our Lady of the Rocks. Ivory. From Mycenae, at the height of Mycenaean power, 14th century B.C.

What happened just four thousand years ago to make this modest island culture, which until then had put out no more than the smallest buds of a special talent, burst into sudden flower? The end of the third millennium saw violent upheavals throughout most of the Bronze Age world. The expansion of the Indo-European peoples set up some of the pressures that were to cause spreading impacts, uprooting whole populations and finally overthrowing the old regimes in the ancient civilizations themselves.

It has already been seen how the Achaeans spread destruction through Greece; at the same time the Hittites, also a largely Indo-European people, were winning themselves a kingdom in Anatolia. There was another violent thrust from Anatolia down into Syria and Palestine, while Amorites and others were making successful onslaughts against Mesopotamia. Most shocking of all, displaced Semites from Asia invaded the Egyptian Delta, and their intrusion, combined with social revolution, toppled the divine Pharaoh from his throne, bringing the established order of the Old Kingdom to an end. The Egyptians had not known that civilization could be an unstable thing, that what had been established by the gods could be overthrown. Their writers expressed their horror and dismay at the social chaos where men had to go armed to plough, where "There is no man of yesterday. The children of princes are dashed against the wall."

The Egyptians' outlook was changed for ever by the experience. They lost their unquestioning confidence in life, but gained a deeper understanding of moral issues. About the year 2000, after more than a century of anarchy, a strong royal house established itself at Thebes and succeeded in reuniting Egypt under its rule. This was the XI Dynasty, which opened the period known as the Middle Kingdom. After further disturbances, the vigorous XII Dynasty succeeded to the throne of Pharaoh in about the year 1990 B.C. The new Dynasty encouraged foreign trade, and it was now that a closer relationship with Crete began.

Although there is nothing to prove it, there is a possibility that during this time of violence and instability, refugees from Egypt and the Levant may have made their way to Crete. The idea that foreign dynasties seized power in the island has almost nothing in its favour. But even if, as is usual, refugees have no political power, they have often had a stimulating effect on the development of cultural life. Conceivably, then, individuals who had been reared in the ways of high civilization may have contributed to the profound social and political changes then taking place in Crete.

At least three royal houses rose to power and built palaces which soon became the centres of thriving cities. It was a turning point in Minoan history to be compared with that which had taken place centuries before in Egypt and Sumeria when the earliest dynasties were established there.

The status and religious meaning of kingship in these two lands differed, although

(f) *top left* Return of stylization. Pottery. From Mycenae, c. 13th century B.C.
(g) and (h) At the dead end of Minoan civilization the Goddess still keeps the ancient symbols – horns, doves, the double axe. (g) Pottery. From Gazi, Crete, 13th century B.C. (h) Impression from a schist mould from Sitia, East Crete, 12th century B.C.

in both it rested on the assumption of a divinely created and controlled world. In Crete the royal rulers similarly stood at the heart of the religious life of their realms: their palaces displayed innumerable religious symbols, contained many sacred rooms and shrines, and were laid out for the staging of games and ceremonies of ritual origin. Yet the whole spirit of Minoan court life was so very unlike either the Egyptian or Sumerian that unquestionably the nature and meaning of the throne must have differed also. It is even possible that it was occupied not by a king but by a queen.

The three palaces that were built soon after 2000 B.C. were all in the central section of the island. There was Knossos in the north, well placed for the Aegean trade, and Phaistos in the south where it prospered on the wealth of Messara - the largest fertile plain in Crete - and was near harbours open to traffic with Libya and Egypt. These two palaces retained their fame long enough for their names to appear in Homer. The third, now known as Mallia (pp. 56, 57), was not so historically cele- brated and has been named after a nearby village twenty-two miles to the east of Knossos. It seems that for the time the importance of eastern Crete sharply declined. But three or four centuries later, when trade with Rhodes and the rest of the south- east Aegean was booming, a fourth palace went up at Kato Zakro on the east coast.

By that time the greater part of the island was dominated by Knossos, and the ruling families in the other palaces were her vassals. But it is uncertain what political pattern prevailed in the days of the early palaces. Probably there was some form of confederacy between them, but Knossos may not as yet have won the hegemony.

The three early-established palaces had certain features in common that were maintained through centuries of alterations and rebuildings. Architecturally all three were dominated by a great central court, rectangular in plan and with the longer axis running north and south. This was overlooked by windows and balconies, and might be approached by columned stairways. Roof lines were fretted with crestings of stone or terracotta "horns of consecration" - stylized bull-horns that were among the sacred symbols of Minoan cult. Each had an informal open court outside the west wall.

Because the axis of the central court determined the orientation of the whole building, all the palaces were alike also in that their four sides faced towards the cardinal points of the compass. The Cretans built their mansions and to some extent their towns with the same orientation, so that it probably had some religious significance for them - as the east-west positioning of his church has for the Christian.

The boldly original architecture of the palaces and the mural paintings that helped to fill them with colour and movement will find their place in the next chapter. It remains here to consider the purposes they served.

At the height of Minoan power and prosperity these palaces became remarkably

Plate 4. Paired hornets with honeycomb? Gold pendant from Mallia, 2000–1700 B.C.

large in relation to the scale of the island itself. They were not quite as extensive as the Oriental palaces with which they are sometimes compared, but then far less of their area was given to open courtyard. Knossos, the largest, came to cover as much as 24,000 square yards. This is only half the area of, for example, Nebuchadnezzar's palace at Babylon, but owing to the ingenuity of the Minoan architects in lighting their buildings, Knossos rose to three, and in one wing to four or even five stories. It could comfortably have accommodated many hundreds of people.

The palaces served as the temporal and religious centres of their modestly-sized domains, with all their country villages and market towns, their ports and fishing villages, their great residential estates, and their sacred shrines among the mountains. Thus they not only housed the royal family and its court and provided the stage for their ritual life, but also accommodated workshops, administrative offices, and great storerooms where subjects deposited their taxes in kind. When Knossos came to exercise a hegemony over the other domains, and presumably exacted tribute from them, her magazines were very much enlarged. The rows of huge, full-bellied storage jars, and the pits, sometimes lined with lead, sunk below the floors, bear witness to the toll of olive oil and grain and wine and precious goods that poured into the palace (p. 59).

The rulers probably also exercised some jurisdiction over foreign trade (in Egypt Pharaoh had control of all major trading ventures), and goods for export, including fine ceramics, may have been stored in the palaces, as well as the exotic products that came in exchange.

Their function as state warehouses and the wealth of goods they must sometimes have contained could help to account for the strongly enclosed and inturned character of these great buildings. In contrast with the later Mycenaean royal citadels they were in no sense forts and the appearance they presented to the world was peaceful and not military. Yet they had substantial outer walls and narrow or winding entrance ways, some of which were overlooked by tower-like constructions. Perhaps this very moderate protection was designed against possible civil disturbances and looting, as well as to screen the sacred lives of the inmates. There can hardly have been a palace in history that did not set a firm boundary between sovereign and subject.

The inner towns surrounding the palaces were well designed for civilized living. The streets were paved and drained, and the neat houses fronting on to them were of two or three floors, flat-roofed and sometimes perhaps with a penthouse where the owners could sleep during the heat of summer. At Knossos there were also spacious, gracefully planned villas that probably belonged to members of the royal family, important officials and other dignitaries. The poorer quarters of the city may have been in scattered districts – including a harbour town two or three miles

Plate 5. Detail of fish on a storage jar from Phaistos, 18th century B.C.

First fruits for the Goddess: stone offering-table that probably served the same purpose as the *kernos*, a ring-shaped cluster of cups used in the cult of the Goddess from Mycenaean to Classical times. The south-west corner of the central court, palace of Mallia.

Approach to the palace of Mallia. A paved way, sometimes called Sea Street, leading to the narrow northern entry.

from the centre. Rich and poor, Knossos at its greatest may have had a hundred thousand citizens. So strong was the sense of security and the peaceful tenor of island life, that they saw no need to protect themselves with city walls.

While most of the rich and powerful lived near the palaces of their lords at Knossos, Phaistos, Mallia and later at Kato Zakro, others built fine houses in more rural surroundings. Some of these people may have been officials appointed from the palace to look after local government and supplies, and so to help maintain the good order of the state. Others again were great landowners made rich by the produce of their soil and their peasants, or merchants making their fortunes either in home towns or through trade overseas. There were at least three large mansions outside the town of Tylissos, to the west of Knossos, whose owners may have prospered from the sale of oil. (The district is still known for its fine olive groves.) Another splendidly furnished mansion, at the sea's edge at Nirou Chani on the other side of Knossos, seems to have belonged to a merchant with foreign interests who kept his merchandise in store until it could be shipped. His vessels would have sailed from the small harbour nearby, and may have been built in adjoining yards. The island port of Pseira also had its well-housed and wealthy citizens.

At Gournia on the Bay of Mirabello some dignitary chose the sumit of a knoll not far from the shore to build a house that suggests a small palace. A humble but well-planned little town grew up round it, served by two ring roads, and packed with the houses of artisans. These potters, carpenters, smiths and oil-pressers lived above their basement storerooms and dealt with the local peasants and fishermen. They were all well equipped with the tools of their trades and must have served the needs of their customers efficiently, while making a decent living themselves.

Late in its history, when the big house had been abandoned by its wealthy owners, a public shrine to the Goddess was set up in the town at Gournia. It can be seen as a very modest forerunner of all the temples to Athena Polios, the Athena of the town, that were to be dedicated in later times. It was also a civic counterpart to those public shrines in the mountains that honoured the Lady of the wild places.

The Cretans furthered their rural economy and their urban trade with an adequate system of roads. A fine paved highway, the first of its kind in Europe, led from the south coast ports and the towns of the Messara across the island to Knossos. Travellers using it would have had a striking impression of the city rising from the Kephala. The way led them first to a comfortable rest house, and then up the flights of a great stepped portico to the south entrance of the palace. Another road forked off to run past the west side of the palace northward through the town towards the harbour.

Further east a main road linked the east coast ports with Mallia, probably enabling that city to dominate the eastern trade – at least until the foundation of Kato Zakro.

The principal sites of Minoan Crete.

The wealth of the palace of Knossos: man-high storage jars (*c.* 1500 B.C.) in the western magazines, with stone-lined storage pits visible in the bottom left hand corner of the picture.

The network of lesser roads may have consisted of no more than roughly-made-up tracks following valleys and ridges. A well-built viaduct on the southern approach to Knossos, however, proves what the engineers were capable of when the lie of the land provided a challenge.

The thoroughfares round the principal cities and ports must have been busy with all kinds of traffic. Officials posting to and fro between Knossos and other seats of government were probably carried in open litters. Where the roads were good enough, merchants and well-to-do farmers transported their bulkier goods in low, ox-drawn wagons. Otherwise goods were tied over donkeys' backs or were carried by manpower – either balanced on a stick over the shoulder or slung on long poles carried by several men together.

The light, horse-drawn chariots, the use of which swept across the ancient world in the middle of the second millennium, revolutionizing travel and warfare, would not have been seen in Crete until the days of Mycenaean domination (p. 216).

The general scene of Bronze Age life in this beautiful and fruitful island is one of ordered prosperity. In all the more cultivable regions of eastern and central Crete, one could not have gone for more than ten miles without coming to a mansion with its gardens and outbuildings, a country town with market and workshops and the large houses of the well-to-do, or a thriving port where foreign voices and ways were gladly tolerated, and where no one could quite forget the vastness and variety of the world beyond the horizons.

Moreover, the life of this countryside must have been constantly stimulated and brightened by intercourse with the palace-crowned cities. Phaistos and Mallia were each less than twenty-five miles from Knossos, and Kato Zakro less than fifty miles eastward from Mallia. In all these places there was not only a lively and sophisticated society, but also the gifted men and women who had won court patronage – artists of genius and craftsmen as skilled as any in the world. The influence of these people and their work helped to raise the standards of taste and craftsmanship throughout the developed parts of the island.

The Goddess of fertility and abundance had certainly fulfilled her worshippers' desires. From her shrines in palaces and caves and on the mountains she presided over a people whose material conditions and civilized ideals could in most respects stand comparison with those of Britain and western Europe over three thousand years later. It is true that there was no written literature and no architectural achievement to equal that of the Gothic cathedrals – but there were many compensations, and for a woman of the privileged class Minoan life might well have been far preferable. The beliefs that did so much to shape and colour existence favoured the full enjoyment of life in this world. War was not glorified, and peace and sunshine seemed secure.

Much of the wealth that supported this civilization-in-miniature came from the natural and cultivated resources of the island. The Messara plain yielded a surplus of grain, and the other small plains and the valleys were highly fertile. There was sufficient pasture for large flocks and herds. More significant because more exceptional, Crete in her small area offered an extraordinary range of climate. Cultivation on slopes and little upland plains thousands of feet above sea level meant a succession of harvests spread over months. Green pastures could be found even at the height of summer.

Although there were no rivers of any size, water supplies were better in those days before the land had been stripped of its forests. Snow lay long on the summits and permanently in the deep clefts between ridges, supplying good springs and some streams that never ran dry. Crete was recognized throughout antiquity as a populous country, and its olive oil, honey, fish and abundant fruits and herbs were renowned. It was "great, fat and well-fed", as one writer put it.

Yet the local economy by itself could hardly have supported luxurious living in so many palaces and mansions. It has already appeared that it was contacts with Egypt and the Levant that brought the first seeds of civilization to Crete. Trade with these countries and others nearer home was needed to maintain and develop it. Here she had a unique advantage, for, as the Greek historian Diodorus was to say, "the island lay in a most fortunate position for travel to all parts of the world".

The pattern of Cretan trade had not changed radically from that of the early phase before 2000 B.C. Her ships still went northward to the Aegean, eastward by way of Rhodes and Cyprus to the Levant, and (very probably) southward to Libya and the Delta. They may perhaps have extended their voyages into the still barbarous west at least as far as Sicily. The position of Crete in the Mediterranean world, however, and the conditions of her trade had altered very greatly.

Crete was no longer a humble semi-barbarous island picking up what she could from more civilized lands, but now, having created her Minoan civilization, was the equal of any people with a stake in Mediterranean commerce. Now her rulers had the resources of wealth and the command of power.

One result of the changed situation was that Crete was no longer limited, like the "underdeveloped countries" of the twentieth century, to the export of raw materials. Her merchants may have continued to send wine, oil, olives, raisins, lichens (for bread) and timber overseas (particularly to Egypt), but they were certainly also able to find eager markets for the more profitable manufactured goods. The fine craftsmen whose workshops were allowed so much space in Minoan palaces certainly contributed to the cargoes of the merchantmen as well as to the luxury of the court. The discovery in a temple at Tod in Upper Egypt of over 150 silver and gold cups, some at least of which seem to have been Cretan made, provides evidence for the probable extent of this luxury trade. They were found in chests inscribed with the name of a Pharaoh reigning in 1900 B.C. The exquisite ceramics (plate 12) made by Minoan potters during the following centuries were also acquired by the Egyptians as well as by Anatolians, Cypriotes and the dealers of Byblos and Ugarit.

As before, much of the Cretan intercourse with Egypt may have been through Ugarit and the other great ports of the Levantine coast. Egyptian influence was now very strong in Syria. Yet in the late sixteenth century B.C. embassies of Cretans were being received by Pharaoh at the Theban capital. Their visits were vividly recorded by Egyptian artists in the tombs of viziers and other great personages of state. The Cretans are portrayed in their customary dress of a loin cloth held by a tight and massive belt, and they are carrying all kinds of sumptuous articles to be presented to Pharaoh. In the earliest of these embassies, which oddly enough dates from the time when Pharaoh was a woman, the famous Hatshepsut, herself a promoter of foreign trade and travel, the islanders are bearing handled flagons and big jars as well as graceful drinking cups. It seems that on this occasion the Cretans were bringing Pharaoh wine and the vessels for serving it in a manner fit for princely palates. In paintings made up to a century later the range of offerings is greater. One man has an ornate vase in one hand and swings a long necklace from the other; one holds a flagon while he balances a huge copper ingot on his shoulder; another also humps an ingot and holds a conical rhyton in his right hand; one has a long dagger carried at the slope with an amphora perched on his shoulder; several bear shallow bowls apparently set with flowers, and have conical vases swung from the crooks of their elbows. In some paintings, too, textiles are being offered. These articles have been so exactly represented by the Egyptian artists that most of them can be identified with their native originals dug out from the ruins of the Cretan palaces or (like the conical rhyton) shown by the Cretan fresco painters on their own palace walls (p. 109).

It is hard to believe that laden embassies of this kind would have reached the Nile by the roundabout Levantine route rather than allowing a north wind to carry them directly to the Delta. As for the nature of their missions, the Egyptians may have called them tribute bearers, but the Cretans themselves, while recognizing the extraordinary power and holiness of Pharaoh, would surely have regarded themselves as the bringers of gifts from one sovereign to another. They may even have been given gold in return. This exchange of gifts between the royal houses of the ancient world was so great and frequent a ceremony that it can be regarded as approaching a form of trade. That it has continued, though on a diminishing scale, ever since, can be appreciated by anyone who has visited surviving royal palaces in Europe or Asia.

Certainly this sudden vision granted through the eyes of the Egyptian painters of Cretans walking through Thebes in their island dress, long locks flowing, seeing the sights, making acquaintances at the court, and prepared to leave behind them quantities of the finest products of their native craftsmen, makes real the intercourse between island people and river people. One can see how much more considerable it was than anything suggested by the scatter of Cretan pots and sherds found in Egyptian soil or even by the treasure of Tod.

It is true that these paintings record events of the sixteenth to fifteenth century B.C., but it is very likely indeed that embassies of a kind went to Thebes much earlier – as soon as Minoan civilization was flourishing and the Pharaohs of the Middle Kingdom firmly in control of Egypt. The sudden fashion for spiral patterns among Egyptian architects, interior decorators, potters and other craftsmen of the XII Dynasty may have been inspired by their admiration for Cretan design. Then again some knowledge of the Aegean and its peoples among cultivated Egyptians is evident in the Tale of Sinuhe, written as early as 1900 B.C. This lively piece of fiction mentions the Islands of the Sea as it follows the adventures of its exiled hero. On their side the Cretans learnt from the Egyptians the idea of making simple records in pictographs and then in hieroglyphic signs, some of which were imitated from the Egyptian script (p. 67).

Of the more substantial returns that must have flowed back into Crete, pitifully little remains. There are scarabs and other seals, a few jars, and a broken statuette remarkable only because it was found at the heart of the Minoan world – in the central court of the palace of Knossos.

Yet taking all the centuries of Minoan intercourse with Egypt as a whole, there is plenty to show how it was that the gifted islanders were able to absorb many things from the older, grander civilization of the Nile. Blending them with their other borrowings from the Levant, and through the Levant from Mesopotamia, they created the first European civilization through the sheer, idiosyncratic force of their native genius.

Another difference in trading conditions that came to the Cretans with their advance in civilized power was the foundation of overseas colonies. With an expanding population, there were plenty of ambitious and adventurous merchants and craftsmen prepared to settle abroad where commercial opportunities were good.

The Aegean in time became very much Minoanized. Most important, because it was a step on the way to the Levant, was the settlement on Rhodes. There were others on Samos and at Miletus – the city which a millennium later was to lead the way in the Greek intellectual revolution.

As for their one-time rivals in the Cyclades, the Cretans came to dominate them

culturally as well as to capture their commercial ascendancy in the Aegean. There
was a Minoan settlement on Thera, and by the sixteenth century B.C. there seems
to have been a large Minoan residential quarter in the walled city of Phylakopi on
Melos. The religious life of this community was identical with that of Crete, and
the artists worked in the pure Minoan idiom. Other islands where Cretans settled
were Kea and Kythera.

There is no certainty of any Cretan colonization of the Greek mainland. The
Achaean invaders, living like uncouth barons in their fortified citadels, for centuries
were hardly interested in the refinements of civilization that were being enjoyed in
the island beyond their southern horizons. As in Crete itself in earlier days, certain
ports had acquired some rudiments of civilized life, and here Cretan traders did a
little business. Then in the Minoan heyday of the sixteenth century the sudden
change began. A still semi-barbarous but strong and wealthy dynasty came to
power in Mycenae (p. 164), and doubtless also in other parts of the Peloponnese
and Boeotia. The civilized elements that they absorbed into their own rough tribal
culture were almost wholly Minoan. Historians no longer believe, as once they did,
that a dynasty from Crete seized power in mainland Greece and was ruling there
when Minoan culture was imposed on the Achaeans. Nevertheless it is incredible
that the artistic and religious life should have been so strongly shaped and coloured
by Minoan tradition if some Cretans had not settled on the mainland under
Mycenaean patronage. Artists and craftsmen probably went there as well as
merchants, proving themselves very ready to execute in their own exquisite style
the subjects – of war and the chase – still dear to their more virile patrons.

In the Levant, Cretan merchant adventurers were active and influential in Cyprus,
but are not known to have settled there in substantial numbers. At the great Syrian
port of Ugarit, already trading with Crete early in the second millennium, they
may have founded a permanent colony. Certainly Ugarit afforded the most vital
meeting-point between the peoples of the Orient, of Egypt and of the developing
lands of the Mediterranean. There the ships from the Nile, hugging the coast as they
came northward, met the ships from the Aegean and from Cyprus; and there these
seafarers could traffic with the landsmen who knew the caravan routes up through
Alalakh into the Cilician plain of Anatolia, south to the Orontes valley and
Canaanite lands, and eastward to Mari and the whole rich, various and changeable
medley of peoples living and contending by the Euphrates and the Tigris.

The Cretans had their place in this sophisticated society with its mixed cosmopolitan culture. While they learnt much there, taking over and adapting artistic
motifs, the planning and decoration of palaces, and perhaps ways of accounting
and other commercial skills, they also contributed to the cultural melting-pot.
The influence of their artistic style, especially in the decoration of ceramics, made

itself widely felt. Records in the palace at Mari on the Euphrates suggest (though there is a doubt) that Cretan textiles, weapons and vases were sent on from there even to Babylon.

It is revealing to compare the Levant with Crete itself. The citizens of Ugarit and of other Syrian cities and the Phoenicians after them were like the Cretans in living at a meeting-point of foreign cultures and in borrowing freely from them. But the results were quite dissimilar. The Levantines were utterly exposed. Foreigners of all kinds settled in their cities. They had to adapt themselves to the great movements of warfare, power politics and cultural domination that swept over them. They became as smooth and worldly-wise, as polyglot and cosmopolite, as the people of present-day Beirut. But for these same reasons they were unable to digest the foreign forms and create something of their own. Their culture remained a magpie one, although the imitative styles they employed to please their customers were often charming and skilful.

The Cretans on the other hand, secure within the stony outline of their island, were able to transmute their borrowings into a native culture that was not only wonderfully distinctive, but vigorous enough to dominate the creative·lives of the Achaeans.

The existence of colonies overseas and the network of their trade must have enhanced the dignity and deepened the understanding of the Cretan people as well as adding to their material wealth. Yet claims for the island as the centre of an imperial thalassocracy can easily be set too high. It is unlikely that there was any administrative cohesion between the Cretan palaces and the overseas settlements. Nor would there have been a navy in the sense that there was to be a Greek navy in the fifth century – or even in the days of the Mycenaean kings.

Merchant ships (with their strong keels projecting below the sternboard and running up to a lofty fish- or bird-headed prow) were designed primarily for ready beaching. But some were large – probably over sixty feet in length and with fifteen oars a side. Such ships carrying fighting men in place of cargoes could have made a formidable marine, and the knowledge that the Cretan rulers could put such a force to sea may have helped to deter pirates or more dangerous aggressors. But it was the wide sea itself that did most to secure the Cretans in their peaceful life, enabling them to live in undefended towns and country houses even at the sea's edge.

Later Greek historians recorded a tradition that Minos of Knossos was the first Cretan king to possess a navy and win command of the Aegean. Thucydides says that he cleared the sea of pirates in order to increase his revenues, and that he colonized the Cyclades and appointed his sons to rule over them.

Minos, the son of Zeus and Europa, patron of Daedalus and stepfather of the

monstrous Minotaur, would seem to reign well on the mythical side of the continuous narrative that passes from myth into history. Yet there undoubtedly were
historical elements in his story. Moreover, he was said to have ruled only three
generations before the Trojan war – and Idomeneus, king of Crete who in Homer
followed Agamemnon to Troy, can be seen, however dimly, to belong to history.

In turning from these Greek traditions, shaped from cloudy memories and
imaginings, to discover what historical events can be deduced from the material
remains of the Cretan past, one is struck by a tremendous contrast. Countless
discoveries of buildings, works of art and personal possessions of all kinds have
made the life of Bronze Age Crete appear most intimately real. Yet the evidence
for historical events during those centuries is tenuous and as easily broken as a
cobweb. Archaeology catches so much of general life, so little of particular events.

What is known mainly concerns two aspects of Cretan history which are very
different and yet not unconnected. One is the occurrence of volcanic eruptions and
earthquakes, the other the relationship between the Cretans and the mainland
Achaeans.

The island has been pictured as a demi-paradise – and so indeed it is. But its
paradisiacal bliss is very frequently disturbed by earthquakes. It is not surprising
that the god Poseidon in his guise as Earth-shaker was greatly venerated among
the Achaeans (p. 234). Probably he had some Cretan counterpart. The findings at
Knossos, Phaistos and many other places suggest that a violent quake occurred in
about 1700 B.C., leaving palaces and cities in ruins.

This date can be accepted as marking the end of the age of the Old Palaces, but
Minoan civilization was still resilient and its rural economy unimpaired. Palaces
and cities were rebuilt more handsomely than before. At Knossos a large new
residential wing was added on the east side of the central court, and the reconstructed
palace at Phaistos was on a magnificent scale. Some new towns, such as Gournia and
then Kato Zakro, were founded, and many of the great mansions were built at this
time.

In about 1570, at the height of Cretan prosperity and influence, another quake
struck the Knossos area. A wall of the palace fell outward, crushing houses that
stood below it. One of these was not rebuilt. Instead two bulls' heads with wide-
spreading horns, together with bronze tripod altars, were carefully sealed inside it
– a placatory offering, it seems, to the angry Earth-shaker.

Once again the Cretans rebuilt what the gods had destroyed. Knossos was
certainly by this time the chief city of the island, with its ruling family exercising
a hegemony among the rest. The palace at Phaistos, indeed, seems to have been
only gradually or partially reconstructed, but meanwhile another very fine royal
residence was built a few miles to the west, quite close to the sea. This sumptuously

decorated place, now known as Hagia Triada, may have served either as an alternative residence for the Phaistos rulers or as their summer villa.

After the quake of 1570, the seismic history becomes both complicated and uncertain. Recent researches have convinced many scholars that a violent eruption of the volcano on the Cycladic isle of Thera did immense damage in Crete – which lies some seventy miles to the south. A tidal wave, it is said, destroyed towns, ports and palaces near the sea. Knossos and Phaistos, situated inland and on higher ground, were spared by the tidal wave but suffered heavily from earthquakes following the eruption. Among those who believe in the importance of the Thera disaster, some would date it towards the end of the sixteenth century, others as late as 1450.

Whichever the date, it has to be said that in spite of the widespread destruction, Knossos (as well as many lesser places) was restored and enjoyed a last period of high prosperity. It is a little difficult to believe that there could be such an immediate revival of wealth and elegant living after the island had suffered a severe economic blow – especially if it were accompanied by foreign conquest or annexation.

Ever since the discovery of the site, it has been very generally agreed that Knossos, and with it the flower of Minoan culture, came to a tragic end. At some time between about 1400 and 1350 the palace was burnt down, and, according to this view, never again knew anything like its former grace. People went back to live among its rooms and courts, but only in an impoverished, or even squalid, fashion.

While this interpretation of events has been accepted, the cause of the final destruction has been much disputed. Was it due to yet another earthquake with resulting fires, to internal revolution, or to sacking by mainland Achaeans?

This is the point to turn to that other aspect of the chronicle of events in Cretan history – the relationship between the islanders and their Achaean neighbours. But first something has to be said (because it is most relevant) of the written records that came into use at first in Crete and then on the mainland. The use of seals with ownership marks in the early days of the Bronze Age has already been mentioned. With the rise of palace civilization, Cretan traders and officials were dealing with peoples who had long practised writing, and they saw the need to imitate them. Preferring the Egyptian hieroglyphic type of script to the Asian cuneiform, they took over a number of Egyptian signs and devised many others of their own. At first these hieroglyphs were carved on seals, and the objects pictured – a walking man, a plough, an eye, and so forth – were realistically shown. As the business of the palaces increased, something more flexible was necessary, and scribes began to incise their records on clay bars and tablets. Not only did they simplify the signs so that they could write more quickly, but they achieved the essential change of using them to represent not things or ideas, but the sounds of syllables.

It seems that while these simplified hieroglyphs remained in use, the scribes also

Examples of the Minoan scripts: Linear A (*left*), on a tablet from Hagia Triada, and Linear B, on a tablet from Knossos.

began to write in a more completely schematized script – now known as Linear A. This script was sometimes written in ink – certainly on pottery, and probably also on paper made from papyrus reed or palm leaves.

Linear A was being used for the palace records at Knossos by the seventeenth century B.C., but it appears to have originated considerably earlier. It was employed extensively only in Crete, for the Achaean chiefs of the mainland had not as yet discovered the uses of literacy. It is one of the few ancient scripts that have still not been deciphered, but it is believed that the texts are in a native Cretan language.

Out of Linear A there was developed a later script: Linear B. Unlike A, which was known all over the island, B was limited to Knossos. But it was also used in the mainland citadels, where economic and social life had now advanced to the point at which written records had become necessary. Linear B tablets have been found at Mycenae itself, at Thebes and, in great numbers, at Pylos.

It is, indeed, with Linear B that questions arise concerning the political relationships between Cretans and Achaeans. When the tablets were first found at Knossos it was assumed that they were in the Cretan tongue; when they turned up on the mainland it was concluded that they represented a Cretan dominance. Then came a great event. The Linear B tablets were deciphered and proved to be written in an ancient form of Greek – the language, in fact, of the Achaean Greeks of Mycenaean times. This discovery confounded those who still believed that Knossos had remained an independent Cretan capital until its final destruction.

The old interpretations had to be modified. The Linear B tablets had always been said to date from the last half-century of palace civilization. It had also been recognized, even among those most devoted to Minoan supremacy, that Minoan art and ways of life were much affected by Mycenaean influence during those last decades. It showed in the greater formality, symmetry and loss of movement in figure painting and ceramic decoration, and in the introduction of various more warlike attributes. Now it was said that if the palace records were being kept in Greek it must mean that either by conquest or marriage an Achaean dynasty had come to power in Knossos during the fifteenth century B.C. The Knossian scribes had adapted their old A script for the writing of Greek, and the resulting B script had spread back to the mainland. Adherents of the volcanic eruption theory suggest that it was this cataclysm that offered the opportunity for the Achaean take-over.

Some version of this story is now widely accepted. But there is one great objection to it. The Linear B tablets from Pylos (p. 209) are very nearly identical with those from Knossos in writing, and similar in content, yet are known to have been inscribed as late as 1200 B.C. At a time of disturbance and rapid cultural change, it seems unlikely that as much as two hundred years could separate them.

An entirely new interpretation has therefore been proposed, and has led to one of the hottest academic disputes of the century. It is being said that the Linear B tablets at Knossos were not written before a destruction of 1400 or a little later, but after a destruction in about 1300; that the Minoan capital had (as was originally thought) remained under its own royal house until that date – when it fell before an Achaean attack. Then, instead of being abandoned as had been said, the Kephala was occupied by a Mycenaean palace and by Achaean rulers who successfully controlled the whole island. Their scribes, naturally enough, wrote in Achaean Greek – using the Linear B script. It follows that "Minos" and then Idomeneus belonged to this Achaean house, which flourished until Knossos was conquered by the Dorians (p. 251) a little later than the same fate overtook Pylos and the other Mycenaean citadels of the mainland.

It is an economical theory, fitting in very well with what is known of the rise and fall of Mycenaean power, and with the Homeric tradition of Idomeneus and the powerful force he led to Troy. But those who know most about Minoan culture say that there are formidable archaeological difficulties in so late a date for the last palace of Knossos.

Perhaps from the point of view of this book it does not matter so very much whether the Achaeans took over Crete in the fifteenth century and abandoned it about 1400, or whether they seized it in 1300 and prospered there until the coming of the Dorians. So much of Mycenaean culture had in any case already been borrowed from the Minoan that it is often difficult to disentangle them. In the next chapter the feminine spirit of Minoan life – its art and religion – will as far as possible be distinguished from the later intrusions of the masculine Achaean spirit – however and whenever this made itself felt.

Plate 6. Fine craftsmanship. A ritual sprinkler in rock crystal, from Kato Zakro, c. 1500 B.C.

Chapter Three

The Grace of Life

A learned German professor confessed that he found in Cretan civilization "the enchantment of a fairy world". This was in the hard days after the First World War. Since then half a dozen equally eminent fellow-countrymen have said that they shared in his enchantment – no doubt all good, sober scholars. Although perhaps only Germans would have expressed their feelings in terms of fairyland, very many scholars have been carried away by the Minoan genius. Sir Leonard Woolley has described its art as "the most inspired of the ancient world". So unenthusiastic a writer as Arnold Hauser has been driven to the use of exclamation marks. Quite against his own convictions he has admitted that the Cretans shared in the "aristocratic social order" of the Bronze Age Orient – "and yet what a difference in the whole conception of art! What freedom in artistic life in contrast to the oppressive conventionalism in the rest of the Ancient-Oriental world!" Mrs Groenewegen Frankfort, normally a minutely analytical art historian, has written of Minoan Crete: "Here and here alone the human bid for timelessness was disregarded in the most complete acceptance of the grace of life the world has ever known."

These testimonies are sufficient proof of an extraordinary quality in Minoan civilization. Through earthquake and pillage, fire and the passage of millennia, and even through the zealous work of the restorers, enough of its creations have survived to convey to us something that can only have come from the quality of the experience of the people who made them.

All civilizations have, of course, been unique; each has grown into its distinctive "form", and its products are unlike all others. Yet, as Arnold Hauser insisted, Minoan culture is exceptional in the essential difference of its spirit from that of its contemporaries. The few thousand gifted men and women of Crete who inspired it seem to have had a way of experiencing life and judging its values quite unlike that of any other Bronze Age people – including those from whom they learnt and those whom they taught.

This is even more striking in the values which they evidently did *not* accept than in those which they glorified. There is first the magnification of the divinely powerful man and the expression of this in grandiose architectural and artistic forms. In Mesopotamia first the Sumerians and then their cultural heirs the Babylonians

Plate 7. A priestess serves at the altar. Detail of a fresco on the Hagia Triada sarcophagus (p. 144), 14th century B.C.

liked to show heavy, static figures of kings and governors praying to or con-
fronting the gods whose stewards on earth they were. When the gods were
represented, as for example on the stele where Hammurabi offers his code of laws
to Shamash, they appear as just the same stolidly majestic human beings as the
kings themselves. Such monuments found their appropriate place in cities dominated by colossal temples and by the massive, temple-crowned ziggurats.

In Egypt, especially in the New Kingdom times that were contemporary with
the liveliest period of Cretan civilization, Pharaoh is everywhere, huge, usually
impersonal and with the curious deadened movement – as though a posture had
been held until all the muscle petrified – so characteristic of Egyptian art. A god
himself, Pharaoh stands or sits among his fellow divinities attended by human
manikins who beside him are as dwarfs. Gigantic statues of Pharaoh, carved in
limestone, or better still granite, and weighing scores or even hundreds of tons, were
dragged over great distances to be set up in rows along temple façades or to form
the towering columns of their aisles. In the XVIII Dynasty, Amenophis III instituted
a statue cult with enormous figures that were worshipped as his "living image".
The building of temples that dwarfed houses, and even palaces, by as much as the
royal statues dwarfed those of ordinary men, was among the principal preoccupa-
tions of the Pharaohs.

The Cretans had absolutely no counterpart to these grandiose images of the
royal and the divine or of the monumental temples that went with them. There
were small shrines in the palaces, usually it seems with no kind of permanent images
but only such symbols as the horns, the pillar or the bird to express the presence of
divinity. The principal places of worship were out in the natural wilds in caves and
on mountain-tops.

In the secular aspect of their lives, the two activities considered most fitting for
the kings of Mesopotamia and Egypt were warfare and the chase. These were the
manly sports, the proof of royal power and virility. On the famous "standard of
Ur" of the early third millennium Sumerian chariots drawn by wild asses are
trampling the enemy underfoot, while above two prisoners are being despatched by
spearmen and a line of wretched-looking captives is being paraded up to the king.
About five hundred years later King Naram Sin appears on a stone stele as a giant
figure standing over a fallen enemy while another begs for mercy. This, unlike the
standard, commemorates a particular historical battle. The theme of the triumphant
royal warlord continues until it reaches its climax under the last inheritors of the
tradition – the Assyrians. In their palaces the monarchs of one of the most martial
and masculine peoples the world has known lived among scenes of battle and siege,
of men done to death and prisoners in bondage.

Hunting scenes, presumably never precisely historical, go side by side with those of war. Of all beasts, the king of men should hunt the lion. Here again the climax comes late, with the Assyrians, in the beautiful, ferocious lion hunt of Assurbanipal.

Among the Egyptians, in spite of their more peaceful life beside the Nile, exactly the same themes were glorified. On the carved ivory handle of a flint knife dating back to the end of the Stone Age, already there is a hunting scene on one side and on the other men fighting one another both on land and on water. On a slate palette carved in the very earliest days of the unified kingdom the idea of the warrior monarch triumphing in the humiliation and slaughter of the enemy is shown in all its assured brutality. On one side the Egyptian king stands over a captive gripping a tuft of his hair and preparing to crush his skull with a mace. On the other side one scene shows the king in the shape of a bull smashing a city with his horns and trampling an enemy, and another shows him marching with his standard-bearers towards a line of corpses, all with their severed heads lying between their legs.

These subjects are repeated through the centuries – only heightened in the New Kingdom by the introduction of the war chariot. Now Pharaoh appears, even more gigantic than before, standing in his chariot with drawn bow while his feather-crested horses gallop over the scrambled mass of enemy bodies. Some temple walls now show huge piles of severed hands, as proof of the triumph of the royal campaigns. Bound prisoners appear as architectural friezes, crouched under thrones, bent round the handles of walking sticks – wherever their helpless degradation can be made apparent. In one tomb in the Valley of the Kings, Pharaoh's sarcophagus confronts a long line of kneeling figures, their necks ending in bloody stumps.

The royal hunts also continue, and in Egypt, too, it is the lion that is accepted as the fitting prey. On a casket of Tutankhamen, the boy-king is galloping his horses against no fewer than eight lions, several of which have already fallen, bristling with royal arrows.

The ideal of the sovereign triumphing in war and the chase was not confined to the Bronze Age Orient. It appears again in no less brutal forms in the New World. Among the Maya and other civilized peoples of Central America once again divine rulers appear in scenes of execution; carvings of bound prisoners, prostrate and writhing, were often set below every step of great ceremonial stairs – where the royal foot would tread upon them.

It would seem, then, that in the first growths of civilization where both economic forces and the human imagination created royal theocracies, it was almost inevitable that the kings would show their godlike power in triumph over foreign enemies, and their godlike strength in killing wild beasts. Yet in Crete, where hallowed rulers commanded wealth and power and lived in splendid palaces, there was hardly a trace of these manifestations of masculine pride and unthinking cruelty. There are no great statues or reliefs of those who sat on the thrones of Knossos or of any of the palaces. Indeed, so far as can be seen, there are no royal portrayals of any kind until the latest phase – and then the sole possible exception, the painted relief sometimes identified as the Young Prince, shows a long-haired youth, unarmed, naked to the waist, crowned with peacock plumes and walking among flowers and butterflies. Nor are there in Minoan Crete any grandiose scenes of battle or of hunting.

The absence of these manifestations of the all-powerful male ruler that are so widespread at this time and in this stage of cultural development as to be almost universal, is one of the reasons for supposing that the occupants of Minoan thrones may have been queens.

Other arguments and intuitions in favour of this rash supposition (hazardous because it is quite likely that evidence will be found to disprove it) emerge from the general quality and inspiration of Minoan life in so far as these can be understood from their expression in art and in religious symbolism and rituals. In trying to

A peaceful prince. Copy of a painted plaster relief, palace of Knossos, south side.

evoke this life, and something at least of the psychic depths from which it grew, it is best to start with its most matter-of-fact aspects, the architectural style and design of the palaces in which Minoan civilization was born and bred. From there an advance can be made on the more difficult ground of art and religion.

First it can again be emphasized that in the Cretan city it was the palace that stood supreme, usually covering the top of a rise with the hierarchy of lesser dwellings below it. In Egypt Pharaoh's residence was of little architectural importance beside the colossal royal temples and tombs. In Mesopotamia and the Levant, although the residential palaces were relatively of greater dignity, they were very much dominated by ziggurat and temples.

There seems no doubt that the Cretans took their original inspiration for palace building from Asia. It even appears that the Old Palaces were, for this reason, somewhat more monumental in style than the later reconstructions, when Cretan fantasy and sense of movement created architectural forms of striking originality.

For this later style, the palace of Knossos of course provides the finest example – also the most complete – although at the present time of fundamental historical disagreements the difficulty of identifying the various reconstructions after the destruction of the Old Palace is very great. However, it appears that the main design of the buildings was maintained even when they were rebuilt, so that a general description need not be misleading.

It has already been said that the palace of Knossos (like other Minoan palaces) was strongly inturned upon its central court. This was as true of its ritual intention as of its architectural plan. The whole existence of the establishment must have revolved round the royal family, and the life of the royal family was divided between the east and west wings of that court. On the west were the ritual and state apartments, and on the east, where the old mound had been cut away above the Kairatos ravine, were the more private and secular apartments.

Anyone with the credentials to be admitted through the main northern gate of the palace would have found the most sacred of all the ritual rooms immediately on his right. Entered through an antechamber, this Throne Room is relatively small, low and dimly lit. It seems to have been designed for a single royal celebrant, and not for a king and queen. One throne alone, carved in gypsum to imitate some more ancient wooden chair, stands between a pair of couchant griffins painted in brilliant colours on the wall. These stiffly elegant creatures, with feathers curled like a duck's tail down the backs of their necks, thrust up their beaks to within a short distance of the top of the throne. The occupant of the throne would therefore have appeared as a figure between two confronted beasts – a ritualistic motif originating in the Orient and often reproduced in Minoan and Mycenaean art. If the royal head were crowned with falling plumes or any other ornate head-dress

The throne of a queen–priestess? The Throne Room at the palace of Knossos.

it would have made a finely contrasting apex above the rising necks and pointed heads of the griffin supporters.

When enthroned, the royal celebrant faced across the room to a stone-lined chamber sunk below ground level and approached down a few steps. This was probably the scene of anointings and other purificatory rites. The descent into the ground suggests an approach to the goddess in her aspect as Earth Mother. There was a modest shrine and other small rooms beyond the Throne Room proper, and it is possible that priests or priestesses maintained a perpetual vigil.

In the great megaron hall of Mycenaean Pylos (p. 209) there were griffins associated with the throne, and it is certain that, whenever they were painted, the Knossian beasts were the product of Mycenaean influence. Yet there could hardly be a stronger contrast in atmosphere, and surely in psychological implications, than between this small, dark room with its earth-fast chamber, and the Pylos megaron with its huge central hearth and general feeling of an Homeric (or northern) banqueting hall.

Immediately next to the Throne Room a wide flight of steps with central columns (of the Minoan shape, tapering towards the bottom) led up to the spacious state apartments on the first floor. These covered a much greater area than the cult rooms below because they extended right over the great block of long, narrow storage magazines behind the west front of the palace. These state apartments could also be reached by a roundabout passage decorated from end to end with two zones of processional figures – young men and girls bearing offerings. It seems very likely, therefore, that these upper suites were sometimes used for the reception of tribute from the Knossian realm. Goods presented could readily be sent down for storage in the magazines below. The rooms themselves were bright with frescoes, and with their coloured columns and probably with balconies opening on both the central and west courts, they would have made a brilliant setting for ceremony.

To the south of the stairs another cult building gave on to the central court. This was a triple shrine, with the central section standing higher than the wings – like a section through the nave and aisles of a church. Two sacred columns stood in the side chambers, and a fifth in the middle. To judge from the model represented by tiny gold plaques from the Shaft Graves at Mycenae, there would have been pairs of horns of consecration in front of the columns and also on the roofs. The shrine, even in its central section, may have been considerably lower than the rest of the façade, and its small scale would have contrasted with the ambitious staircase that rose beside it. Variety, the breaking up of wall surfaces and the avoidance of any approach to symmetrical formality were characteristic of Minoan architecture and seem appropriate to the whole spirit of the culture that produced it.

Sunk below ground level not far from the shrine were two large stone cists that probably held the treasures and cult figures belonging to the shrine itself. One of them contained the two faience snake goddesses, together with a small, equal-armed marble cross, artificial sea shells and ritual vessels. It can be imagined that for special festivals of the Household Goddess, these intensely vital little figures would have been set up on shelves within the triple shrine.

Not far behind the shrine were two darkish crypts, their roofs supported by square pillars. Even these functional pillars were evidently charged with divinity, for runnels and cavities were cut at their base to receive libations. Women may have descended to raise their hands in prayer before them – as is shown on a vase painting.

This west side of the central court of the palace of Knossos can be seen as forming the very heart of the sacred power of the Cretans. In the throne, the lustral basin, the sacred columns and pillars, the double axes and horns of consecration, the Great Goddess was present in many manifestations. And here she was served by the supreme rulers of the Minoan world.

When the rituals of the throne room were over, the royal celebrants and their followers must often have left the dim sanctuary, stepped into the dazzling light of the court, passed by the shrine – perhaps pausing to pay some observance there – and crossed to the private apartments at the southern end of the east wing. This building was the most brilliantly original piece of domestic architecture of its time.

The principal access was itself a masterpiece – a grand stone staircase, two flights to each floor, supported on massive, tapered columns of painted wood, rising round an open court which served it as a light-well. This unique stair, one of the bold inventions of the Minoan architects, served four or even five stories – one on the level of the court, two below, and either one or two above. Those below court level had been built into a terrace cut into the side of the ancient mound, and this device must have served to protect them from the extremes of midday heat. At each floor the stairway gave access to a hall and further rooms extending eastward – on many different levels and all ingeniously lit by windows opening on to light-wells, and ending with colonnaded verandahs looking out over gardens to the Kairatos ravine.

The finest of these halls, on the floor below court level, was in effect a splendid reception suite, each part opening to the next by sets of three or four doors which could be kept closed for small gatherings, opened for great ones. A wooden throne stood in this suite, and it seems certain that it must have been the scene of many of the gayest, most brilliant hours of Minoan courtly life.

In contrast, the royal living quarters were of modest size, convenient and private. Tucked away on the same floor as the reception hall was a set of rooms that may have belonged to the Queen. A moderate-sized room that was once charmingly decorated with a fresco of swimming dolphins, fish and sea urchins, and later by a frieze of dancing girls, could have served as her bedroom and boudoir. Adjacent to it were a bathroom, a strong closet or treasury for valuables, and a room that seems to have had running water and a flushing lavatory with a wooden seat of a kind which has since become universally familiar, but must then have been a minor wonder of the world. It was, indeed, one of the marvels of the palace of Knossos that it was supplied with running water, and had an excellently-planned drainage system both for rainwater and for sewage.

It appears that a second suite of similar plan and presumed to have been the king's (or should one say the consort's?) lay above the queen's apartments and was connected with them by a small private staircase. These arrangements heighten the already strong impression that in its later phases the palace of Knossos had a residential style, a domestic civility and convenience that seems already to anticipate European palaces of the Renaissance and after, rather than imitating its contemporaries in Egypt and the Orient.

The fact that the workshops of the potters, gem-cutters and others faced on to the central court and were only separated from the royal quarters by a passageway, suggests that artists and craftsmen held an honourable place in the palace community. Indeed, it seems almost inevitable that the royal family as well as courtiers must often have visited the workshops and studios of these talented subjects.

Plate 8. A mixed audience at Knossos. Fresco. After 1600 B.C.

Overleaf Plate 9. Youths and girls bull-leaping. Fresco at Knossos, after 1600 B.C.

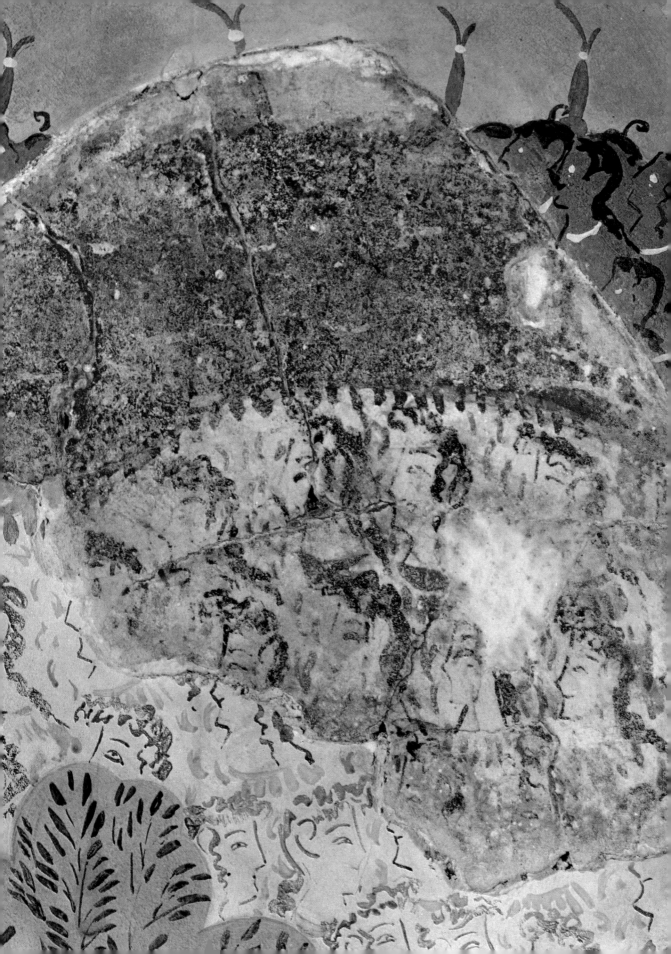

One of the most evocative of all the features of the palace of Knossos lies just outside the north-west corner of the building. In the Old Palace it had been a long narrow paved court, but in the later reconstructions the designers built two banks of very shallow steps – or narrow platforms – meeting one another at right-angles. These banks form two sides of a paved area measuring about thirty-three by forty-eight feet; at the outer angle of their junction there is a large rectangular stone plinth (p. 86).

This stepped area (which can properly as well as conveniently be called a theatre) cannot be understood in isolation, for it formed the terminus of a carefully made-up and paved road leading some two hundred yards to a building known as the Little Palace. This is a mansion of accomplished architectural grace. It has an entrance hall leading up flights of stairs through a hall with a central peristyle court into a large reception room at the end. This building has all the appearance of a palatial establishment designed for courtly functions, but some parts of it were dedicated to ritual use. It had a series of pillar crypts comparable to those at the main palace, and it was beside one of these that the magnificent bull-head libation pourer (p. 88) was found.

The picture which the imagination irresistibly presents is of processions passing along the road, justifiably known as the Sacred Way, perhaps sometimes down-hill to the Little Palace, but more often up to the theatre. The palatial, semi-secular atmosphere of the Little Palace seems to lend colour to the idea (p. 121) that although religious meanings and purposes certainly underlay the royal and courtly life of the palaces, this had become lightened to produce a unique blend of religion, serious play and social entertainment. If, as is in itself very likely, the royal family were sometimes borne by palanquin along the Sacred Way, the procession may have been only slightly more sacred in purport to the watching citizens than the procession of the Queen of England when she drives in a gilded coach to open Parliament.

What, then, took place in the stepped area? It has always been recognized as having some "theatrical" purpose, usually connected with "cult performances" and sometimes, temptingly, identified with the famous dancing place which, as Homer tells, Daedalus built for Ariadne.

From the analogy of theatres and stadia of Classical times, it has been assumed that the steps were intended to hold an audience – indeed, they are often referred to as seats. Yet they are of quite different proportions from the high steps that form the seating in the later buildings, and would have been extraordinarily inconvenient to sit upon – although they could have served a standing audience. Is it not quite conceivable that they were designed not for viewers, but for participants in per-formances that were still ritualistic, but in which choreographic and dramatic movements had come to play an important part? The use of shallow platforms to

Plate 10. "An eye as big as a hen's egg". The "Parisienne" fresco, Knossos, after 1600 B.C.

secure a range of heights in the grouping and movement of figures is, of course, a commonplace of the modern stage.

If part of the performance took place on the two banks of steps, then the plinth at their junction might have been intended for musicians, or for individuals reciting words to accompany the movements. Or it could have been occupied by royal performers who might well have played a central but static role.

Two facts add some slight support to this explanation. One is that at Knossos anyone on the steps and the plinth would have had direct access to the Throne Room quarter through a private entrance. The other is that at Phaistos, where a comparable theatre was furnished with only one bank of steps, the paved crest of the Sacred Way continued up this bank as a distinct narrow flight with raised treads. This looks as though leading performers following the Sacred Way were expected to mount immediately and with formality on to the steps.

At Knossos one objection to this scheme is that it would seem to leave no space for an audience except on the paved court itself. There might have been a stilted stand to the north of the court. Or again it might be that an enactment taking place at the end of a procession need not have involved many others in addition to the participants.

The idea that this finely constructed theatre can be recognized as the famous dancing floor of Ariadne is certainly attractive. If memories of the importance of bulls in Minoan life, reinforced by surviving representations of bulls, inspired the legend of the Minotaur, then surely the legend of the dancing floor could have been inspired by memories of the Minoan passion for dancing reinforced by the survival of the theatre? Knowledge of the Sacred Way must have survived, for a new road was laid exactly above it in Roman times.

The immediate surroundings of the palace of Knossos are not without significance for any understanding of its life. Probably the inmates of the great eastern residential wing could walk out into a well-tended garden – and somewhere near the palace there was a dancing place with a line of fine old olive trees. There may have been another garden to the south of the palace. If so, it would have added to the pleasures not only of those entering by the south road and the long portico, but also coming in through the west court and the Corridor of the Procession. Any visitor entering by the west porch would have been greeted by bull-leaping frescoes, and then have passed into a dimly lit length of the Corridor with its figured friezes. On turning to the left along the south side of the palace, he would emerge suddenly into brilliant light on a kind of verandah, perhaps with the south garden just below him. From here there was a lovely view of the valley and the conical summit of Mount Juktas. This small but shapely mountain must itself have been a feature of the iconography of the palace. It was the traditional burial place of the Cretan

A fine setting for ceremonies: the stepped area at the end of the Sacred Way, palace of Knossos.

Sacred horns and sacred peak: southward view to Mount Juktas from the palace of Knossos.

Zeus, and on its western face supported a peak sanctuary that was probably of very ancient origin. At sunset Mount Juktas seems to draw nearer to Knossos, and glows with a serene radiance more than worthy of Zeus.

The deliberate creation of light and shade, of enclosure and sudden release, are characteristic of the lively movement of Minoan architecture. As for the gardens, many works of art reveal how much the Cretans loved flowers and a cultivated and formalized nature as well as the free and uncultivated. Indeed, the "Young Prince" or "Priest King" of the fresco walks among his lilies and butterflies not far from the Juktas verandah. Perhaps real lilies spired not far away, and real butterflies - living symbols of the soul - fluttered above them.

In this account of the palace of Knossos as the setting for Minoan courtly life, one omission is obvious. The feature of that life that left the deepest impression on posterity was its involvement with bulls - as we now know with the bull-leaping game. Was there a fixed place for this extraordinary manifestation of "serious play"? It seems that some kind of arena would have been needed for the manage-

A symbol of power. Rhyton in black steatite with rock crystal eye and wood-gilt horns. From the Little Palace, Knossos, 1550-1500 B.C.

ment of the beasts before and after the leaping, and to keep them from the audience. Both the central and west courts would appear unsuitable for various reasons – most of all because they were paved. To practise this game on a stone floor would enormously increase the hazards. On the whole it is most likely that the arena lay to the east on level ground near the ravine – where it was easily accessible from the residential wing of the palace and also from the town.

Many features of the design of the palace of Knossos, then, can be said to express a feminine spirit. It had domesticity, privacy, lightness of touch and domestic amenities. It was probably set among gardens and flower beds. Yet it must have been its interior decoration, and above all the frescoes that enlivened so many of its rooms and passages, that did most to determine its character. In both style and subject these tended to enhance the feminine quality implicit in the building.

One general characteristic must have been the contrast between the sober exterior, much of it built of limestone ashlar, and the bright, pale colours of the interior. To imagine it in the days of its perfection suggests a seashell (and the Cretans loved seashells) in which a horny outside conceals irridescent beauties within.

In turning from architecture to art, it is necessary to look back for a moment to the middle phase of the Bronze Age before the earthquake of 1700 B.C. Very little of the interior decoration of the Old Palaces has survived, but it is unlikely to have included scenes from life. Probably friezes of running spirals, rosettes and other formal patterns were freely used to give colour and emphasis. The decorators also liked to paint panels of imitation marble, an unpleasing convention that was to remain in favour all through Minoan times – and which, indeed, has always been popular in Mediterranean lands.

Animal art was left largely to the seal-cutters, whose skill was increasing. The plastic arts still hung fire. Such clay figurines as there are from this time are chiefly of interest as illustrations of the current fashions. Already these showed a startling contrast between the minimal dress of the men, who appear naked except for a penis sheath, and the voluminous clothing of the women in full bell skirts and bulky hats and head-dresses. In the latest of these figures, votives from the shrine of Piskokephalo, greater feeling has begun to be expressed. The woman praying, with her right arm laid between her breasts, has a graceful carriage and a pervasive tenderness. At this date the women evidently liked to wear their hair piled on the top of the head and held in place with a broad bandeau.

The only considerable artistic triumph of the age of the Old Palaces was in its ceramics. The study of pottery, so often a dry affair of archaeological interest only, here encounters a decorative art hardly bettered at any other time or place. This highly distinctive pottery seems to have been created by a vigorous school of

Fashions at the time of the Old Palaces: stark dress for men, and women's dress still unsophisticated.
Clay figures from the mountain sanctuary of Petsofa, 2000–1850 B.C.

potters working in the royal workshops of Knossos and Phaistos. The potter's wheel had come in with palace civilization, and its use, together with exceptionally careful preparation of the clay, made it possible to produce very thin walls and pure and elegant shapes.

The finest wine-cups and bowls were as thin as porcelain. The coating of glossy black paint, irridescent like a rook's feathers, characteristic of this pottery was probably intended to simulate bronze or more precious metals. Indeed the gold cups from Vaphio and a wavy-edged silver cup from a Cretan tomb certainly represent the forms from which the potters were working.

However, they secured a wholly ceramic effect in painting the dark surfaces with bright, pale colours – red, white and yellow being the commonest. The little egg-shell-ware cups were usually decorated in an appropriately refined and delicate

Fashions at the time of the Old Palaces. The bandeau. Clay. From the sanctuary of Piskokefalo, 1850–1700 B.C. The big hat. Clay. From a sanctuary, probably Kofinas, *c.* 1900 B.C.

Plate 11. Gold pendant from a grave near Hagia Triada (2.7 cms), *c.* 1500–1450 B.C.

style with combinations of rosettes, and daisy and other stylized flower patterns (p. 97). Occasionally they were given more dynamic spirals and whorls.

These dynamic patterns appear with their full whirling and explosive force on the larger vessels – fat, spouted jugs looking like gaping birds (plate 12), handsome jars, fruit or cake stands, and pedestalled bowls intended, like the Classical crater, for mixing wine. Particularly festive-looking are a huge crater with white ceramic blossoms projecting from stem and bowl and a chain to attach a wine ladle, and a fruit stand with a fringe of leaves round the rim and inside a really magnificent four-armed spiral design in which geometric designs exuberantly sprout leaves and tendrils (p. 98). Both these vessels come from the Old Palace of Phaistos, and the mere sight of them is enough to evoke the scene of a royal banquet. The picture is heightened by a fragment from another dish which shows a woman dancing with hands on hips and curls bobbing above her nose.

The Phaistos potters liked on occasion to include representations among their patterns – sometimes the shellfish and other marine creatures that were to swarm on the ceramics of the later palaces. They were also skilled at producing a kind of surface rustication which added richness of texture to the accomplished perfection of colour, decoration and form.

The extraordinary skill and sensibility of these potters arouses curiosity as to their sex. It is very likely that, as in most simple societies, Cretan women had been the potters in the days before the first palaces were built. But often it happened elsewhere that with the coming of civilization and with the adoption of the wheel, the old feminine craft was taken over by the men. Had this transfer already taken place in Crete before 1700 B.C.?

The type of ornamentation – mainly geometric and freely laid on over the whole surface of the pot – was certainly within the range of women potters. Decoration falling into a similar category is executed with great ability, for example, by the Pueblo Indian women of the South-west of the United States. This is hand-made village pottery – but it is notable that it has been kept in the women's hands even now when it is prized and can be seen for sale in the great cities.

In Crete the pretty eggshell cups and bowls are strongly feminine in taste. The large vessels may seem less so, but the Pueblo women used to turn out jars that were big and bold enough – and who shall say that women who played with bulls were lacking in boldness? A hand-over from one sex to the other would account for the very sharp difference there is between the pottery of the Old Palaces and that of later times. Altogether, it is a reasonable guess that in these early days of Minoan civilization it was still the women who turned the potter's wheel and laid on the slips and pigments – unless, of course, men and women collaborated in the craft as they did in playing bulls.

Plate 12. Masterly ceramic art of the Old Palaces. From Phaistos, 18th century B.C.

Beetles as votives. Perhaps the horn of *Rhinoceros oryctes* made it a sexual symbol; some were shown climbing on female figurines. From the peak sanctuary of Piskokefalo, 1850–1700 B.C.

"Pretty eggshell cups . . . strongly feminine in taste". From Knossos, 18th century B.C.

Handsome painted pottery of the Old Palaces; from Phaistos, 18th century B.C.

Fit for a palace banquet. Fruit stand (?) in painted clay. From Phaistos, 18th century B.C. Diameter 54 cms.

Egyptian influence and the beginning of naturalism. From the palace of Knossos, c. 1700 B.C. Height 57 cms.

Although wine cups and mixing bowls, great stands for piling fruit or sweet-meats, can go far in suggesting the good life of the first palaces, while their beauty is proof of the extraordinary artistic talent of the Cretans, it is not until the time of the later palaces, and particularly for the period from about 1550 B.C., that the work of the Minoan artists suddenly opens the door on to the Minoan world. Kings and queens, priests and viziers, may live and die in honour and glory, but always it is the artist whose power is of the kind to endure.

Artists working in many different media contributed to this particular Bronze Age miracle: sculptors in ivory, stone and bronze; seal-cutters, workers in faience, goldsmiths and vase painters – all these people have left works of art that also reveal much about the feelings and doings of the Cretans and about the spirit of Minoan life. Yet more than any other artists it was the fresco painters who saved a brilliant but transient moment of history from oblivion. They employed the true fresco technique of painting on to wet plaster.

Lifelike wild goat in bronze. Votive from the sanctuary at Hagia Triada, 16th century B.C.

Minoan influence in the Aegean: flying fish in blue. Fresco from a house in Phylakopi, Melos, 16th century B.C.

The dating of wall paintings is always difficult, for they may be new or already centuries old when a building is destroyed; and they may hang on to ruined walls and fall into later deposits to the confusion of the archaeologist. Moreover, in the case of Knossos there is the doubt as to whether the last phase of the palace and many of its paintings belonged essentially to the later Mycenaean world or whether it was a Cretan palace briefly and peacefully taken over by a Mycenaean dynasty in the fifteenth century B.C.

It seems best first to look at those works of art which, whatever their exact age, are in style and spirit most purely Minoan. Most of these works do in fact belong, either certainly or very probably, to the earlier rather than to the later period of the palaces and mansions restored or built after the earthquake of 1700 B.C.

The unique quality in this art was its feeling for nature. Nothing at all like it had ever before been created by man – for he had never been able to look at nature in that way. It is true that some ten thousand years earlier the Palaeolithic hunters had made wonderful animal studies. But in these each animal was seen in isolation and with an intensity of feeling that went with the hunters' desire to possess and to kill. The Sumerians and Babylonians had made little use of nature in their art, and where they did it was entirely subservient to the great Bronze Age god-man symbiosis. The Egyptians often made accurate portrayals of plants and trees, birds and fish, and animals both wild and domestic. But they, too, were seen as part of

 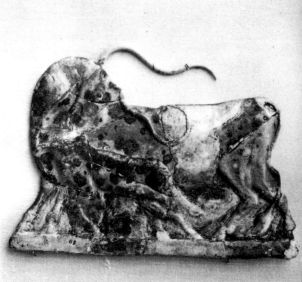

The goddess as animal mother: "the goat wild and watchful, the cow domestic and tender". Faience. From the palace of Knossos, *c.* 1600 B.C.

the furniture of human and divine life, to be cultivated, milked, sacrificed, netted, hunted or deified. Moreover, with few exceptions they were seen both prosaically and statically, frozen to resist the stream of time.

Some of the simplest and perhaps the earliest of nature studies by Cretan painters show the glittering and darting creatures of the sea. Nothing could better suit the Minoan desire to express the fleeting moment (in total contrast to the Egyptian ideal) than the leap of the flying-fish. They appear with dolphins and small fish in the room that may have been the Queen's boudoir at Knossos and, in a sky blue with gauzy black wings, at Phylakopi in Melos. Quick, full of life, mouths agape, they flutter there for an instant, in their own element quite free from man and his purposes.

Flying-fish were made also in faience, an art presumably learnt from the Egyptians. Some were found in the treasury of the shrine at Knossos together with the snake goddesses and two faience bas reliefs that are unquestionably the finest animal studies in all known Minoan art. One is of a wild goat with a sucking kid, standing on rocks, her head raised, alert and wary; the other a dappled cow, her head turned back to watch her calf tugging eagerly at the dug. The bodies are finely modelled, so far naturalistic, and yet at the same time they are formalized, each based on the S-curve which always seemed to fascinate Cretan designers. These two superb animals face left and right, and it is tempting to suppose that they were intended to confront one another, representing two opposing forms of motherhood under the aegis of the goddess, the goat wild and watchful, the cow domestic and tender; one from the mountain, the other from the cattle byre.

These studies of marine and animal life in faience and in fresco are remarkable enough, and it is true to say that no artist before had looked at nature with an eye that was so observant and admiring, and yet also detached and undemanding. The creature is appreciated, and intensely, for itself alone. Yet they and others like them would not be enough to fulfil all the claims that have been made for the originality of the Minoan genius. This appears at its height in later frescoes that are still completely free from any touch of Mycenaean influence. Few compositions of any size survive, but scores of fragments remain to show what delights there must have been in the houses of the royal and rich at this time at the beginning of the late Bronze Age – about 1550 B.C.

The best of these frescoes come from a mansion standing beside the Sacred Way at Knossos and from the villa or summer palace of Hagia Triada. In one blue monkeys are picking flowers among a profusion of rocks and plants – iris, yellow roses, crocus and wreathing ivy. In one a blue bird (plate 15), perhaps a roller, seems to be just poised for flight from a fantastic rocky outcrop with various slender plants waving round it and enhancing the suggestion of rising flight. In another a cat is stalking a large bird that sits unaware, with its back turned, on the far side of some swirling vegetation. The cat is so intent, setting its paws so cautiously, that one is made aware of its silence and stealth. In a fourth the painter is once again catching the fleeting moment, and a rising movement: against a background of plants and rocky spires, a deer is springing through the air.

The quality in these scenes of nature that is most wonderful because it was quite new is that they have been painted to create an atmosphere, and an atmosphere charged with a sense of all-pervading-moving-springing life. The animals and birds, although brilliantly suggested, are not very exactly drawn or anatomically analysed; the plants would not satisfy a botanist, or the rocks a geologist. And the scenes as a whole, though spacious and evocative of Mediterranean ground, have been painted without any desire to express depth or structure.

Yet the veining and softly marbled colouring of the rocks, the cumulative effect of the intertwining of the plants and flowers, and the creatures going their own ways among all this delicate richness of colour and shape, evoke a country that is quick with life and yet as much a poetic dream as the blue, remembered hills. If Artemis dreamed, this might be the country of her dreams.

These unique works, then, form the heart of the Minoan artistic achievement. There are other paintings which lack their quality but still help to show the Cretans' love of nature both wild and cultivated. In a mansion at the harbour of Amnisos

A new formality. Probably a ritual vessel, painted with stylized nautilus and papyrus designs in red-brown on buff, c. 1400 B.C.

(near Knossos and traditionally the naval headquarters of King Minos) the walls of a reception room were decorated with tall spikes of flowering lilies growing from stone basins of a kind that might be expected in a formal garden. Almost identical lily spikes were also painted on tall vases. The pleasant building outside the south entry to the palace of Knossos that probably served as a rest-house for travellers was enlivened with friezes of red-legged partridges (plate 14) and hoopoes – painted with more than usual specific accuracy.

A distinct use of natural forms appears on the pottery of the later palaces. In the sixteenth century leaves and other plant forms were painted with a highly practised simplicity suggestive of Chinese brush work (plate 2). Then after about 1500 the potters developed a manner of painting that would have suited their wares to the submarine halls of some Minoan Neptune. Using rich browns and red-browns on a pale background they painted dolphins, fish, seashells, sailing nautilus, staring and tentacle-brandishing octopuses, all over their pots, filling in the gaps with seaweeds, corals and rock formations. Sometimes the effect was over-crowded and rather heavy, but at its best, as in the magnificent octopus jars, this marine style could hardly be bettered. Although lacking in sensitivity or poetic feeling, it was still very Minoan in its combination of decorativeness with intense life and move-ment (pp. 103, 104). It is not surprising that this vigorous and unsubtle style was particularly popular in the Mycenaean world.

The Minoan artists were perhaps most remarkable for their new vision of nature. But they also looked at man through fresh eyes. Their extraordinary good fortune in not having to devote most of their energies to stereotyped portrayals of royal personages and gods or their supposed victories has already been made clear. In the work that can fairly be said to be most purely Minoan the artists seem to have regarded human beings in much the same spirit as they regarded animals: like the springing deer or the stalking cat they were to be caught fleetingly, doing those things that it was natural for them to do. For the Cretans those things were dancing, bull-leaping, boxing, acrobatic tumbling and chattering together in a crowd – all well suited to the Minoan artists' love of life and movement.

Again, as with the animals, the human beings and their activities are deftly suggested with little concern for anatomical correctness. The women are imbued with charm, chic and sexual allure, and if to suggest this it helps to give them eyes as big as hens' eggs, then – as in the instance of the famous "Parisienne" (plate 10) – they are given eyes as big as hens' eggs. The men appear tanned (in paintings) and very muscular (in modelling and sculpture), but often in positions impossible for the human body.

Freely impressionistic effects were also used more broadly. In frescoes showing crowds (plate 8) watching various spectacles, patches of pale colour in pleasantly

"Tentacle-brandishing octopus". The naturalism of the Late Palace period, 1550–1500 B.C.

undulating shapes have been blocked in where women are to be shown, with similar reddish-brown shapes for the men, the individuals' heads then being drawn on top after the fashion of Raoul Dufy. This same combination of detailed representation with bold overall colour-effects was also often used to suggest backgrounds – zones of vegetation, rock, and perhaps sky, always with the undulating shapes.

In renderings of the human body there was a sharp contrast between the most typical work of the fresco painters and that of the sculptors. Even when depicting dancing, bull-leaping and other vigorous actions, the painters did nothing to suggest that the human body had a bone or muscle in it. The sculptors, on the other hand, whether they were carving reliefs or working in the round, liked to make an exaggerated play with muscles and tendons and rib lines – often making them stand

Left The worshipper; possibly the young god before the Goddess. Bronze. Cretan style, provenance unknown, 1550–1500 B.C. *Right* A Cretan child, possibly playing with knuckle-bones. Ivory. From Palaikastro, 1550–1500 B.C.

out in bulging lumps. As there is no consistent difference of date between them, it seems that painters and artists must each have rejoiced in exploiting their own medium – for colour and for plasticity.

One piece of sculpture stands out from the rest for its purer naturalism. It is the little ivory figure of a flying acrobat, probably part of a bull-leaping group, from the palace of Knossos. Although the main figure is slightly elongated to heighten the sense of movement, it is not in the least contorted, nor is the musculature exaggerated. It has a naturalism and grace that are Classical, but with an immediacy of movement that is Minoan. The placid baby from Palaikastro can be compared with it in naturalism.

The palace of Knossos contained a number of paintings in another, different,

An almost Classical naturalism. Bull-leaper or acrobat. Ivory. From the palace of Knossos, 1550–1500 B.C.

Bull at the royal gate. Life-size plaster mural from the north portico, Knossos, *c.* 1600 B.C. (?).

Queen-priestess or goddess? Much-restored fresco of tribute-bearers from the Corridor of the Procession, Knossos, 15th century B.C. (?).

manner. These are the lines of tribute-bearers in the south-west corridor, also perhaps the "Young Prince" and the powerful head of a bull, the principal surviving fragment of a scene probably showing the capture of wild bulls, that decorated a colonnade near the north entrance. These last two are not ordinary frescoes, having been modelled in low relief in stucco before the paint was applied. They have usually been dated back to as early as 1600 B.C., although it has always been recognized that the bull relief was still on the wall when the palace was abandoned and probably helped to give rise to the legend of the Minotaur.

The tribute-bearers may have numbered several hundred, but with the exception of the handsome, curly-haired youth carrying a conical rhyton, only their feet, or here and there a whole leg, and the bottom of the women's skirts have survived. However, there is enough to show that although these figures had more life and individuality than comparable Egyptian processional figures, they manifest just that sense of timelessness, of arrested movement, that is contrary to the whole spirit of Minoan art. The same is true of the "Young Prince", truly Cretan though he is in his dress and ornaments and garden setting. These figures are supposedly walking, but their steps are frozen, their muscles passive, both feet flat on the ground. This static quality, and indeed the whole idea of a monotonous procession, seem miles away from the fleeting, dancing mood of most Minoan art. Just the same stance is found in murals in the Mycenaean palace of Pylos, in the Mycenaean warrior in ivory from Delos, on the late sarcophagus from Hagia Triada, and, in decadent form, on the Warrior Vase from Mycenae.

As far as can be judged, the bull relief from the north entrance, in spite of its majestic force, shares in this sense of arrested movement. If style and feeling are sufficient guide, these Knossian works of art were executed at a time when the Minoan spirit had been stiffened and confined by Egyptian influence and Mycenaean discipline.

The fondness of the Minoan artists for showing scenes of human life gives their work an extraordinary historical interest. As well as recording many details of dress and ornaments and changing hair fashions, it also provides a remarkable record of the social life of these Bronze Age Cretans. From this point of view, the most important paintings and sculptures are frescoes large and small from Knossos and Hagia Triada and some marvellous carved steatite vessels from Hagia Triada.

The way in which Cretan men and women dressed themselves is particularly significant because it suggests a frank encouragement of sexuality such as would be appropriate to the high status of women in Minoan society, to their uninhibited liveliness in public and the freedom with which they mingled with men.

The bulky, gathered skirts of the Old Palace days, with their touch of rusticity, were soon supplanted by two graceful and elegant styles that stayed in fashion with only minor changes for as long as palace life continued. Both fell from a narrow, belted waist and were close-fitting to the hips. Below the hips one style had a varying number of brightly-coloured flounces sewn to the underskirt, while in the other the skirt flared out to an ornamental hem. Occasionally, in place of the more formal design, the hemline was embroidered with flowers (p. 114). On occasion an ornamental double apron or divided overskirt might be worn – as is very clearly shown on the snake goddess figurines (plate 13).

The same frontless jacket was worn with both styles of skirt; it had short, rather full sleeves above a tight-fitting stomacher that may have been laced up below the naked breasts. It appears to have been prevented from slipping back off the shoulders by a strand or chain linking the upper edges above the breasts. Perhaps some of the delightful gold necklets with links in the form of flowers, leaves and other natural shapes may have served for this necessary liaison. In all portrayals of women, the breasts that were so provocatively supported and framed by these jackets were made large and prominent. Evidently big breasts were as much admired in Minoan Crete as in modern America – and for the same reason: love of the sustaining female.

Blues, yellows, soft reds and greens were the usual colours for women's clothes. It has sometimes been said that the material was of wool, but voluminous woollen skirts would have been intolerably hot for the greater part of the year. It seems far more likely that these rainbow garments were made of linen – either homegrown or imported from Egypt. At this time Egyptian craftsmen had become highly skilled, and used a tapestry weave to produce beautifully patterned linens.

The palace ladies usually went bare-headed but had their hair gracefully dressed.

Plate 13. Goddesses of the palace of Knossos. Faience figurines, c. 1600 B.C.

There were various fashions, but most often the long wavy hair was loosely gathered on the top of the head, then fastened behind with a tie or in a loose chignon and allowed to fall down the back. Curls, sometimes small and tight, sometimes romantically free, were arranged across the forehead, often with a fillet, while long, wavy side locks dangled in front of the ears. No wonder that the ladies had ivory-handled bronze mirrors among their more precious possessions.

Hats were certainly still worn on ritual occasions. Although the tall head-dress worn by one of the snake goddesses may not have been found among mortal millinery, the round, pancake hat of her companion undoubtedly was. It might have a tassel or plumes flowing from the centre of the crown.

In the dress of the men, all emphasis was placed on the narrow waist (enhanced by a massive metal belt) and on the codpiece or penis sheath – a combination at least as provocative as the revelations and concealments of the women. The multi-coloured loincloths were short at the back but at the front came down to the knee, where they seem sometimes to have been weighted by a long narrow fringe – possibly of beads. On some occasions, and especially for sports, the men wore the codpiece with a much shorter, apron-like garment which exposed the side of the thighs right up to the waist belt. They set off their bare torsos and limbs by intricate gold necklaces, armlets, bracelets and anklets. A gold signet ring might be worn on the finger, but more commonly the personal seal was hung from wrist or neck. At least from the time of the later palaces the men usually kept their hair long, allowing it to fall down their backs, and often, like the women, bringing locks forward to hang in front of the ears.

Although the general fashion was for a strong contrast in the dress of the two sexes, there appears to have been a tendency to ritual transvestism. Thus when taking part in the bull games, the women donned the short loincloth and codpiece, and in funerary rites men and women might both wear identical skirts of sheepskin. In celebrating a form of communion, in which both sexes took part, the men put on long, flounced robes.

As in Egyptian paintings, the Minoan artists always showed the ladies with pale, moon-like complexion, and the men with a ruddy brown sunburn. One would like to know whether the Cretan women, active as they were, did in fact shield themselves from the sun, or whether these colourings largely depended on an artistic convention.

The surviving fragments of frescoes and reliefs afford glimpses of Minoan life that suggest a lantern lecture with many slides broken and missing.

Ladies in blue-bordered red jackets and with richly braided hair are displaying their fine breasts, toying with their necklaces and gesticulating with their slender white hands. . . .

Plate 14. Nature and art. Fresco of red-legged partridges from the Rest House, Knossos, c. 1500 B.C.

Dancer with flying hair; red-brown dress, trimmed with blue. Palace of Knossos, *c.* 1500 B.C.

A man's hand reaches out to place a necklace round a lady's throat. . . .

A woman dances with her right arm extended horizontally and her left bent back; she is moving so fast that her long, wavy hair is flying out round her shoulders. . . .

A large audience of men and women is assembled (plate 8) to watch a dance. At the back some men are waving their arms; in the front women are seated below a line of olive trees, their legs, discreetly covered by flounced skirts, drawn up beneath them. The dancers are all women, and they are moving in one direction, their right arms raised in front of them (p. 116). . . .

"The hemline embroidered with flowers." Votive robe with crocuses. Faience. From the Treasury, palace of Knossos, *c.* 1600 B.C.

An audience of several hundred men and women is crowded round a threefold shrine – possibly the one in the central court. It has red columns in the middle section, blue in the side ones. In spite of their proximity to the shrine, the ladies seated in the front row appear to be gossiping in a very lighthearted way. . . .

The bull game is in progress (plate 9) in which a man and two women are taking part. The man has already completed the first stage of his leap and is poised on his hands on the bull's back facing the tail, his legs tumbling over to complete the somersault. Just beyond the beast's hindquarters a woman is waiting with arms outstretched to receive him. The other woman is lightly on her toes at the bull's head; she has his left horn under her left armpit and appears to be holding on to it; her white left breast stands out against the horn. . . .

A figure in a white robe is seated in a palanquin carried by other white-robed individuals. . . .

Youths are seated on campstools, two by two facing one another and passing a two-handled goblet, probably a "loving" or communion cup, between them. They are wearing blue and yellow flounced robes down to their feet. A large-eyed girl in blue with a sacral knot at the back of her neck (La Parisienne) appears to be with them. . . .

One scene cannot be described without comment. It has been restored to show a man in a yellow loincloth and cap with horns, assumed to be a Cretan officer, leading a file of black troops running at the double. On the actual fresco fragment the Africans are represented only by one knee seen against a blue ground, and the back of one head against white. While it is not at all impossible that the Cretans, with their unmartial spirit and close contacts with Egypt, might have employed Nilotic mercenaries, this evidence seems insufficient to establish the fact.

In these Knossian frescoes, the interest is predominantly with the women. In the marvellous reliefs from the black steatite vessels of Hagia Triada only men are represented.

On a tall conical rhyton four separate registers represent strenuous physical action: Wrestling in the upright manner; one man has dropped on to one knee. . . . Bulls galloping with heads thrown right back; one appears to be tossing a man whose arms are flung above his head. This is usually referred to as a bull-leaping scene, but it seems much more likely to show the capturing of wild bulls (p. 118). . . . Boxers wearing gloves and helmets (p. 119); two have been knocked down and crawl groggily on all fours. . . . Another form of wrestling in which men are being violently thrown. As others are in a punching attitude, this could represent the *pancration*, a combination of wrestling and boxing practised by the Classical Greeks. . . .

A relief on a cup is hard to interpret. A figure holding a long staff before him

"The dancers are all women." Detail of miniature fresco, palace of Knossos, 16th century B.C.

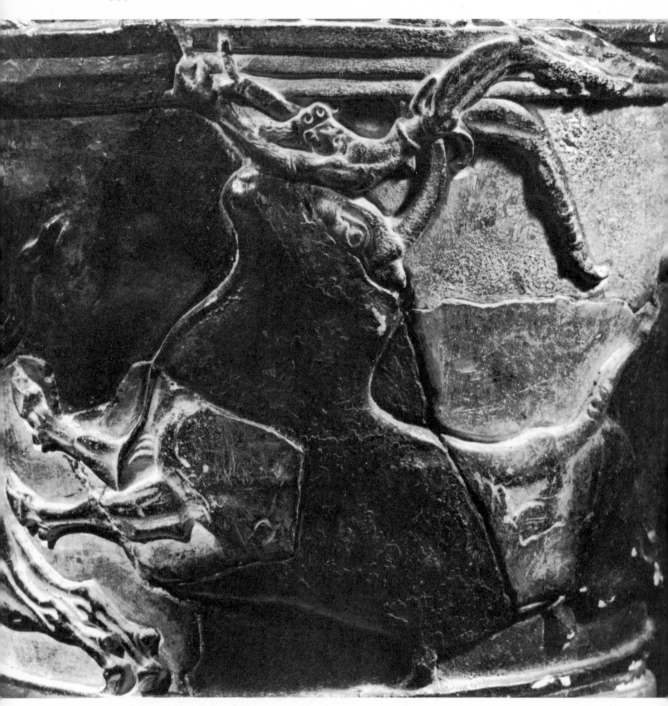

"A horn in his crutch." Scene from the capture of bulls? Detail from black steatite conical rhyton, Hagia Triada, 1550–1500 B.C.

Boxers in helmets and gloves. Detail from black steatite conical rhyton, Hagia Triada, 1550–1500 B.C.

confronts another with a sword held sloping against his shoulder and an object that may be a cult sprinkler in his left hand. In their slack stance and slight physical development there is a suggestion that these figures are intended to represent young boys. It is impossible to be sure what they are doing without understanding what is going on behind them, where two other young people are hidden except for their heads behind two huge balloon-shaped objects.

One of the most remarkable scenes in all Bronze Age art is carved round the curved cheek of an ovoid rhyton. A crowd of countrymen is returning from work – probably, as some of the implements they carry over their shoulders seem to be winnowing fans – from the threshing floor. They are utterly unlike the courtiers and athletes, with rolled headcloths or round flat caps, short hair, and coarse, mobile, humorous faces.

Perhaps they have been drinking at a harvest festival, for they are all very jolly and one man is laughing uproariously over a friend who has fallen down. They are led by an older man dressed in a very odd-looking tunic that may have been peculiar to the occasion. Among them a group is singing lustily, conducted by an enthusiast who is shaking a sistrum and beating time with the other hand. The whole party is stepping high as though stamping time to the music. The noise and heat and sweat and hearty good spirits are all there, and with them a rough sense of comedy that is unique. Is it justifiable to say that already it is clearly European?

All these varied scenes from Minoan life have two things in common. In none of them (in startling contrast with their Egyptian counterparts) is any work or other practical activity to be seen. In all of them there is a mingling of the secular with the sacred, of play and sport with ceremony. Even the boxing and wrestling which appear to be most nearly secular may have a ceremonial setting. There are pillars behind the competitors that could be accepted as cultic.

Like the Jongleur de Notre Dame, the Cretans must have felt that they could serve their Lady through the excitement, exercise and delight of their bodies. In the sophisticated palace and urban society, however, these activities no longer involved the universal participation of simpler times, but had become entertainments watched by large, light-hearted audiences of men and women. The same kind of evolution from the religious rite towards the secular entertainment has been made familiar and understandable through the history of Greek drama and athleticism. The unanimous testimony of so many works of art must express much that was essential in the Minoan experience of life and justify the claim that, more fully than any contemporary people, the Cretans expressed the idea of *Homo ludens*. It was a part of the inheritance, surely, that they left for the Greeks?

Bull-leaping must have been an important and immensely popular element in the life of the Cretan *Homo ludens*, and it would seem that performers and audiences

Three details of harvest scene – the falling man, the leader, the sistrum-player – on black steatite ovoid rhyton, Hagia Triada, 1550–1500 B.C.

Capture of bulls by force: two scenes from the first of a pair of gold cups from Vaphio, Laconia, *c.* 1500 B.C. *Above* The would-be captors are tossed and gored. *Right* The bull is caught in a tree-anchored net.

would never have lost their sense of the religious potency of the game. The great beasts themselves moved in an aura of ancient holiness. It has been seen how already for the Palaeolithic hunters the personification of feminine divinity was associated with the symbol of the bull's horn. In Anatolia primitive wall paintings at Çatal Hüyük dating back to the sixth millennium B.C. already showed men touching the horns of a colossal bull as though to receive its potency. In the contemporary Bronze Age world a supreme sky god was often identified with the bull, and the Egyptian sacred Apis and Mnevis bulls were greatly venerated. Pharaoh was identified with the Bull of Heaven. The Cretan games cannot have been unaffected by this sacred taurine ambience.

The games have occasionally been called bull-fights, and it has been pointed out that there is a faint but pervasive religious feeling in the modern Spanish bull-fight. This is true, but it flows mainly from death on the sword and its erotic symbolism. Dangerous though the Cretan bull-leaping must have been, it was not essentially associated with death and was in no sense a fight. All the many portrayals of the leaping show a perfectly successful union of human skill and spring with taurine strength. It is in the rounding up and capture of the bulls that death seems to have been anticipated. In the scene of this kind on one of the Vaphio cups a helpless man is being tossed, his arms flying above his head. On the Hagia Triada rhyton the man is in a similar position and the bull's horn is in his crutch (p. 118). It is

Capture of bulls by sex: decoyed by a cow (right), the bull is tethered by the hind leg. Scene from the second of the Vaphio gold cups. 10.8 cms in diameter, the cups are probably of Cretan manufacture.

possible that the tossing was repeated in the great charging bull relief at the north entrance to the palace of Knossos.

As it was a subject chosen by artists, it can be guessed that the capture of the free bulls was itself a significant operation – as it is to some extent in connection with the modern bull-fight. It is usually considered that the Greek tradition of the sacrifice of the Athenians youths and girls to the Minotaur embodied a memory of their being despatched as forced tribute to take part in the bull games. If the witness of the artists is to be believed, it is more likely to have referred to the capture with its driving, netting and roping.

For the bull-fight the most aggressive beasts are selected from among the rest to go into the arena; for the totally different ideal of bull-leaping it is quite possible that the mildest and most biddable were picked out. Nor is it impossible that between their capture and their appearance in the arena the bulls underwent some training to accustom them to human beings and even to collaborate with them in the leap. One seal-stone shows a man holding a bull's horns from behind while the animal is lying down.

In spite of the number of times that it was represented by painters and sculptors, leaping as it was practised in the arena is not altogether easy to understand. One great difficulty has been the fact that bulls charging and tossing in anger always move the head sideways in a manner that would make the graceful vault between the horns totally impossible. Here again it is very significant to find that this sideways attack is most truthfully rendered in the scene of the murderous bull on the Vaphio cup, whereas in the bull-game scenes the animals are always holding their heads perfectly straight. It would seem, then, that in the arena the bulls were not in fact attempting to toss the players, but were either running forward or swinging up their heads. It is even conceivable that they had been taught to rear their heads in this way. The acrobats themselves evidently executed as great a variety of somersaulting leaps as a modern athlete on the vaulting horse. Although they may usually have grasped the two horns in the first stage of the vault, this was not their invariable method. The painting in which a woman is holding one horn under her armpit has already been described, and in several scenes the vaulter is so close to the bull's neck that it is hard to see how he could have somersaulted from the horns.

In trying to imagine the general atmosphere and expectation of the bull-leaping occasions, it may be helpful to recall a great circus tent or hall where trapeze artists are performing without nets. The tension and excitement are stimulated by awareness of mortal danger, yet it is assumed that all will be well, and death is in fact a most rare visitor. The simpler enjoyment of the audience is in supreme skill and grace of movement. The fact that men and women perform together and entrust their lives to one another adds a distinctive flavour.

In the Cretan arena to emotions of this kind there has to be added the stronger religious and numinous significance. Civilization is young; mankind has not as yet been affected by the intellectual revolution of the Greeks, and all the external world is charged with divinity and symbolic meaning. The bull himself is sacred, and a universal symbol of potency. The performance may perhaps begin and end with libations or other ritual observances, and the play may be expected to serve the divine power and bring fertility and well-being to society. At the same time all this is an accepted thing, well below the surface, and the audience gives itself over to an enjoyable excitement not so far removed from that generated below the Big Top.

Dancing, which it is clear the Cretans also loved, is so much a universal form of human expression that it does not call for the same attention as the extraordinary bull game. Nevertheless it is known that the Cretan involvement with the art was exceptional, so much so that later Classical tradition associated the island with the origin of dancing. One version of the story was that it all began with the goddess Rhea, who taught the Corybantes in Phrygia and the Kouretes in Crete (p. 133) to dance and clash their arms on their shields to conceal the birth cries of the infant Zeus and so save him from his devouring father Kronos.

The Cretans danced to music – and there again the Greeks recognized their skill, telling that several of their own most important musical forms, including the hymn to Apollo that was sung and accompanied on the lyre by a single musician, had been introduced from Crete. A triangular harp and double pipe were being played in the Aegean a thousand years before the heyday of the palaces, but now, although the pipes continued and probably the harp as well (as it was played by the Greeks), the seven-stringed lyre was most popular as an accompaniment to dancing. This graceful instrument, too, survived to be played in Classical times.

To judge from the record left by Minoan artists, the women did most of the dancing. In the fresco scene already described they seem to be moving forward in an irregular line, but in a little pottery group from Palaikastro (plate 1) they are holding arms and doing a ring dance round a woman playing the lyre. It is possible that this is the classical Cretan dance known as the *hyporchema*, and that a version of it is still danced in western Crete today.

These dances in turn may have been connected with the famous *geranos*, or crane dance, which Theseus was said to have seen being danced by Cretan maidens, and which he then introduced to the island of Delos. This Delian *geranos* became one of the dances performed in the Athenian theatre during intervals in the regular drama. It was supposed to symbolize Theseus's rescue of the Athenian youths and maidens from the Minotaur – and must have served to keep thoughts of the Cretan past alive in the minds of the Athenians.

In the famous Homeric description of one of the scenes on Achilles's shield

Naked dancers. The religious setting is shown by the horns of consecration. From the tomb of
Kamilari, near Phaistos, c. 1500 B.C.

"Fumy with poppies." Here and on seals (p. 139) the goddess is associated
with three seed pods; it seems that opium must have been used in her rites.
From Gazi, 1400–1200 B.C.

(*Iliad*, Book XVIII) two movements – of approaching lines and the ring – are described, but here men and women take part together.

> . . . the god depicted a dancing floor like the one that Daedalus designed in the spacious town of Cnossus for Ariadne of the lovely locks. Youths and maidens were dancing on it with their hands on one another's wrists, the girls garlanded and in fine linen, the men in finely woven tunics showing the faint gleam of oil, and with daggers of gold hanging from their silver belts. Here they ran lightly round, circling as smoothly as the wheel of the potter when he sits and spins it with his hands; and there they ran in lines to meet each other. A large crowd stood round enjoying the dance while a minstrel sang divinely to the lyre and two acrobats, keeping time with his music, cart-wheeled in and out among the people.

This description, in spite of all that separated the *Iliad*, Achilles and the Trojan war from Minoan Crete, seems to give a true idea of the dances and acrobatics enjoyed at Knossos and still continued in a rustic setting by islanders who on every holiday are to be seen circling tirelessly on their village dancing floors.

Even more than the bull-leaping, Minoan dancing merged with religious rites. The performances given in front of palace audiences seem to have involved small companies dancing formal figures, though occasionally whirling at speed. Religious dancing in sacred groves and before the goddess and her altars was far more abandoned and ecstatic. The seal cuttings, where this religious dancing is often shown, leave no doubt of that. Again it is largely though not exclusively women who participate; they wear the same long flounced skirts and raise their arms above their heads, but it is always evident that their bodies are swaying with every appearance of trance-like abandon (p. 132).

They are, indeed, very strange glimpses that can be caught through the gem-cutter's art. Here are females dressed as though for an Edwardian garden party going into the countryside and abandoning themselves to rites usually associated with primitive, or at least more rustic, societies. However, to find this surprising is perhaps allowing too much to modern associations of the flounced skirt. The orgiastic dances of women celebrating Dionysus and Bacchus are a familiar enough part of Classical history (p. 282), and were probably descended from these Cretan rites – the continuity being maintained partly through cultural tradition, partly through an unchanging psychological need.

It is quite likely that, as today, drugs were sometimes taken to encourage a sense of revelation, possession and trance. On one seal the seated goddess is holding three poppy seed-heads, and in a late figurine she is wearing three seed-heads, cut as for the extraction of opium, set in a crown above her forehead (p. 127). The growing of opium poppies has a very long history in Anatolia.

Plate 15. "Something entirely new – painting to create atmosphere". The "Blue Bird" fresco from the House of Frescoes, Knossos, *c.* 1500 B.C.

Inevitably the dance has led straight into the heart of Minoan religion. Although a good deal has already been said about the goddess and her worship in the greatest of her island realms, it is necessary to consider it more coherently before it can be possible to win any understanding of the psychological foundations of this strangely feminine society.

The first essential is, of course, that the Cretans saw the supreme divine power in terms of the feminine principle, and incarnate in a woman whom they portrayed exactly like one of themselves. Although she had many aspects, and one at least of them was virginal, this dedication to a goddess involved also a glorification of the meaning of sex. Fertility and abundance were the purpose and the desire, sex was the instrument, and for this reason its symbols were everywhere. The dove was presumably chosen for the goddess because it was always supposed to be the most amorous of birds.

The free-standing columns and the pillars that were anointed, the sacred trees, the horns of consecration that made holy the altar or shrine or building on which they stood, the horns of the living bulls, the mountain peaks, the stalagmites to which offerings were made in the cave sanctuaries, all expressed phallic power. Some would say that the snake did also, although it certainly had other meanings.

All these masculine symbols would be seen in relation to the goddess, and it was probably for this reason that feminine symbols were less varied. The cave was one, and perhaps the tomb-chamber and crypt in which the pillars stood. It is being suggested here, however, that the most famous and frequent symbol of all – that of the double axe (plate 16) – was itself a feminine symbol as well as being one of the emblems of the goddess. It may have begun its evolution from a practical tool into a religious symbol as an instrument of sacrifice comparable to the cross. Its shape, the double triangle, was widely used as a sign for woman, and the shaft thrust through the central perforation afforded an effective piece of sexual imagery. It is striking that the double axe was very often set between the horns of consecration or of the bucranion or on the top of a tall shaft. In vase paintings the shaft hole was frequently penetrated by the sacred branch or the knot (p. 132). Double axes had been thrust into the phallic stalagmite in the cave of Psychro. Always and everywhere they are associated with the goddess, never with any male divinity.

The double axe came to have the supreme significance in Crete appropriate to a symbol of the goddess. It was known as the *labrys* from its Lydian name, and the palace of Knossos was known as the Labyrinth in the sense of the House of the Double Axe. It was only later, when visiting Greeks saw the bewildering ruins of the ancient palace, that the name came to be applied to the maze, and the sign of the maze was set upon the Cretan coinage. In the palace as everywhere else the symbol was displayed as frequently and conspicuously as the cross in Christian

Plate 16. The sacred symbol of the *labrys*. Miniature gold double axes from the cave of Arkalochori, *c.* 1500 B.C.

Left A symbol of the Goddess: the sacral knot. Often associated with the double axe. Priestesses probably wore it at the back of the neck (plate 10). Faience. From the Upper Grave Circle, Mycenae, 16th century B.C. *Right* An ecstatic dance; seal-stone from the domed tomb of Vaphio. Carnelian, *c.* 1500 B.C.

buildings. It might be made in bronze of gigantic size, or very often in gold. The way in which it must have been set up to dominate shrines and altars appears very clearly in a scene on the Hagia Triada sarcophagus where a priestess is pouring a libation into a vessel standing between two towering obelisk-like shafts, set on stepped bases and crowned with ornate double axes in gold.

Minoan worship, then, was shot through and through with sexual imagery and meaning. This related to the goddess in many of her aspects, but in particular as the deity of vegetation and spring renewal – and of the idea of rebirth in general. When she is shown in this manifestation she is accompanied by a youthful male deity, a Year Spirit who is her consort and offspring, who dies and is born again – the Cretan version of Adonis. In Minoan Crete this young god was always subject to the goddess – he was the instrument of her fertility and is shown in humble and worshipful attitudes. He was indeed the leader and embodiment of those young

Kouretes, native spirits who, with their female companions, the Kourai, made flowers bloom and nourished the flocks and herds. Or, in the more orgiastic aspect of the worship of the goddess, he was perhaps the Minoan Dionysus with his rout of maenads.

It has already been shown how, when the high civilizations of the Bronze Age developed in Egypt and the Orient, the goddess who had ruled in prehistoric days had to take a humbler place in the pantheon. Although in Crete she maintained her rule until the last light of Minoan civilization was fading away, and established a remarkable ascendancy for a time even among the Mycenaeans, it was inevitable that she would have to surrender in the end to the masculine Indo-European religion and in particular to the father-figure, Zeus. One part of the Cretan mythology is so significant from the point of view of this meeting and mingling of the Minoan with the invading Indo-European gods, and so relevant to the theme of the Minoan contribution to Greek culture, that it has to be recounted here. It has already been touched upon in connection with the dancing of the Kouretes.

Zeus was, of course, an Indo-European god introduced to Greece by the invading Achaeans. Yet the poet Hesiod, living about a century after Homer, accepts the legend that he was born in Crete. The story was woven from ideas of the Cretan goddess of the caves and her Year Spirit and from a primitive myth that appears to have been known to the pre-Hittite peoples of Anatolia and also in Asia. The legend was that the god Kronos, having betrayed his own father, feared that his children by the goddess Rhea would in turn destroy him. To prevent this he devoured his offspring as they were born, until at last Rhea hid away her last-born, the infant Zeus, fobbing off her husband with a swaddled stone. According to Hesiod, the infant was hurried off to Lyktos, where his grandmother Gaia (Earth) hid him in a cave on Goat's Mountains. Various developments of the story suggest that the birth took place in the cave, and tell how the Kouretes danced and struck their shields to conceal the baby's cries. In some versions he was suckled by the goat, Amalthea, but in others Amalthea was a nymph.

Evidently, then, by the time of Hesiod the name of Zeus had already been given to the Cretan goddess's young male companion or Year Spirit – one of whose island names was Velchanos. (In several seals this young god is shown with one of the huge figure-of-eight shields of oxhide – which would certainly have made a thunderous sound if beaten upon with spears.) This identification was made even clearer when the text of a hymn was found on the site of the temple of the Diktean Zeus at Palaikastro in eastern Crete. The hymn had been written down as late as the third century A.D., but contained ancient material. In it the Kouretes invoke the young god not by the name of Zeus but as "the greatest Kouros". He is reminded how at his birth the Kouretes had danced with their shields, and is begged to rise from below to the upper world of crops, beasts and men. The sexual imagery employed in this hymn has encouraged the belief that the spring festival of rebirth may have been the occasion for human rites of copulation.

These mythical tales can easily become tedious. But this group affords a great testimony to the lasting power of the Cretan goddess. So strong was it that the Greeks allowed her to capture the origins of their Sky Father, to pull him down from self-created majesty on Olympus to wailing infancy in a Cretan cave. It was another of those traditions that kept the Greeks always conscious of the ancient and mysterious importance of Crete. Euripides wrote:

> Hail thou, O nurse of Zeus, O caverned haunt,
> Where fierce arms clanged to guard God's cradle rare,
> For thee of old some crested Corybant
> First woke in Cretan air
> The wild orb of our orgies . . .

One can say that the goddess in her wider sphere even survived to influence ideas about the infancy of Jesus. The manger is as often set in a cave as in a man-built stable.

The site of the Diktean cave has in fact always been disputed. The most popular have been the Psychro cave above the plain of Lasithi in the eastern mountain range which has now been named, or re-named, Dikte, and the Idaean cave on the north flank of Mount Ida. The latter was famous and much-visited in Greek and Roman times. Psychro was one of the most important of the Minoan cave shrines; it was furnished with great storage jars and with offering tables, and worshippers went there with their votive gifts over many centuries. Recently it has been suggested that the cavern of Arkalochori, not far from Lyktos, was the original birthplace of the Cretan Zeus, and that the venue was only changed when the roof of the cavern collapsed. Certainly it must have been a rich sanctuary, for it contained more than two dozen fine golden double axes as well as rapiers and spears of bronze.

Perhaps the truth is that, as with many mythological sites, each region had its own birth cave. The cave has always been a womb image, and it seems very probable indeed that those in great mountains were not only chosen as birthplaces for the young god, but were visited by women who wanted children, or protection in childbirth. One cave was certainly used in this way – and it is one of those places where archaeological discovery is touched by Homeric light. In his lying tales to Penelope, Odysseus spoke of having landed at Amnisos, the harbour near the cave of Eileithyia. Eileithyia was the goddess of childbirth. When the cave was identified, it proved to have been the home of Stone Age families at the time when, a few miles

Left A poor man's votive offering. Double axe in pottery from the cave of Eileithyia, after 1400 B.C. *Right* A plea to Eileithyia for a child? Clay votive, from the cave of Eileithyia, after 1400 B.C.

away, the settlement was flourishing on the Kephala. Then, as early as the third millennium B.C., it became a cult centre and remained so until the fifth or sixth century A.D. The suppliants who went there seem to have been humble folk, for they left no rich offerings. The goddess of the palace or of the wild woods may seem remote and strange, but through the universal and unchanging sympathy of women in childbirth, Eileithyia of the cavern is brought very near.

There has been much argument as to whether the divinity of the Cretans was one goddess or many. It is puzzling that people who can understand a monotheistic religion in which the divinity may be represented as a young man, an old man and a dove, and in which this three-in-one enjoys an obscure and changing relationship with a woman who is both mother and virgin, should expect to find a precise intellectual answer to this question.

The Cretans had a sense of divinity as an all-pervading creative power that for them was feminine. Below that level they personified different aspects of the divinity according to their practical and psychological needs. They would have felt no more difficulty in their goddess being the one and the many than they would have in identifying her with foreign goddesses – or their young Velchanos with the invading Zeus.

Much has already been said about the Minoan goddess and the various names under which she emerged into history. To try to tell the whole story, to follow the distinct yet always mingling and varying manifestations with their attributes and epiphanies would be as bewildering as to describe the shifting cloud shapes of a windy day. There have already been hints that the many aspects of the goddess tend to fall into two companies that are complementary and opposite – both possibly represented at the centre point of Minoan life: the royal shrine of the palace of Knossos.

On the one side are the domestic divinities, dominated by the household goddess who was to emerge most clearly as Athena. To this domestic and orderly company, appealing to the conscious mind, should presumably also be added those more sober and home-keeping personifications of the maternal aspects of the goddess who, like Rhea and Hera, were to become the wives and mothers of the Classical pantheon.

On the other side were the divinities of the wild places and the unconscious mind, some of them concerned with vegetation and its spring rebirth, others with wild animals. The Cretan vegetation goddess is shown again and again on the seals, dancing in meadows and groves with her Kourai or her young god (p. 138), perhaps fumy with opium, pulling down the bough from the sacred tree, receiving blossoms, fruits and poppy seeds (p. 139). This goddess is not so easily discovered under later names because her role was largely usurped by the god. She is most nearly recognizable in the divine (as opposed to the humanized) Ariadne who became Dionysus's spouse and was often shown seated with him below a vine.

Equally of the wilds, but chaste and free, was the mistress of wild animals, huntress and later tamer of the beasts. She can certainly be found in the Cretan Britomartis (sweet virgin), and in Artemis of the stags, and in Diana.

The attributes of the Cretan goddess help to reveal her as both the one and the many. The horns of consecration and the pillar and the tree belong equally to the palace or house and to the wilds; so, too, does the double axe, although it was perhaps more strongly associated with the domestic divinities. The snake belonged to the household goddess. It represented the friendly reptiles that were kept in shrines, palaces and humbler houses – and are still kept in peasant homes in many parts of the world. Accommodated sometimes in dark tubes, or lurking in hearth-

Mother and child, one of the undying forms of the Goddess. Pottery. From the cave of Eileithyia, after 1400 B.C.

Vegetation rites: a lament for the death of the year? Gold signet ring, Minoan in character, from a chamber tomb at Mycenae, *c.* 1500 B.C.

side holes, the snake expressed something of the chthonic aspect of the goddess, but essentially was the guardian genius of family or house. Yet snakes, perhaps in their sexual meaning, did also have some small part in the rites of the wild ones.

Most interesting is the place of the bird, and particularly of the dove. The dove, of course, became the emblem of the goddesses of human beauty, love and fertility – Aphrodite and Venus. These ladies one would expect to be divided between the two companies according to whether they stood for untrammelled passion, or love and marriage. Undoubtedly Aphrodite was sometimes both wild and dis-

"Receiving blossoms, fruits and poppy seeds." A summer festival? The young god descends with shield. Gold signet ring, Minoan in character, from Mycenae, *c.* 1500 B.C.

reputable (she became the goddess of prostitutes), and at different times and places could be identified with almost all aspects of the goddess. However, it is conspicuous that a bird that appears to be a dove is resting on each of the three pillars in a miniature shrine of the palace of Knossos, and in other shrines in the island, some-times together with snakes - as well as being perched on the little threefold gold shrines from Mycenae (p. 140). Yet they are quite absent from all the scenes of the wild ones whether in meadows, groves or on mountains. So it seems that in Crete the goddess who could appear as a dove was closer to the household goddess, and the

Threefold shrine with sacred horns, pillars and doves. Gold ornament from the Upper Grave Circle, Mycenae, 16th century B.C.

doves were of the kind that perched on the palace roofs and horns of consecration and made love in the embrasures, rather than the turtles of the woods. In fact they can be seen as Athena's bird before some influence perhaps from Mycenaean Pylos (p. 241) turned it into an owl.

However, Aphrodite was also a goddess of gardens, so the garden-loving Cretans may have recognized her under the name of Antheia, goddess of flowers, worshipped in the island in later days. Then there is the element of the sea: Aphrodite, born of the god's semen in the sea-foam, may have been identified with the aspect

Man-made triton shell. Cut from very hard liparite. Probably a rhyton, but tritons were blown, perhaps to evoke the Goddess. From Hagia Triada.

of the Cretan goddess concerned with the ocean. Water, like the earth, has always been recognized in the human psyche as a feminine element – in contrast with the air and fire of the masculine. For islanders so lovingly familiar with the Mediterranean and its creatures, and so far dependent on it and its moods for life and prosperity, it is unthinkable that their divinity did not extend her rule to the sea. It will be remembered that there were seashells, painted and also artificial, in the shrine treasury with the snake goddesses. Triton shells, again both real and carved in stone, were probably used for summoning the goddess on ritual occasions. Yet

The funeral of a prince? The sarcophagus may have been made for an Achaean conqueror or for a native Cretan. Fresco on plastered limestone, from Hagia Triáda, 14th century B.C.

there is a dearth of material, and it seems that shrines to a Lady of the Sea may have been destroyed by the waves.

There are, it is true, seals that show the goddess in a boat with shrines. In one (a gold signet from Mochlos) she appears to be naked, and a tree or bough sprouts from the shrine. Probably, however, this is not an Aphrodite-like manifestation; the rings may well be funerary and the boat concerned with the voyage and resurrection of the dead. There is no question at all that the goddess was as much responsible for the human dead and their rebirth as for the return of life to the vegetation.

The Cretans did not normally make lavish provision for tombs or cults of the dead – even of the royal dead – as the Achaeans were to do. The old communal tombs of pre-palace times gave way to individual or small family graves, the corpse often being pushed into a big jar, or into the painted clay troughs that were also used as baths. Decent offerings were granted the dead and libations poured, but Minoan society, devoted to the life of the passing moment, did not squander its resources on death.

Their trust was in the goddess who took the dead back into herself. The Roman historian, Diodorus, records that in the legendary tomb of Minos in Sicily the burial vault lay below a temple of the goddess – whom he calls Aphrodite of the Doves. A tomb of the same plan was unearthed at Knossos and proved to have a pillar crypt inscribed with the double axe. In the burial chamber a single column rose from a square hollow intended to receive libations. The sexual imagery was even more striking in another Knossian tomb which was itself cut out of the rock in the plan of a double axe, and contained a pillar carved in relief on a pier of rock projecting from the inner wall.

These somewhat dusty archaeological evidences of burial rites and the hope of rebirth through the goddess are suddenly brought to life by pictures of such rites painted by an artist who had witnessed them. Unfortunately the famous Hagia Triada sarcophagus was painted as late as the fourteenth century, and both the style and some elements of the scenes show strong Egyptian influence. Yet it does vividly recall a scene from Minoan religious ritual in the full detail of its performance

Bull sacrifice and sacred tree. Detail from the second side of the Hagia Triada sarcophagus.

and setting. The burial was that of a man, and to judge from the fact that his sarcophagus was made of stone instead of clay, and finely painted, it is likely that he was royal or noble.

Of the panels of figures on the long sides of the chest it seems that one (pp. 142–3) represents the burial of the dead man, the other his hope of rebirth. On the first the corpse is represented by a stiff, armless and legless figure upright outside a small tomb. Egyptian influence appears in the three men, clothed in what look like sheepskin skirts, who are walking towards him carrying the models of a boat and two bulls, presumably for furnishing the tomb. Between the dead man and his servitors is a half-flight of steps similar to the steps that symbolized the throne in Egyptian hieroglyphs, but apparently approaching a cyprus tree or branch. On the same panel but moving in the opposite direction is a man wearing the usual women's garb of flared skirt and short jacket, playing on a large lyre as he walks behind two women, one dressed exactly like the lyre player but wearing a flat hat with a tassel and carrying two bucket-shaped vases on a pole on her shoulder. Immediately in front of her a woman wearing a sheepskin skirt and jacket is bending forward to tip the contents of another vase (water? wine? blood?) into a larger vessel which has been set up between two tapering pillars crowned by golden double axes and perched birds.

On the other panel all the figures are moving or facing in the same direction – towards a sacred tree sprouting from a shrine with horns of consecration, and with a single double axe pillar in front of it. Here the bird on the axe is black and relatively large. Gazing up at the bird with her hands extended to touch an altar, and probably making offerings, is a woman in a sheepskin skirt (plate 7). Behind her a dappled bull is lying bound on a sacrificial table with two frightened-looking goats beneath it. The bull (which has close Egyptian equivalents) is past fear, for an artery has been cut and the blood is pouring into another bucket-shaped vessel. Behind this sacrifice, but apparently leading a procession of five women, is a jaunty-looking man in a knee-length tunic playing a double pipe. The leader of the procession of women is dressed like the vase-carrier of the other panel (except that her hair is confined in a net), and she stretches her arms towards the bull. The four other women follow her in pairs; unfortunately their upper bodies have been destroyed, so that the nature of their headgear will never be known. In this scene the pipes, the life-giving sacrificial blood, the large bird and the green, springing tree, all suggest a resurrection. Conceivably, the large bird could be the risen dead, though it is usually interpreted as representing the presence of the Goddess.

It seems certain that all these celebrants in their interestingly varied dress were intended to be human beings, and probable that the fleece-skirted men and women were professional priests and priestesses, while the women in long skirts and jackets were courtiers and relatives of the deceased. It would be interesting to know whether the crown-like tasselled hats of the two ladies (worn also by the "Young Prince" of Knossos) were a mark of royal birth.

The Goddess herself appears only on the narrow ends of the sarcophagus. In both she is driving in a chariot with a female attendant, but at one end their chariot is drawn by a pair of horses, at the other by griffins with a dark-winged bird flying above their backs. Is it possible that this bird represents the dead man being borne off by the Goddess to his new life? If so, it may be to the happiness of the Elysian

The Goddess in her horse chariot and in her griffin chariot. Two details from the ends of the Hagia Triada sarcophagus.

Fields. In Homer there is a contradiction between the usual view of the afterworld as a dim place of twittering ghosts, and a single mention of a green Elysium. It has been thought that the lively, light-hearted Cretans with their love of flowers and gardens and their trust in the Goddess may well have contributed the vision of a blissful land of the dead.

This long and speculative account of the Hagia Triada panels is justified because scenes so complete and, in a sense, prosaic, make the worship of the Goddess seem nearer and more real. Different though the rites enacted at a prince's or a nobleman's funeral would be from many other Minoan religious ceremonies, they do make it possible to visualize the kind of figures that once served at the shrines and altars of the palaces and great houses, and the manner in which the symbols of the Goddess may have been set up there and in many country sanctuaries – by the roadside, by sacred groves and springs, or even among the mountains.

The scenes are also of particular significance here because they prove quite conclusively the dominant rôle played by women celebrants – even in the burial of a man. Whether they appear to be priestesses or court ladies or princesses, it is they who carry out the sacred acts of the libation, the sacrifice, the offerings at the altar. The men (wearing skirts) merely carry the heavier offerings and provide the musical accompaniment.

There is no need to say very much more about the active worship of the Cretan goddess of many names, except to give some account of the cave and peak sanctuaries which, characteristically, the Cretans preferred to monumental temples in urban settings. These were the places of public worship, in contrast with the private shrines and sacred pillar crypts and snake abodes in which families of every kind from the royal house downwards paid their domestic tribute to the household goddess. Many of them are set in the neighbourhood of towns and cities, and must have served the citizens. One cannot be sure, but it seems likely that the palaces would have had some patronage of the more important, and that royal figures would have visited them at least on special festivals.

The caves were used as sanctuaries before the peaks – which came into fashion only with the founding of the palaces. It has already been suggested that many of them may have claimed to be divine birthplaces and that, like the cave of Eileithyia, they may have been specially associated with human childbirth and the maternal aspects of the Goddess. Sometimes they were enclosed by walls, and contained altars and little chapels. Those of them which had fine stalagmites and stalactites and other concretions must have been awe-inspiring to the visitants who left the familiar sunlight and warmth and saw these strange shapes glimmering in the light of lamps against an unfathomable darkness.

These natural temples of the Mother Goddess did not lose their sanctity in Classical

Plate 17. A lion of Mycenae. Rhyton of thick plate gold. From the Upper Grave Circle, Mycenae, 16th century B.C.

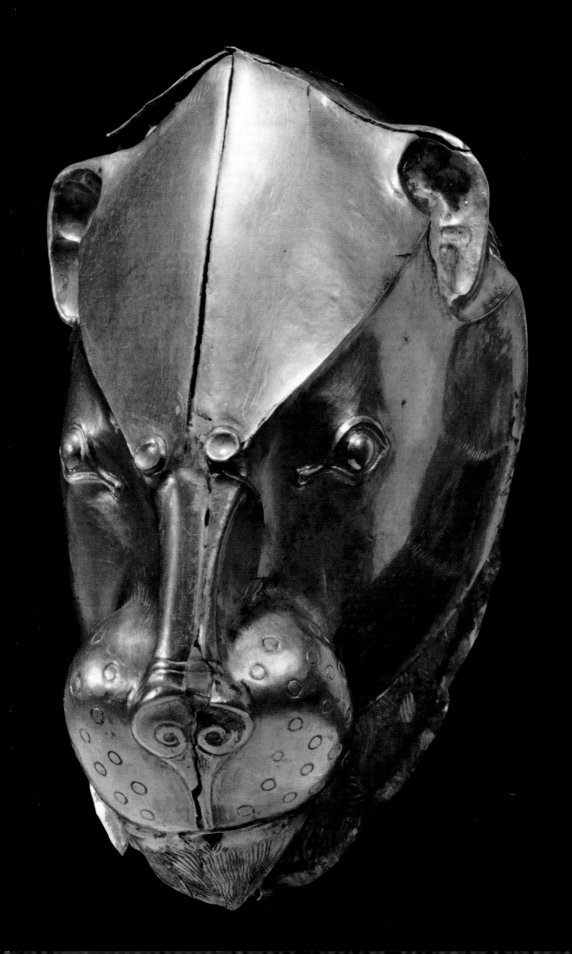

times. According to tradition they became centres for priestly colleges and were used for religious instruction and even for initiation into "Mysteries". Pythagoras and Epimenides are said to have been associated with the Idaean Cave. Even if these traditions are in part legendary, they show the lasting power of the caves, as do the vast number of votive offerings left in their depths by some hundred generations of pilgrims.

Because of their exposed positions, the remains of the peak sanctuaries have eroded away, but a fine impression of one has been carved on a conical rhyton from Kato Zakro. This shows a bird flying over horns of consecration, and ibexes on a spiral-carved shrine (p. 152). It seems possible that the ibex, with its noble horns, may have served as an equivalent to the bull in the iconography of these mountain-top sanctuaries.

From the simple sexual imagery running through much Minoan religious symbolism, it would be expected that the peaks would be particularly identified with the young male god, the Cretan Zeus. That this appears to have been the case is shown not only by the identification of the sanctuary overhanging the west face of Mount Juktas with the burial-place of Zeus, but also by the fact that when the peaks came to be Christianized, most of the chapels were dedicated to the Lord Christ.

Torn and blurred though the record is by time and earthquake, and inadequate though the effort to communicate it must be, it is hoped that something of the unique quality of Minoan civilization has come through. It remains to look more closely at the claim that this quality, which has enchanted and turned the heads of so many scholars, is expressive of the feminine personality.

To say that a culture is dominated by the feminine principle does not necessarily mean that women will dominate men in the society concerned – still less that the men will be effeminate. There is much that is feminine in Japanese culture, and, to a lesser extent, in its Chinese parent. The love of nature, and the intense identification with it found in the poetry of the Haiku, the strong sense of the seasons, the cult of children and the delight in making toys, the aestheticism and secular ceremonial of domestic life – all these could be said to be feminine in spirit, and yet outwardly Japanese women were subservient to their husbands. On the other hand, it may be significant that in this other famous island the supreme divinity remained feminine, a rare state of affairs under civilization.

As for the legal and customary position of women in Minoan society, it is difficult to reconstruct it from what remained after the overrunning of the island by patriarchal Achaeans and Dorians. It seems, however, to show a perverse prejudice in scholars when they are unwilling to allow significance to the fact that in western Asia Minor, with its close and persistent contacts with Crete, matrilineal inheritance

Plate 18. Seal stones. (a) Woman offers lilies at a horned altar. Carnelian (1.7 cms), from tomb at Pylos, c. 1500 B.C. (b) Priest leading griffin. Jasper (2.1 cms), from the domed tomb at Vaphio, c. 1500 B.C. (c) Lion killing bull. Onyx (4 cms), from the domed tomb at Dendra, c. 1400 B.C. (d) Bearded Achaean. Amethyst (1 cm), from the Lower Grave Circle at Mycenae, c. 1600 B.C.

Attitude of worship. Detail of the figure illustrated on p. 106. Bronze, 1550–1500 B.C.

The offering-bearers. Model shrine. Clay. From the tomb of Kamilari, Phaistos.

persisted until the fourth century B.C., and that in Lycia, adjacent to Crete, children were always named after their mothers. Herodotus attributed this to the Lycian inheritance from both Carians *and Cretans*. There would appear to be a probability that in pre-Achaean Crete family inheritance went through the mother.

As for the part played by women in religious offices, the testimony of the Hagia Triada sarcophagus is plain enough: at least in some ceremonies, the priestesses were set above the priests. If this was still true in the fourteenth century, its prevalence in earlier days must be as nearly as possible certain. It is supported by one section of the figures in the great Corridor at Knossos where a woman, more likely to be a priestess or queen than a goddess, stands at the centre between two approaching lines of men – presumably bearing tribute (p. 109).

From the point of view of the social structure, and of judging the sex of the occupant of the throne at the apex of that structure, this pre-eminence of the priestesses may be of more significance than the dominion of the Goddess herself. She could, after all, be a masculine dream. Yet Cretan men and women were everywhere accustomed to seeing a splendid goddess queening it over a small and suppliant male god, and this concept must surely have expressed some attitude present in the human society that accepted it? Moreover, it was a concept strong enough to hold out against the contrary ideas that the Cretans encountered in Egypt and the Levant.

Again, there is the intimate love of nature and gardens (most women in their poetry identify themselves with plants and flowers and birds); the devotion to the fleeting moment and the neglect of history; the passion for dancing; a certain light-mindedness that, so far as can be judged, apparently went with an absence of any strong sense of guilt or thoughts of punishment. Most striking of all, perhaps, is the lack of the martial spirit that was so much in evidence in the Bronze Age world. The only item of military equipment symbolically displayed was the protective shield.

In addition to these characteristics, there was another which much more strongly implies the self-confidence of women and therefore their secure position in society. This is the fearless and natural emphasis on sexual life that ran through all religious expression and was made obvious in the provocative dress of both sexes and their easy mingling – a spirit best understood through its opposite: the total veiling and seclusion of Moslem women under a faith which even denied them a soul.

Are all these manifestations of the social and psychological ascendancy of women in Minoan Crete enough to put a woman on the throne – or at least a high priestess, who would presumably have been a queen, as the supreme figure in the ritual life of the palace? It has to be said at once, not necessarily. It is quite possible that a reigning prince might have played the part of the god, the Cretan Zeus, in relation

Ibex at a peak sanctuary. Detail of a steatite rhyton formerly covered with gold leaf, from the palace of Kato Zakro, *c.* 1500 B.C.

Enthroned goddess and demonic servitors. Was the filling of her cup to bring rain for the growing corn? Gold signet ring from Tiryns, 15th century B.C.

to the goddess who was ritually present in his palace. It is undeniably possible, yet psychologically it would have been an extraordinary state of affairs. Nowhere, so far as is known, was there any representation of a prince or his divine counterpart receiving royal honours. Instead a king would have been confronted on all sides by representations of his part as the subservient one – of the god as the mere instrument or worshipper of the goddess. Would this have been tolerable for a sovereign prince of great worldly power?

In the scenes from the seal-stones, not only is the Goddess always the central figure, being served and honoured in a variety of ways; she is sometimes shown seated on a throne. Supposing that a king did rule as consort of the Goddess, one would expect at the very least that at the royal court, which elsewhere, in Egypt and the Orient, was seen as the human reflection of the divine order, there would have been a throne for the queen as the counterpart of the Goddess. Yet in the sacred room at Knossos, and apparently also in the state apartment in the residential quarter, the throne stood single and alone.

If it were not for the tradition of King Minos, and the corresponding absence of any recorded memories of Cretan queens, and perhaps also certain strong if un-conscious assumptions among Classical scholars, it seems that the archaeological evidence would have been read as favouring a woman on the ritual throne at Knossos.

The idea has received some support from features in the Throne Room. On seals and elsewhere griffins are shown accompanying the Goddess, and on one seal-stone in particular (from Psychro) she is flanked by a pair of these fabulous creatures. It has been suggested that this scene represents a living enactment witnessed in the Throne Room at Knossos, where a priestess-queen representing the Goddess appeared between confronted griffins (p. 77).

This would make a more telling argument if it were not for the fact that painted griffins also flanked the throne at Pylos – and the notion of a queen enthroned in the great hall of a late Mycenaean kingdom would be as unwelcome as it is improbable. Moreover, although the date of the last phase of the Knossian Throne Room is doubtful, it was certainly decorated at a time of Mycenaean influence.

The actual remains of a woman who could have sat on the throne have recently been found at Arkhanes, a few miles from the palace. She had been buried in a gold-adorned gown, with gold rings and necklaces, and two tiny gold boxes, perhaps amulets, lying on her breast. One of her rings showed a vegetation rite, with the Goddess, in a dress much like her own, male dancers, butterflies, and a tree set in a triple shrine.

The most likely hypothesis would be that queens exercised some temporal power in the days of the Old Palaces, but that this became less as the wealth and worldly importance of Knossos grew and spread, and suffered a further setback with Mycenaean dominance or conquest. Yet to the end a queen might well have remained a high priestess presiding over the ritual occasions of the palace. The low, dimly lit apartment which has been given the name of the Throne Room is clearly part of a ritual quarter (p. 78) contrasting with the reception room suites on the upper floors.

The hypothesis of queenship is a fascinating one, but even if it were ever proved it could not do more than enhance appreciation of the unmistakably feminine quality of Minoan culture. Are there any reasons why this quality should have prevailed in Crete and led to the creation of so extraordinary a civilization? First it will be rashly suggested that the small, delicately-boned Mediterranean race with its relatively slight body and facial hair may have tended also towards a more feminine metabolic balance. Human evolution has moved in the direction of the prevalence of female and infantile characteristics, and this has been more marked in some racial types than in others. There is a persistent belief that the Mediterranean peoples, much mixed though they now are, tend to possess lively, volatile and emotional temperaments.

Historical explanations are also available. Crete was first settled by Stone Age peasants at a stage of culture when, on the whole, women tended to have an equal place with men in responsibilities and esteem. They did not have to fight for the island, but occupied it quite peacefully. In Anatolia, whence probably the bulk of these original colonists and subsequent settlers were derived, the Oriental cult of the Goddess had been strongly implanted and continued to flourish in the worship of Cybele and other goddesses even after the Indo-European penetration. Forms of matrilineal society were known there, and persisted in the regions nearest to Crete.

Most important of all, the geographical situation of the island made it an ideal forcing ground for these seeds. In the security of another island, Malta, the worship of the Mother Goddess was intensive and long-lasting and produced some curious blooms. But Malta was too remote from Egypt and the Levant to receive the fertilization needed to produce high civilization. Crete was open to it, yet at the same time sufficiently isolated to remain secure for several centuries. The protection of the sea enabled the islanders to seek trade rather than war, and to hold on to their wealth without the burden of great military strength. Peaceful security made it easier for the women to retain their social position and their influence on cultural and religious life.

This influence, together with the cultural inheritance, must have helped to save the Cretans from developing a martial spirit from within. For although the sea made armed force less necessary, it did not prevent it: the Achaeans of the Mycenaean Age were not unduly threatened from without, and yet they developed a passionate love of arms. The Cretans seem to have reduced and diverted their aggressiveness through a free and well-balanced sexual life, and through their enthusiasm for sports, games and dancing. It has recently been said of the Nuba people of the southern Sudan that their "distinguishing feature is their lack of aggression. They love music and dancing. . . . Their fighting instincts are released in the wrestling matches which are the centre of their life." The Cretans were living at a far higher level of civilization in a society that could offer a variety of satisfactions. Small Nuban boys have only one ambition: to become master wrestlers. Cretan children would not have had any such monomania imposed upon them. Yet it is obvious that the capture and playing of bulls must have assumed tremendous importance for many young people, and that, together with boxing and wrestling, it made an outlet for the aggressive urges more usually directed against an imagined external enemy.

So Minoan Crete, which the islanders called their motherland, enjoyed peace and was able to nourish a culture that gave full expression to some of the best elements of the feminine principle. It was ready for the marriage with the vigorous and masculine Achaeans now rising to power in their fatherland across the sea.

Plate 19. A princely wine cup. Beaten gold. From the Upper Grave Circle at Mycenae, 16th century B.C.

Overleaf Plate 20. "Mycenae rich in gold". The citadel at sunset, seen from the Perseia Spring.

Chapter Four

Graves and Kingdoms

A gold mask from the corpse of a king of Mycenae; a massive gateway leading into the royal citadel; the great circular hearth of a royal banqueting hall: these three things evoke the essential character of the Mycenaean Age. The times at which they were made span its greatest centuries.

The severe golden face (plate 23) with strong brows, narrow straight nose, thin straight lips, curling moustache and full beard represents a dead man. The line of the lids shows that the eyes are closed in death, yet they still seem to stare. This mask deserves its fame, for more sharply than anything else it expresses the beginning of Mycenaean civilization.

It seems also to express the contrast with the Minoan ideal. There is the warrior king, the bearded northerner, the man of authority who would have no natural sympathy with flower gardens, elegant ladies, aestheticism and young men in flounced robes. This king died in about 1550 B.C., at a time when Minoan influence had recently begun to make itself strongly felt in Mycenae. His own possessions already showed this influence, and it was soon to go further in softening the rough Achaean traditions. Yet, looking at that face, it is hard to believe that the man behind the mask would have approved what was happening. . . .

The path climbs up the lower slopes of the hill and narrows at the square hole of the gateway. Above it the pair of heavy-footed, heavy-muscled lions flank the sacred column, their forefeet resting on the altars at its base. Beyond the gate the path mounts more steeply than before toward the summit of the acropolis of Mycenae, once crowned by the royal hall of the line of Agamemnon. The huge stones of the citadel walls, and the gate itself with its twenty-ton lintel, seem to proclaim an heroic primitivism, like the dream of some German romantic for a backcloth to Wagner.

The Lion Gate of Mycenae (plate 21) is perhaps the second most famous relic after the gold mask – which came from a cemetery lying just inside the gate itself. Again its fame is appropriate, for this architecture expresses something enduring in the Mycenaean tradition: its aggressive masculinity and ingrained militarism. When these blocks were cut and piled into the mighty defences, the prehistoric king had been lying in his grave, the gold mask pressed against the dried flesh, for

Plate 21. Royal Mycenae. The Upper Grave Circle inside the Lion Gate.

The hearth in the great hall. "Palace of Nestor". View from behind the hall with oil store in foreground. Epano Englianos, near Chora, accepted site of ancient Pylos; 13th century B.C.

about two centuries. The Achaeans, under the leadership of Mycenae, were masters of the sea, had absorbed much of Minoan culture and were trading with the civilized peoples of the eastern Mediterranean as well as with the barbarous west. Yet they still enclosed their citadel within these rugged walls, and carved the confronted lions and pillar, probably the emblem of the royal house, in the same primitively martial spirit. The king's dwelling, which rose high above the walls, was decorated with frescoes derived from those of Knossos; yet it was relatively small, without domestic spaciousness. Mycenae was still in its general ambience more a warrior lord's stronghold than a palace.

The third handiwork of the Bronze Age Achaeans to convey with exceptional force something of the essence of Mycenaean life is less well known than either the gold mask or the Lion Gate. It is a little later in date even than the portal, and was in use when the invaders brought Mycenaean greatness to an end. It is a huge, circular hearth that fills the centre of the great hall of the "Palace of Nestor" at the site identified with ancient Pylos. The disk, of clay coated with stucco, is thirteen feet across and boldly decorated in black, blue and yellow. Round the vertical edge a stylized flame pattern licks upwards to where a ring of spirals runs round the rim of the hearth, framing the space where the royal fire once burned. The smoke, and perhaps sometimes the fumes of a roasting ox, seem to have been drawn up through a chimney of terra-cotta pipes, to be carried out through a clerestory that was supported immediately above the hearth on four big columns of fluted wood.

The king sat on his inlaid throne to the right of the hearth as one entered the hall through its one doorway. Painted stiffly on the wall behind him were a pair of griffins, and outside them a pair of lions. In the corner another fresco showed a man in a long robe playing on a lyre. If, in Homeric fashion, the king wished to pour a libation to the gods, a channel and shallow basins sunk into the floor beside his seat could have carried away the wine. While all the rest of the floor was covered with a painted chequerwork filled with abstract patterns, one square between the king and his hearth was charged with an octopus, its eyes staring out between eight serpentine tentacles – a symbol, perhaps, of his far-reaching power.

Halls of this kind, which to judge from Homer can legitimately be called banqueting chambers, formed the heart of most if not all Mycenaean royal houses. They can be distinguished among the ruins of Mycenae and of Tiryns; but nowhere else except at Pylos, in its distant south-western corner of the Peloponnese, does enough remain to make them and the life that went on round the hearth fire an easily imaginable reality. The contrast between a relatively small and compact royal house centred upon a great hall where the king sat among his companions, and the spreading Cretan palaces with their domestic suites and reception rooms centred on an open court, is plain enough. Equally unmistakable is the difference in the social ordering and conduct of the royal household that it must represent.

These halls are called *megara* after the banqueting chambers of the Homeric heroes. They are entered through a pillared porch and vestibule, a plan which is thought to have been derived from a type of house that already had a long history in Greece itself and in Anatolia. This derivation may well be correct, and in so far as the porched entrance and certain other features are concerned the halls of the Mycenaean princes may have been native to this part of the world. Some architectural features are certain to be quickly adapted to temperature and rainfall.

Yet at the same time it would seem to be no better than scholarly masochism not to recognize in the "high hall" with its great hearth and its throne the survival of a tradition that stretched back into the ancestral past of the Achaeans. Northern kings had halls like this where they banqueted with their followers and poets recited while they plucked upon the strings. In the north they were high-roofed and gabled against the snow, the hearth was in a trench along the centre and hangings and tapestries might take the place of frescoes. So much else was the same. Even as late as Viking times the chief or king sat in his "high seat" in the centre of the long side of the hall. The most celebrated example must be Heorot, or Hart Hall, built by the Danish king Hrothgar in the Anglo-Saxon epic, *Beowulf*. "It towered up steep, with gables wide", and there Hrothgar handed out gold to his followers as they banqueted, his queen carried round cups of mead, and all heard "the string, the twining of the harp, the clear song of the minstrel who told of the creation of man from most ancient days".

If the Mycenaean halls with their brilliant frescoes and other refinements borrowed from the Cretans were a little more splendid and civilized than the memory of them pictured in the "shadowy" halls of Homer, and if Heorot and its like were darker and more barbarous again, they are all given a significant unity by the kind of society they were built to serve. They were built for warrior kings who lived and feasted among their followers, giving them patronage and expecting them to follow the royal arms into battle. These royal residences of the Mycenaean Age were so essentially different from the Cretan palaces that they will be referred to here as halls – a name often given to great English houses that were centred on a banqueting chamber.

The bearded face of a fighting king buried with his arms, the massive fortifications and gateway at Mycenae, the mighty hearth at Pylos, have been chosen to represent the dominant spirit of Mycenaean life. A more balanced picture will be drawn in round them, but it is claimed that they justly represent the enduring core of Achaean tradition which was never lost in spite of the softening influence of Minoan culture.

Having suggested the qualities which were to distinguish the mainland civilization from that of Crete, it will be best to give an outline of what is known of the five or so centuries during which that civilization rose to power and wealth, and then, like so many others before and since, collapsed through external pressures and growing internal weaknesses. Afterwards an attempt will be made to describe the life of those centuries, using archaeological material, and occasionally appealing to Homer to bring more light to the scene. The earlier phase will be treated in this chapter; the later, imperial, phase of Mycenaean history, about which much more is known, will be the subject of the next.

The Mycenaean period can be said to have begun by the middle of the sixteenth century B.C. This date has also been chosen as marking the beginning of the late phase of the Aegean Bronze Age. It was a flourishing time for the Cretans both at home and in their enterprises overseas – of which their tremendous impact on mainland Greece was, of course, a significant part. It is not known whether the dynasty ruling in Mycenae included newcomers, or whether the old Achaean ruling family became more prosperous and more able to respond to the Minoan influence. Certainly they rose rapidly to a new level of affluent civilization, leading the way for the other Achaean kingdoms. It was one of these early kings of Mycenae who was buried near the citadel in the golden mask.

After this initial upsurge, the fifteenth and early fourteenth centuries can be seen as a middle period of consolidation, when the Mycenaean kingdoms absorbed the civilizing influences which at first had been superficial. The barbarous elements so noticeable before died out. The early trading ventures to the north and west were now followed by a more substantial expansion of interest in the eastern Mediterranean. The Cretans still dominated the sea routes, but Mycenaean settlers established themselves in Rhodes (where they seem at first to have been on peaceful terms with the existing Minoan colony), and began to develop trade with the Levant and Egypt. There was another settlement at Miletus. Mycenaean power was in fact following almost exactly along the lines already long ago opened up by the Cretans.

The date at which the Achaeans overtook the islanders and became the leading marine power in the Mediterranean is involved in the mists of doubt at present obscuring the history of Knossos. If it is true that Knossos had accepted a mainland dynasty as early as the mid-fifteenth century (p. 69), and was destroyed some fifty years later, then it follows that the Mycenaean traders and colonists would have been free of all Cretan rivalry soon after 1400 B.C. But if, on the other hand, Knossos kept its independence until it was seized by the Achaeans towards the end of the fourteenth century, then their absolute ascendancy would have been delayed until then. This date fits quite well with the complete Mycenaean domination of Rhodes, where the old Minoan colony was abandoned, with increased trading activity in Cyprus and with the establishment by 1300 of a Mycenaean commercial settlement at Ugarit on the Syrian coast.

As for Knossos itself, if in fact the palace was taken over by an Achaean dynasty in the later fourteenth century, if an Achaean "Minos" controlled a still prosperous island, then local ships manned in part by islanders and carrying Cretan cargoes would have sailed and rowed the sea-ways together with those of the mainland kingdoms. Fine Cretan bronze work was certainly finding foreign markets in the thirteenth century, for the palace accounts at Pylos (p. 221) record the purchase of Cretan cauldrons.

Whether or not Knossos was contributing to them, there is no doubt of Achaean power and prosperity for many decades after 1350 B.C. This was the Mycenaean heyday. While the fall of Minoan Crete particularly affected the position in the east Mediterranean, the Achaeans were also developing their commerce round the Aegean, including Troy, and westward to Italy. Although other Mediterranean peoples, notably the Phoenicians, had a share in maritime trade, their pre-eminence was probably recognized all the way from central Italy to the Levant. How far their power was centralized it is difficult to judge, but it is likely that the king of Mycenae enjoyed something like the power of leadership and command allowed to Agamemnon in the *Iliad*, and that he could claim to speak on equal terms with the Hittite king and with Pharaoh.

Here a slender shaft of historical light comes from the Hittite archives. Some

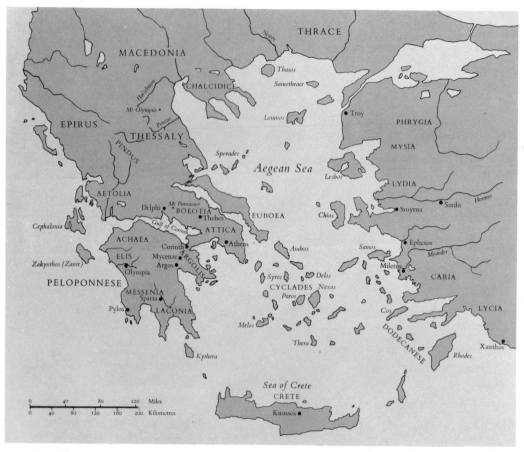

Greece and the Aegean Sea.

documents refer to a maritime kingdom of Ahhijawa – which can be read as Achaea. The most illuminating is a polite letter addressed by a Hittite sovereign to a king of Ahhijawa over a trouble involving Miletus, which the Hittites had temporarily occupied but still recognized as lying within Ahhijawan territory.

This policy of distant co-existence was characteristic of the relationship between the two peoples – or between their warrior élites. Although the maritime power had settlements or trading depots at Miletus and elsewhere on the coastal fringes of the land power, there was very little intercourse between them. Hardly a Mycenaean potsherd has been found within the perimeter of the Hittite realm.

It was quite otherwise in Achaean relations with Egypt. Mycenaean products, perhaps most of all perfumed oils, were popular by the Nile, while reciprocal Egyptian influence on the art and architecture of mainland Greece was at least as strong as it had always been in Minoan Crete.

The Achaeans had reached the summit of their power by 1300 B.C., and yet by the end of the century it was to collapse with extraordinary speed, and afterwards existed only in fragments. Although internal weaknesses and aggression from outside were largely responsible for this breakdown, the strain of the campaign against Troy may have helped to speed it.

According to the estimate of Eratosthenes, a Greek historian accepted in his day, Troy fell to the Achaeans in the year 1184. The date is now usually pushed back to about 1250, precisely the date calculated by Herodotus. This is a proof of the soundness of Greek tradition and historical methods – except, of course, for the few scholars who refuse to allow any reality to Homer's Trojan War, seeing it as no more than a late version of a long-lived heroic siege legend.

According to tradition, there was instability in the royal houses of the Mycenaean kingdoms in the half-century or so before the heroes sailed for Troy. The hall at Thebes was destroyed towards the end of the fourteenth century. A new dynasty was said to have been set up in Mycenae itself – and by an outsider coming to Greece from Lydia in Anatolia. This was Pelops, grandfather of Agamemnon. Agamemnon's father, Atreus, was involved in a struggle with his brother which would have involved grave disturbance in the kingdom. Meanwhile, on the other side of the Peloponnese, another new royal house was supposed to have been established when Neleus, having quarrelled with his twin brother in their northern kingdom of Iolkos in Thessaly, came south to Messenia and took the throne of Pylos. He was father of the good Nestor who sailed with the Argonauts, lived on to be the doyen of the Greeks at Troy, and returned home to receive Telemachus in the great hall at Pylos.

Archaeological confirmation for such instability is not forthcoming because of the uncertainty of dates. Houses destroyed, and never rebuilt, outside the citadel at Mycenae may be the results of civil disturbance at this time. Perhaps taken together there is enough evidence to show that the Achaean power, although still great both at home and overseas, was already a little shaken even before the exhausting venture of the Trojan War.

However this may be, there is no doubt that an external threat followed by invasion afflicted the Achaean kingdoms some two generations after the survivors had struggled home from Troy. The first threat, probably with minor raiding, was met by the strengthening of the defences of the main citadels and the protection of their water supplies. A massive stone wall was built across the Isthmus of Corinth to protect the Peloponnese against attack from the north. Tablets preserved at Pylos reveal some of the desperate last-minute movements of men and ships that were made in an effort to defend the whole kingdom.

It was hopeless, however. Pylos itself was burnt and deserted. Mycenae, Tiryns,

Midea and other lesser citadels and fortified refuges were destroyed, and failed ever fully to recover. Only Athens, at that time a relatively small and poor kingdom, contrived to hold out against the enemy – a feat which later Athenians never allowed to be forgotten. This great disaster is believed to have taken place at the end of the thirteenth century or a little later, and may have been the work of the Dorians – a still barbarous branch of the Greek people, who had been living as shepherds and warriors among the northern mountains.

These invaders were to the Achaeans what the Achaeans had been to the Cretans. But now the fabric of high civilization could no longer stand the strain. Indeed Mycenaean civilization had never had so broad a social base nor such deep psychological foundations as the Minoan, and was therefore more liable to collapse. Also this time round about 1200 B.C. was one of great ethnic disturbances comparable to that of eight centuries before (p. 51). Once again peoples were on the move, and each movement was liable to set off another. This time, too, some took to the sea. The Hittite empire collapsed, the pressures on the Levant and on Egypt were very great, so that their peoples could offer little cultural support to keep civilization alive in the Aegean.

As the invaders spread southward through the Peloponnese, then overseas to Crete and the rest of the south Aegean, and even on as far as south-west Anatolia, many Achaeans themselves migrated. Some did not go far, but, taking advantage of the islands of country left unsubmerged by the Dorian tide, found refuge there – especially in the rugged hills of Arcadia and in Attica. Many of the refugees who chose Attica came from the kingdom of Pylos, and by some means or other a Pylian dynasty came to power in Athens. This admixture of two vigorous and gifted peoples – native Athenians and incoming Pylians – was to make an important contribution to later Greek history. Other refugees went overseas, as far away as Tarsus and the Cilician Plain. Some went to Cyprus, or joined the "People of the Sea" in their attacks on Egypt and the civilized states of the Levant. Later, many crossed the Aegean to settle in Ionia.

Meanwhile in Greece itself Mycenaean civilization was not dead, but flickered on in decadence for another century. Mycenae was re-occupied, although in a sadly diminished style. Life for ordinary people may not have changed profoundly, but there were no rich kings or royal households, no overseas trade, to support artists and fine craftsmen and make a focus for civilization. After about 1100 B.C. the end of the Mycenaean tradition began to be transformed into the beginning of a new Greek way of life. Athens was at the heart of the new development (p. 268).

After this summary of the five centuries that saw the rise and fall of the first Greek-speaking civilization, the Mycenaean way of life must be examined in greater detail. The central theme of this book must, of course, be kept in mind. In the

The ritual hearth was an ancient tradition. A hollowed hearth-stone from Lerna, *c.* 2000 B.C.

marriage of Cretan with Achaean traditions, how far did the offspring favour either parent and how far did it come to develop its own mature individuality?

In the days before the rise of the first great dynasty at Mycenae, the citadel may have consisted of a chieftain's hall protected by a wooden stockade or a simple wall and with a small settlement loosely gathered round it. Living conditions were probably quite rough, although the ruling family would have enjoyed the same kind of honour and service as was paid to King Hrothgar at Heorot. On the slopes below the rocky eminence of the citadel there stretched a cemetery where the dead of Mycenae were buried in modest style.

Then about 1600 B.C. contacts with Crete increased, and the chiefly rulers began their rise to royal wealth and power. These earliest kings and queens were buried in a concentrated area in the lower part of the cemetery. The funerals were now grander affairs, and the dead, laid at the bottom of shafts cut into the rock, were supplied with valuable and finely wrought weapons, ornaments and other worldly goods (p. 175). When the funeral celebrations were over, the grave roofed with wood and the shaft above it filled with earth, carved gravestones were often set at the top to mark them. This is the first sculpture of Greece – and it is crude in both workmanship and style. Where figure subjects appear they are just such as would be expected of the Achaeans: men going to fight or to hunt in chariots drawn by galloping horses.

Above left A survival from a simpler past. Vessel of traditional character from the Lower Grave Circle, Mycenae, *c.* 1600 B.C. *Above right* Establishment of a Mycenaean style. The ivy leaf is of Minoan derivation, but the style is typically Mycenaean. Upper Grave Circle, Mycenae, *c.* 1500 B.C. *Below* Superb carving in rock crystal. The realistic duck's head may show Egyptian influence. Upper Grave Circle, Mycenae, 16th century B.C.

The Achaean love of battle. One of the earliest Greek stone-carvings. Grave-slab from the Upper Grave Circle, Mycenae, 16th century B.C.

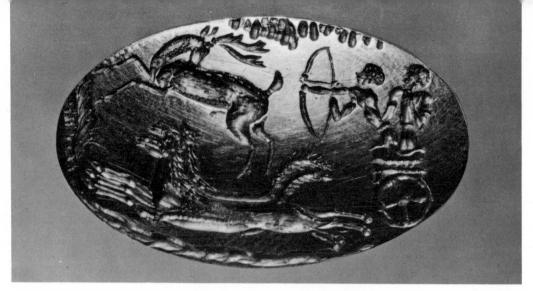

The Achaean love of hunting. Gold signet ring from the Upper Grave Circle, Mycenae, 16th century B.C.

One of the richest of these graves had received altogether the bodies of three men and one woman – the first two bodies having been pushed to the wall to make room for two later interments. One of these was a six-foot man with bandy legs; the other a man who seems to have suffered a fractured skull and to have died from a trephining operation. What, however, brings these skeletons an imaginable life is a tiny seal cut in amethyst (plate 18). It shows a man with a strong beard, a shock of hair falling over his forehead and behind his ears, clearly marked brows, a nose with a sharp, upturned tip and lips full and well marked. It is a face that suggests a countryman and soldier rather than a palace prince, and it shows all the vigour that must have been needed by the generation of men who began to lay the foundations of Mycenaean power.

About half a century after the earliest of these graves had been filled, a second group of royal burials was begun much higher up the slope although still, at this time, outside the citadel. Some of the shafts were very large and deep, and the grave furnishings very splendid indeed. The two royal cemeteries remained in use side by side, and this may possibly mean that there was a dual kingship at Mycenae like that later established in Sparta. Round each group a circular wall was built to isolate the royal dead from their less exalted subjects. Certainly they were greatly venerated, for when in about 1300 B.C. the Lion Gate and the contemporary Cyclopean fortifications were built, a very special effort was made to enclose the upper grave circle within the walls, so making it a part of the citadel (plate 21). As by this time, after centuries of accumulation, the graves were well below ground level, the ring wall had to be heightened so that from this time onwards visitors looked down on the royal tombs, distinguishing them, no doubt, by the various grave stones that still stood above them.

Their ancient sanctity and the veneration in which they were held lasted long after the Mycenaean world had collapsed. The Greek historian, Pausanias, visiting Mycenae in the second century A.D., was evidently shown the upper circle and told that the graves belonged to Agamemnon and those who were murdered with him. The tradition was that they had been buried inside the walls, while Agamemnon's unfaithful queen, Clytemnestra, and her lover, Aegisthus, were condemned to lie outside the citadel. Through the remarkable persistence of this story, two large vaulted tombs not far from the walls are still attributed to Clytemnestra and Aegisthus.

This picture of the Greek tourist visiting Mycenae reveals the continuity and wholeness of Greek life as it lay extended in time. Names and dates slipped, periods were telescoped, legends were woven round slender facts, yet the essence of the matter was there and never lost its inspiration.

When Pausanias saw the royal graves of the upper circle, the treasure that had been buried with the remains of nine men, eight women and two children still lay at the bottom of the shafts protected from robbers both by the veneration in which the dead were held and the depth of soil which covered them. Now, together with the lesser treasure from the lower grave circle, it is in the National Museum in Athens and assails the eyes of modern tourists with a blaze of gold. There are in fact thirty-three pounds of gold, much of it beaten thin and therefore affording a maximum show. It brilliantly justifies the recurring Homeric epithet for Mycenae as "rich in gold". Yet the first impact is undoubtedly one of a barbaric splendour quite unlike any of the subtle Minoan displays to be seen at Heraklion.

Oriental motifs in Mycenaean art. The lion leaping on deer amid palm trees is of Levantine and Nilotic origin. Panel from one side of a hexagonal gold-mounted wooden box, from the Upper Grave Circle, Mycenae, 16th century B.C.

A closer examination of the extraordinary wealth of objects does not dispel this impression of barbarism, yet shows that it is only a part of the truth. These early kings and queens owned many things that were beautiful and made with admirable skill. The bronze dagger blades (plate 32) inlaid with patterns and scenes in silver, gold and niello, for instance, are marvels of craftsmanship. The bronze mirrors and sumptuous jewellery, both of which were enjoyed equally by men and women, suggest at least the beginnings of sophistication in the royal household.

Gracefully stemmed gold goblets (plate 19) with one or two handles, fluted gold cups and quantities of gold and silver vases give some idea of the splendour of the service in the banqueting hall; strong, shapely bronze utensils (plate 37) suggest well-stocked kitchens and pantries. The love of both men and women for personal finery, and perhaps the need for the royal family to wear the metal of the sun, appears in crowns and diadems (plate 22), ornate gold ear-rings and hairpins (plate 44) for women and massive upper arm bands for men, in linked gold necklets (plate 30)

Left Lions on a royal wine cup. Thick sheet gold. From the Upper Grave Circle, Mycenae, 16th century B.C. *Right* "Quaint and clumsy-looking." African ostrich egg mounted by a Mycenaean craftsman. From the Upper Grave Circle, Mycenae, 16th century B.C.

Lions and spirals in gold embellish a sword hilt. The bronze blade is engraved with griffins. From the Lower Grave Circle, Mycenae, 16th century B.C.

and heavy necklaces of amber, and in gold roundels about two inches across (plate 26), their shining disks showing butterflies, octopuses and a variety of spirals and whirligigs, that may have been attached, like showers of huge sequins, to the ladies' skirts.

The gods were served as splendidly as the king in his hall, and even with more refinement. The graves yielded some fine rhytons in gold and silver – perhaps at that time more precious than gold. One, in the form of a bull's head, is only a little inferior to the masterpiece from the Little Palace at Knossos. The head is of silver with horns, eyes, nostrils and a rosette on the forehead in gold. There is a maned lion's head (plate 17) in thick plates of beaten gold, extraordinarily strong and noble, and rhytons of mounted ostrich eggs, as quaint and clumsy-looking as their counterparts in Elizabethan England. There is a base of a silver rhyton in the form of a stag, also rather clumsy and with an air of the Caucasus in its style. There is a conical silver rhyton of classical Cretan shape carved with a scene of a violent assault by Mycenaean warriors against a fortified citadel.

This siege scene, made some two and a half centuries before the Trojan war, leads to the armaments which are so conspicuous among the royal possessions. As well as the famous inlaid daggers the men had great numbers of bronze swords – as many as twenty-seven in a single grave. The design of the best has an exceptional force, the blades sweeping out into wings (protecting the grip) that seem to give them a sense of movement like that of a modern aircraft. Often these horns and the hilts were covered with gold, and the pommels were of gold, ivory and alabaster. The blades too were sometimes ornamented with griffins, horses or abstract patterns, and there is no doubt that some of these swords were intended for ceremony and not for war – the military insignia of kings who were war leaders.

All these rich and much-wrought objects are likely to have belonged to their owners while they were alive: to have been used in the hall on the top of the hill before they were carried down with the corpses to the cemetery. But the dead were also dressed in a fashion they had not known during life, and it is this funeral gear more than anything else that gives the air of barbarism to the assembled treasure. The most important of the men were buried with gold masks and breastplates, the most important of the women with colossal diadems or rayed crowns, and the tiny bodies of two infants had been completely sheathed in gold – cut-outs that survive like little gold spectres of brief lives.

Apart from the bearded face, which has a certain austere strength, the other five masks (plate 23) are roughly made and in every way uncouth. Two of them represent a totally different physical type from the rest, having round, fat faces, and roundish eyes.

The pre-eminence of the bearded prince is emphasized by the fact that he alone had been supplied with an ornamented gold breastplate, or pectoral. (His companion had a plain one.) This pectoral is a curious affair, for while the remainder of the surface is covered with running spirals, two plain circles are embossed to represent nipples (p. 182).

Two ornate diadems (plate 22) found in a grave reserved for women were so large, and so flimsily made, that they could have been worn only in death. One of them, over two feet in length, is topped by nine feebly designed flowers, the other by seven embossed rays, each well over a foot long – an extraordinary anticipation of the rayed sun crown of later times. In the patterns on both diadems the numbers seven and nine seem to be significantly repeated.

Nothing quite like these royal cemeteries has been found elsewhere in Greece. Although further discovery may always alter the balance, they seem to prove that already in the sixteenth century Mycenae was ahead of the other kingdoms that were then beginning to take shape and to rise in culture and prosperity. These were Iolkos in Thessaly; Thebes and Orchomenos in Boeotia; Athens, still relatively small, in Attica. The greatest concentration of Mycenaean power, however, was, and remained, in the Peloponnese where Pylos commanded Messenia and, more important still, Mycenae dominated Tiryns and other strongholds in the Argolid.

Although there is so much that can never be recalled, the burials of these precursors of Agamemnon do reveal something of the early days of Mycenaean history. The first and most obvious thing is the tremendous debt that was owed to Crete. The finest of the royal possessions were all of Minoan inspiration. The bull's head and conical rhytons both have close counterparts in Crete, while the designs on the

Plate 22. Tiaras made for the grave. Flimsy gold (62 and 65 cms across). From the women's grave in the Upper Grave Circle, Mycenae, 16th century B.C.

Overleaf Plate 23. Masks for dead princes. Five gold, one electrum. From both grave circles at Mycenae, 16th century B.C. (bottom left, the so-called Mask of Agamemnon).

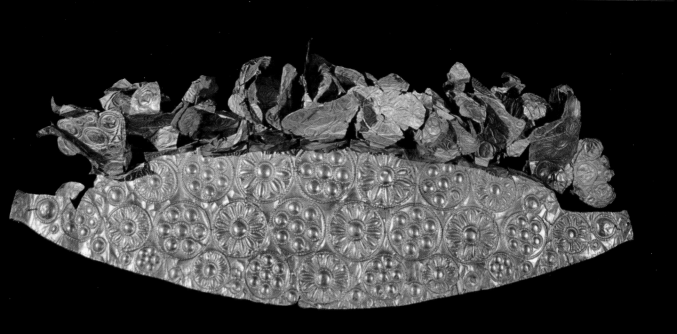

daggers, especially the lilies, the cat hunting ducks and the running spirals (plate 32), show the movement of Minoan art as well as some of its favourite subjects. They are perhaps rather stiffer in effect, but this may well be due to the difficulty of inlaying metals. All these things and many others must either have been shipped from Crete or have been made by Cretan craftsmen who had come over to work for *nouveau riche* Mycenaean patrons. Some of the painted pottery that accompanied the more precious vessels had been brought from Crete and the Cyclades, and luxury goods are far more usual items of foreign trade than bulkier and less valuable objects. Moreover, it seems significant that those things which must have been made locally because they were intended expressly for funerary use are precisely the things which are most barbaric. These are the masks, pectorals and diadems designed for dressing the corpses, and the carved grave slabs set above them.

In spite of the cultural influence of Crete which prevailed at this time and continued during the fifteenth century, the evidence of the graves supports that of hearth and hall, and stronghold, and later tradition, to prove that underneath the veneer of Mediterranean civilization the Achaeans maintained a considerable part of their old social structure and values. Although it would be unwise to over-emphasize this, it appears that even Cretans working for Mycenaean lords chose subjects of battle, animal combat and the chase that they knew would be pleasing to their patrons. More convincing is the testimony of the large quantities of weapons laid with the dead, and most of all that of the sculptures carved as their lasting memorials in the eyes of all men. There was the prince in his chariot intent on the slaughter of men and beasts.

The other very significant fact revealed by these Mycenaean treasures is the extent of the foreign contacts – through trade, or royal gifts, or piratical raids – that must have added to the luxury of the king's household. In addition to goods and materials acquired from Crete and other parts of the Aegean, there were ostrich eggs from Africa, ivory probably from Syria, Anatolian silver, lapis lazuli from Mesopotamia, and northern amber – including beads undoubtedly manufactured in Britain. The gold is presumed to have been of Egyptian origin, probably from the Nubian mines that brought the Pharaohs so much of their wealth. A few objects, such as the stag rhyton, may have come from the north-east, perhaps the Caucasus.

The idea of the Mycenaean princes commanding from their halls a network of trade stretching from Britain and Scandinavia to the Caucasus, the Tigris and the Nile is a fascinating one. And of all these foreign involvements, those with the barbarians to the north and west may have been the most important in furthering the Mycenaean rise to wealth and power. Faint echoes of the doings of such merchant adventurers may be heard down the centuries in the stories of Odysseus and of the Argonauts. More substantial news of it comes from the barbarian lands

Plate 24. The irresistible spiral. Stray find from Kalamata, Peloponnese, 15th century B.C. (See also plates 29, 32 and 33.)

Armour for the grave. Breast-plate, with nipples, worn by the prince with the bearded mask. Gold. From the Upper Grave Circle, Mycenae, 16th century B.C.

themselves, where at just this time in the sixteenth century the veils of prehistoric darkness were beginning to lift. Though literacy was so long delayed that their names and heroic deeds died with the bards who sang them, in these remoter parts of Europe, too, there were chiefs who were well armed in bronze and not without gold.

There are clear traces of Mycenaean contacts along the Danube and with eastern and central Europe. Peoples living in Jutland and elsewhere near the Baltic, and benefiting from the boom in the southern markets for the amber which was so providentially washed up on their shores, began to embellish their bronze ornaments with running spirals, a fashion that almost certainly came to them from Greece along the tracks of the amber route.

It is hard to say how far the Mycenaean traders themselves followed these over-land routes, how far they depended upon intermediaries to bring them the precious resin from the distant north. They certainly sailed in some numbers westward to

Sicily and southern Italy, establishing trading posts along coasts where Greek colonists were to follow them many centuries later. These voyages to the central Mediterranean seem to have led on to what is the most surprising of all Mycenaean relationships with Bronze Age Europe – the ties that certainly existed with Britain.

At just this time when Mycenaean kings were rising to a new wealth and power, a rather similar advance, although on a smaller scale, was taking place in southern England. There, too, a warrior aristocracy was ruling over peasants and herders and beginning to trade and to prosper – and to be buried with appropriate extravagance. Among the possessions so buried were a few objects that prove these chieftains to have had contacts with the Mycenaean world – most striking among them a fluted gold cup that might well have been filled with wine in a Mycenaean hall. These things, however, are of no great moment – the usual fruits of trade and of local imitation. The unique event was the building of the great sarsen-stone circle and trilithons of Stonehenge.

This sanctuary, constructed from colossal yet carefully-shaped blocks that make the cyclopean masonry of Mycenae look like childrens' bricks, has nothing to compare with it in all prehistoric Europe. Some of the local lords controlling the pastures of Salisbury plain, and perhaps, like Odysseus, owning twelve herds of cattle, may have had the wealth and authority needed to turn what had been a modest sanctuary of Stone Age origin into a noble and unparalleled work of megalithic architecture. It has always seemed that some individual must have initiated it – through swollen ambition or religious obsession – but because the whole design and method of the building is so far advanced on anything known in the island before, it has seemed likely that ideas drawn from a more civilized tradition might also have been involved. Known contacts with the Mycenaean world make this appear to be the most likely source of such inspiration. The probability is strengthened by the Mycenaean affinity of certain valued objects buried with the chieftains whose graves lie clustered round Stonehenge. One of these men, for example, carried a patterned rod, probably a sceptre of chiefly rank, identical with another carried by a near contemporary interred in the lower circle at Mycenae. A dagger carved on one of the huge sarsens is certainly foreign to western Europe, and can be likened to one carved on the gravestone of the prince of the bearded mask.

Homer makes it plain that architects, like poets and singers, could be wanderers – independent characters who liked to sell their talents from town to town and court to court. Perhaps, then, some Mycenaean "Daedalus", more reckless than the rest, took ship with a merchant sailing for those distant isles of Ocean. Perhaps he had heard tell of an ambitious British chieftain who would employ him. Or, conceivably, he may have left Greece with a restless or exiled Mycenaean prince who, settling among the rich cattle men and traders of Salisbury Plain, galvanized and directed their native energies. These are tales woven as fancifully as any ancient legend, yet here, too, there are unmistakable threads of fact. Some history there was, and perhaps some day it will be understood, linking the smooth chalk grasslands of southern England with the harsh hills and rich sea plain of the Argolid.

It was probably a search for tin and copper, needed in such quantities for arms, armour and chariot fittings, and for the great cauldrons and other vessels that were a recognized element in princely riches, that took the Mycenaean adventurers into barbarian Europe. They must have turned in that direction because the Cretans and other long-civilized peoples had a stranglehold on sources of metal nearer home. It was not until the Achaeans conquered Crete that they were able to move with full force into the eastern Mediterranean, and win access to the copper mines of Cyprus.

Mycenaean commerce with Europe may have done very well, for in dealing with backward areas stronger and more civilized peoples generally have the better of the bargain. But is it enough to account for the sudden influx of wealth that made Mycenae "rich in gold" as early as the sixteenth century? If thirty-three pounds of the precious stuff was given to the dead, how much more remained in the hands of the living – perhaps to be worked and re-worked with changing needs and fashions? If this was in fact Nubian gold, could the Achaeans possibly have supplied the Egyptians, who were far from being extravagant users of bronze, with enough tin and copper to pay for it? It is possible but not very likely.

All kinds of explanations are plausible. One, which is particularly pleasing because it would account for the fact that the Achaeans acquired so much of the root of all evil without apparently giving anything tangible in exchange, is that what they sold was themselves. In the early sixteenth century the Egyptians under Theban leadership were fighting hard to expel the Asiatic rulers, the Hyksos, who had usurped the throne of Pharaoh. The warlike Achaeans might well have served them as mercenaries and returned weighed down with golden wages. Yet the supply of gold seems to have lasted much later than the campaigns – and it is hard to believe that successful warriors would have returned to Greece without bringing jewellery or other Egyptian luxuries, some of which would have gone with them into their graves.

On the other hand, it looks as though the whole idea of making much of royal tombs was the result of Egyptian example. It was an idea which would appeal to the Achaeans with their glorification of kingship in a way which it never had to the Cretans.

Another explanation might be that the gold reached Mycenae by way of Crete. If gifts or tribute had for some time been going to Pharaoh on the scale suggested by the earliest of the Theban tomb paintings (p. 62), then substantial return gifts of gold would be customary. Much of it might then have been transferred from the treasury of Knossos to that of Mycenae as gold to buy off attack, as dowries (given on a magnificent scale between royal families of the Bronze Age) for Cretan princesses wedded to Achaean princes, or as payment for some services rendered.

The fate of gold in human hands has been unlike that of any other substance. Because it is imperishable and passionately desired it has never been discarded but always handed on. It is only the custom of giving it to the noble dead that has saved some small part of ancient goldwork in its original forms. Even today traces of prehistoric gold from the Old World and the New must be present and in current use. Who shall say what weight of gold once wrought by Mycenaean smiths into the winecups, jewels and glittering weapons dear to their lords is now incorporated in our own jewellery, watches and cigarette cases, our currency hoards and our dental bridgework?

Not unconnected with the source of their wealth is the question as to who these early kings of Mycenae may have been. Were they the descendants or direct in-heritors of chieftains who had been living there in barbarian style ever since the Greeks entered the Peloponnese? In some of the early graves, survivals from the older tradition show that there was no complete break with the past. Yet the many signs of far-flung foreign contacts, the mixture of barbarism with borrowed civilization, and above all the introduction of the horse-drawn chariot to the Aegean, suggest that these princes were no settled stay-at-homes content to advance slowly along the ancestral ways. Their own bearded faces show that they had not as yet adopted Aegean habits, but this may have been an old Achaean fashion, and cannot be used to prove that they were newcomers.

Probably these dynasties were mainly of local Achaean descent, but this was a time of change when there must have been many warriors on the move seeking gold and places of power. Some may have won a foothold at Mycenae. Nor must it be forgotten that there are scholars who believe that the first truly Greek-speaking invaders did not arrive in southern Greece until this time, and that these are the burials of their conquering leaders.

On the civilizing side, the possible influence of Cretan brides cannot be ignored. The influence of women taken into the royal houses in this way could help to explain the surprisingly rapid assimilation of Minoan fashions, Minoan domestic amenities and religious forms that was already happening in the sixteenth century and which was so profoundly to affect Achaean cultural life during the fifteenth.

Whatever the origin of these early dynasties, there is no doubt that Mycenaean civilization, which might be personified as having an Achaean skeleton and Minoan flesh, began its growth here in the Argolid and in Messenia, and soon spread over the many small kingdoms that composed Mycenaean Greece. Probably it was diffused through that brotherhood of princes, with its visiting, gift-exchanging, intermarrying and quarrelling which was to be so characteristic of the Heroic Age.

Unfortunately the material sources of evidence for the succeeding middle phase of Mycenaean history are very patchy. The royal graves at Mycenae have already given a good idea of how things began. The remains of great buildings, and above all of the royal halls and their archives, have much to tell about the days after about 1350. But for the century and a half in between, a time when in many ways Mycenaean culture was at its best, a scatter of tombs provide most of the information.

However, at least the tombs themselves are very relevant to an appraisal of the differences between Minoan and Mycenaean values. It has been seen how before they came under Achaean influence, the Cretans characteristically did not make much of death and funerary rites. The attitude of the Achaean élite was quite otherwise. The pride of the warrior kings and their sense of family, encouraged perhaps by what they knew of Egyptian funerary pomp, led to a great expenditure of wealth and labour on provision for the royal dead. Their example was soon followed by the nobility. To the extravagant provision of grave goods already seen in the early period at Mycenae was added the building of splendid tombs. Outside every royal citadel these mausolea were cut and built, and probably near every nobleman's house as well.

These tombs were usually cut into hillsides. A roofless, more or less horizontal passage was driven in to meet a cylindrical shaft sunk from above; a circular chamber was built within the shaft, the walls being brought in by corbelling to form a lofty, pointed dome, the top of which projected above ground level and was covered by a mound. It seems that this mound was often crusted with white lime plaster, so that visitors approaching a royal town were made to realize the king's grandeur not only by the sight of his hilltop megaron rising above the citadel walls, but also by the ancestral tombs shining like half-buried eggs among the rocky slopes.

At Mycenae the use of these domed tombs did not begin until about 1500, when burial in the grave circles was coming to an end. Further south in Messenia it seems to have been introduced earlier. What, however, makes them of far more than archaeological interest is not only their expression of kingly self-assertion, but also the really extraordinary architectural development they underwent between the fifteenth and thirteenth centuries.

There can hardly be a better demonstration of the skilful inventiveness of men whenever they are confronted with precise and soluble problems. The open sides of the entrance passages were found liable to collapse – until they were lined with masonry; seepage through the dome weakened it – until layers of waterproof

The greatest royal tomb at Mycenae: the "Treasury of Atreus". The gateway, 18 feet high, was enriched with half-columns and running spirals. The corbelled vault is 45 feet high. The tomb probably dates from about 1300 B.C.

clay were introduced into the covering mound; the monolithic stone lintel was very much inclined to shatter from the pressure of the dome – until this was relieved by the construction of a false arch, an open corbelled triangle, immediately above the lintel. While these technical improvements were being made (and the kingdoms were growing richer), a corresponding advance was made in the scale and excellence of the workmanship. Rubble walling gave place to well-fitted ashlar, larger and larger blocks were used, and the corbelling of the dome was made perfectly smooth – with even the lintel stone curved to fit into it. Fine ornament was also added – though rarely. In the Treasury of Atreus at Mycenae (so called because, after it had been robbed and left open, later observers did not recognize it as a tomb), the great portal was enriched with carved half-columns and low reliefs and provided with bronze-covered doors with gilded bosses, while the vast interior dome was banded with bronze and pinned with hundreds of gilded rosettes. The ceiling of a side chamber in the "Tomb of Minyas" at Orchomenos in Boeotia was finely carved all over with running spirals and rosettes (p. 192).

The evolution of these tombs through the centuries is best seen at Mycenae – where there were at least nine of them. They reach their architectural climax in the Treasury of Atreus, a truly monumental work which for a combination of style, technical skill and size is one of the masterpieces of architectural history. The passage is 118 feet long; the portal nearly 18 feet high with a lintel weighing quite a hundred tons, and the chamber nearly 50 feet across below a 44-foot-high dome.

Standing at the entrance and imagining it when the façade had its neat, formal ornamentation and its huge bronze doors, and looking up at the Pantheon-like perfection of a dome which has stood fast for about 3,300 years, it is very easy to feel that here was a premonition of the spirit of the Graeco-Roman age. If this is too fanciful, then at least one can say with complete conviction that in manner, purpose and monumental feeling the Treasury of Atreus is as remote as it can be from the spirit of Minoan Crete.

This great tomb is usually dated to about 1300, and the simpler but architecturally more advanced "Tomb of Clytemnestra" well into the thirteenth century. However, the absolute dates are not at all surely fixed, and it might well be that tradition was right in assigning the "treasury" to Atreus while the later tomb was that of Agamemnon.

The pursuit of this extraordinary development in funerary architecture has led on into the late phase of Mycenaean history. These splendid late tombs were in fact all long ago robbed of grave furnishings which can safely be assumed to have been of fabulous richness. A few more modest examples built during the middle period have been found more or less intact. Helped out by such hints as can be picked up elsewhere, the picture they give of the fifteenth and early fourteenth centuries is very much what would be anticipated from the general historical situation. During this time there must have been something like a balance of forces between Crete under the leadership of Knossos, rich, deeply civilized and still holding on to her ascendancy in the eastern Mediterranean, and Greece, under the leadership of Mycenae, gradually extending her sea power and her trade abroad, while becoming more widely civilized, and probably more socially and politically coherent, at home.

It looks as though outwardly the relation between the two powers was friendly. The Cretans did nothing to fortify their exposed cities and palaces, and it is therefore improbable that the fine Cretan gold work and other treasures acquired by

Plate 25. Gold bites gold. Dog's-head handle of drinking cup. From the acropolis of Mycenae, 16th century B.C.

Achaean princes and nobles were obtained by raiding. If there was indeed an Achaean dynasty in Knossos during the second half of the century, then the influx of such luxuries could sometimes be explained in this way, but if Knossos kept its independence for another hundred years, then it would seem that its peaceful rulers lived in their good fools' paradise, imagining that with so many of the other elements of their civilization, their neighbours were also absorbing their unwarlike spirit.

As for the Achaeans themselves at this time, there are many later analogies (for example the Russians of St Petersburg and of Moscow in the nineteenth century) to suggest that some individuals would in fact have been eager to fling themselves into the ways of the more refined civilization, while the majority held out for the sterner virtues of their ancestors. There is evidence of this in a small but not insignificant matter of fashion – some men continued to wear beards and shortish hair (p. 192), while others adopted the Cretan styles. In general, however, it would be true to say that this century saw the Achaeans completing the process of adapting the Minoan civilization to their warlike and masculine-dominated society. Indeed, before its end their stiffer, more formal artistic ideals began to have a reciprocal influence in Knossos.

The glimpses of the men and women of this period that are afforded by the domed royal tombs and the slightly more modest chamber tombs of the nobles confirm this general picture of the middle phase of Mycenaean history. Nearly all of them come from the Peloponnese.

Although the "Palace of Nestor" at Pylos belongs to the thirteenth century, the tombs round it prove that there was already a royal hall there in these earlier times. One of these tombs had been plundered, but the robbers overlooked an exquisite gem which lay hidden at the bottom of a grave pit. It is a gold seal, perhaps worn at the king's wrist, bearing a most regal griffin (p. 192), with intricately feathered wings and fanlike crest - in every way a superior creature to the stiff and gawking griffins which were later to be painted behind the throne in the great hall.

If this royal seal, and the scatter of gold leaf trampled into the tomb floor, are enough to hint at the lost riches of the kings of Pylos in the fifteenth century, a second, smaller tomb in the neighbourhood helps to evoke the lives of minor members of the royal house. The vault had been in use for over a century, and skeletons had been bundled into both pots and pits to make way for fresh corpses. One of these pots looks purely Cretan; others show the stiffening of the naturalism of Cretan vase-painting that expressed the native Mycenaean spirit. These stowed-away burials had been allowed to keep numbers of daggers and rapiers, and one of them pieces of a gold diadem like a smaller, more wearable, version of those from the women's grave at Mycenae.

Plate 26. A shower of huge sequins? Gold discs from the women's grave in the Upper Grave Circle, Mycenae, 16th century B.C.

Top A finely carved ceiling over the side chamber of the domed tomb known as the "Treasury of Minyas" at Orchomenos. Limestone, *c.* 1300 B.C. *Above left* A bearded Achaean. Gold and niello. From Pylos. *Above right* "A most regal griffin". Gold seal. From a domed tomb at Epano Englianos, Pylos, late 15th century B.C.

Men as well as women used hand mirrors. Polished bronze and ivory. From tomb at Routsi, near Pylos, *c.* 1400 B.C.

Last of all a man had been stretched out below the centre of the dome, a dagger by his side, an arrow between his legs, a bronze mirror at his waist, and a bronze cup, from which, perhaps, he had liked to take his wine, standing near his head. Here, surely, was the average loyal member of the royal entourage, the man who would follow his lord to battle or the chase according to the duties and pleasures of the household. It is therefore interesting that he evidently sought the intervention of the Goddess, for he had a little stylized figure of her placed on his breast.

In tombs at Routsi, still not far from Pylos, the ever-present influence of Cretan style among the élite is even more conspicuous. Achaean women often carried daggers, and here one had been interred with two fine specimens (plate 32), probably made as early as 1500. One shows the marine life dear to the Cretans: nautili are swimming among branching corals and sea plants. The other is inlaid with golden felines, long and lithe, hunting among silver plants and rocks. In this scene the artist succeeded in overcoming the limitations of space and technique to convey a sense of animals moving freely within a natural setting. His was, in fact, a Minoan sensibility, going against the Mycenaean tendency towards fixity, symmetry and division.

Here again the Cretan Goddess was present. One of several beautifully cut seals shows a full-breasted woman in a flounced (but very much divided) skirt holding out lilies towards an altar where olive branches sprout between horns of consecration (plate 18). Whatever hand cut this gem, the scene and its meaning are wholly Minoan.

The Mycenaean capital of Laconia has not yet been found, but a domed tomb near modern Sparta has yielded a proof of the splendid vessels that might have been used in the banqueting hall. The pair of gold cups from Vaphio are an example of archaeological finds so deservedly famous that they become undeservedly tedious. Perhaps, indeed, the contrasted scenes of free bulls being gently captured with decoy cows and violently captured with nets are, in spite of their real magnificence, somewhat over-muscled, over-emphatic and generally overdone. If they are of Cretan workmanship, perhaps the artist was striving too hard to please his Achaean patron. Still, the prince who drank from such handsome cups as these was a man of substance who would with propriety have claimed descent from a god. When in the Odyssey the young Telemachus visits the hall of Menelaus, the Laconian king, he is overcome by its splendour in comparison with the rusticities of his own home in Ithaca. The cups suggest that the kingdom was already wealthy in the fifteenth century. The picture is added to by seals from the same tomb at Vaphio. One shows a man setting off briskly in a chariot drawn by two fine horses, another a boar hunt and a third a stout, truly episcopal-looking figure, presumably a priest, in volumin-ous vestments (plate 18). The other aspect of religious life is well represented by a woman with arms raised and head thrown back in an ecstatic dance (p. 132).

It is, however, back in the Argolid, nucleus of the Mycenaean world, that the most surprising news of the fifteenth century has been made known. Midea, the modern Dendra, was one of the many lesser centres in the region which must have been affected by the wealth and power of the high king of Mycenae. Here in a domed tomb a prince – a small man – had been buried in a deepish pit with his wife beside him, and another woman, presumed to be a daughter or attendant, in a separate pit nearby. This arrangement has inevitably raised the question as to whether at this time the Achaean lords expected their womenfolk and servants to be put to death in order to attend them in the next world. They were both provided with elegant drinking cups, hers in inlaid silver, his a shallow golden bowl embossed with dolphins, nautili and the most sinuously lifelike of octopuses. This bowl, itself a wonderfully fine example of the Cretan feeling for seascape, contained some of the most exquisitely cut seals of the whole range of Minoan and Mycenaean gems.

At the time of the funeral a fire had been lit beneath the dome and many precious possessions burnt there – among them a dog, probably a favourite hound. The prince had also been lavishly supplied with weapons – a gold-hilted sword and three others at his side and a heap of swords, daggers and knives at his feet.

While this royal grave helps to fill in the general picture of the Mycenaean rulers acquiring fine possessions of Cretan inspiration while at the same time indulging their natural love of warfare and the chase, it is another Midean tomb that revealed something startlingly new about the equipment of an Achaean warrior. This was a simple rock-cut chamber of the kind considered appropriate to a minor noble rather than one of royal blood.

The body of the nobleman, and probably his sword, had been removed by modern members of the ancient profession of grave robbers, but they failed to discover various massive bronze objects that had been laid at the side of the chamber. Among them was a complete set of bronze plate armour (plates 35, 36).

Few things could have caused more excitement among those scholastic champions who wage their own version of the Trojan War. What is disputed has nothing to do with Helen, but with how far the *Iliad* and *Odyssey* truly reflect the life of Mycenaean times.

Again and again Homer describes how his heroes dressed themselves for battle – for instance when Menelaus prepares for his duel with Paris. "First he put on his fine greaves with silver anklets. Next a cuirass across his chest, his brother Lycaon's which fitted him. Over his shoulder he slung the sword with silver knobs, then a strong, broad shield, and upon his head a fine helmet." Those who wanted to make as little as possible of the surviving Mycenaean elements in the epics liked to point out that, but for a few fragments of greaves, no evidence for body armour had ever turned up. The Homeric descriptions, they said, obviously dated from much later times. Even those who wanted to make as much as possible of the Mycenaean elements were extremely cautious. It was better not to use a word like "breastplate" that implied metal armour, but rather "cuirass" or "corselet" which could be of reinforced leather.

The weight of the argument suddenly thrown in to confound the anti-

Mycenaeanists and fulfil the secret hopes of their opponents could hardly have been greater. The Midean armour is very heavy indeed. Above the breastplate are a gorget, and huge shoulder-pieces like the pouldrons of the fifteenth century A.D., while below it are broad overlapping bands of bronze that are clumsier versions of the medieval taces. Whenever warriors long to chop and not to be chopped, they are liable to weigh themselves down with very similar devices.

Achaean warrior in boar's-tusk helmet. Ivory. From a chamber tomb at Mycenae, 14th century B.C.

With the armour was found the remains of a helmet banded with sections of boars' tusks. This kind of helmet is described in some detail in the *Iliad*, where Odysseus was given one said to be laced with thongs inside "while without the white teeth of a boar of flashing tusks were arrayed thick on either side". Far more often the Homeric helmets were of bronze. The discovery at Dendra was no surprise, for boars'-tusk helmets were already familiar both from actual specimens and

The helping hand. Carving of the Divine Child and his attendant "nurses" or goddesses. Ivory. From Mycenae, 15th century B.C.

from paintings and carvings (p. 196). Indeed, they had long been one of the favourite items in the pro-Mycenaeanists' armoury – made all the more effective by the fact that they had probably gone out of use even before the end of Mycenaean times. Sheet bronze helmets with pendant cheekpieces have also been found. Both boars'-tusk and bronze helmets are provided with holders for "nodding plumes" like those of the Homeric heroes.

If a minor nobleman of fifteenth-century Midea could drive to war armoured cap-à-pie in this fashion, then it is only reasonable to suppose that by the time of the siege of Troy kings would have had very fine armour indeed. Even the cuirass of Agamemnon seems possible, with its bands of blue enamel, tin and gold and its "blue dragons which reached upward to the neck". The discovery at Dendra has scored a decisive if limited win for those who believe that Homer reliably preserved many memories of the Mycenaean past. It also supports the general principle that archaeology tends to underestimate the material wealth and skills of the peoples whom it studies.

One marvellous work of art believed to have been carved in the fifteenth century will serve to balance this martial aspect of Mycenaean life. It is a miniature ivory group from a shrine in the citadel at Mycenae. Two women dressed in the Cretan style are squatting (but gracefully) side by side, a single long stole drawn across their backs. One has her arm round the other's shoulders, and her hand is being caressed by her companion. This second woman is holding out her other arm to steady a plump little boy who seems to be essaying his first steps at their knee (p. 197).

This charming ivory is usually accepted as Mycenaean work. If so, the Cretan inheritance is still very strong. It shows in the studied asymmetry, the immediacy of movement, the returning curves of the design – and in the posture of the "nurses", so reminiscent of the seated women in Knossian frescoes. The religious meaning of this trinity will be considered later. Here it only needs to be said that it leads back to the realm of the Goddess, where the clanking Midean warrior would seem brutally out of place.

Chapter Five

The Imperial Age

While the central stretch of Mycenaean history, the period of growth and consolidation, has to be pieced together from a few scattered clues – most of them picked from the grave – the last phase, the imperial age following the overthrow of Minoan Crete, is far more coherent. Light falls on it from all sides. There is architecture military and domestic; there are paintings secular and religious; there are the inscribed tablets which, for all their narrow limitations, do help to bring their world to life – even uttering the names of individual citizens. Also there are the *Iliad* and *Odyssey*: in spite of all dispute no one can deny that they do flood this period with the light of imagination, and moreover allow modern man to share the vision of it that was to mean so much to the Greeks.

The castle-like appearance of the later Mycenaean citadels made a characteristic contrast with the Cretan palaces. Not only were most of them protected by massive walls and towers, but the natural sites chosen were usually more formidable. There are no parallels to the sheer natural walls of the Athens acropolis, but at most of the Achaean strongholds the natural defences were good. One of the most striking from this point of view is Gla, the largest of all Mycenaean citadels, where on the north-west side the fifteen-foot-thick wall follows the edge of a cliff dominating a dead flat plain – once the lake of Copais (p. 200). The ancient name of this Boeotian fortress is unknown, and it may be that it was not a royal capital like the rest but that the two-mile circuit of the walls was intended to provide a temporary refuge for the surrounding countryside.

At the site believed to be ancient Pylos there are sheer, though not very high, cliffs to the north, and on all sides the hill of Epano Englianos provides good protection. The earlier citadel had a circuit of walls, but when the hilltop was flattened for the thirteenth-century hall no fortifications were added. This was probably due to the general geographical situation, for here on the south-west coast of the Peloponnese the threat from either hostile neighbours or invading foreigners was far less than in the north. Because of the absence of walls and the relatively gentle approach, Pylos has more of the atmosphere of a Cretan palace than any other Mycenaean site. Yet the king's hall occupies only one quarter of the area of the palace of Knossos.

Gla, largest of all Mycenaean citadels. Its cliffs rise from the ancient bed of Lake Copais. The nick at the right of the picture is the South Gate.

Less than fifteen miles to the north of Epano Englianos, at Peristeria, a hilltop fortified with massive walls of Mycenaean type has recently been discovered. Richly furnished beehive tombs prove it to have been a place of importance in the Pylian kingdom. The relationship between this stronghold and unfortified Pylos is not as yet understood.

The citadels of Mycenae and Tiryns were by far the most formidable. If today thousands of tourists pour in from all over the world to see them, they were already admired by the Greeks of Classical times. Pausanias found the tremendous walls of Tiryns as remarkable as the pyramids of Egypt – but in this, it must be said, he showed strong nationalist bias.

The acropolis of Mycenae is in fact quite a steep hill, although as usually seen from the seaward side its proportions are dwarfed by the peaks of Mounts Elias and Zara. Viewed from the Perseia Spring, the source of the city's water supply, where the citadel can be seen standing out above the fertile stretches of the coastal plain (plate 20), it is easier to imagine what a proud and princely place it must have been when the royal hall crowned the summit above the lofty, jutting walls. Other houses, many connected with the royal establishment, crowded round both inside the citadel and without.

As usual, the walls follow the contours. They average about fifteen feet in thickness, the space between the masonry faces being filled with earth and rubble. Some sections are built of huge, irregular stones skilfully fitted together without mortar. This work does not compare in exactness with the similar masonry of the Peruvian Incas – where, as the guidebooks say with more than usual truth, it is impossible to insert a knife blade between the blocks. Nevertheless it is impressive work, and one can sympathize with the Greeks who fancied that this mighty building of their ancestors could only have been raised by a race of giants such as the one-eyed Cyclops.

In some places, and most strikingly in the walls flanking the Lion Gate (plate 21), the irregular Cyclopean masonry gives way to a still massive but regular ashlar. The local conglomerate rock splits easily along its horizontal bedding, and can then be sawn into rectangular blocks. Once this method had been mastered, the Mycenaean architects could achieve the dignity of ashlar building both in the citadel and, as already seen, in the Treasury of Atreus and other royal tombs.

The military details of the fortifications are well devised. The deep insetting of the Lion Gate made it possible for attackers to be enfiladed from both sides. In the northern extremity a sally-port was provided by constructing a corbelled tunnel through walls which at that point were as much as twenty-two feet thick. Not far away the architects showed exceptional skill in securing a secret water supply for the garrison. They made three long flights of stone steps, the first, again with a corbelled roof, sloping down steeply through the walls, the other two making an elbow bend underground and outside the defences. At the bottom was a cistern assumed to have been supplied underground from the Perseia Spring. In time of siege the capacity could be vastly increased by flooding the lower section of the stairway – which was coated with a waterproof cement for the purpose. Above ground the whole reservoir was quite invisible – and could only be betrayed to the enemy by treachery.

The exact date when the people of Mycenae built these defences is not sure, but probably the greater part was completed soon after 1300, a generation or more before the time when Agamemnon could have mounted the throne in the high hall on the top of the hill. But there were additions – one of them the water stairs which may have been constructed a century later at a time when all the Achaean kingdoms were under threat from the Dorian invaders or other disturbances. It was in this situation that the Athenians, too, took the precaution of securing their water supply against a siege by sinking a deep well inside the walls.

A man setting out by chariot from Mycenae, through the Lion Gate (where the wheels would find well-worn ruts to accommodate them) down the ramp and southward, bowling along between fields and groves, could easily reach Tiryns in an hour or two – having passed by Argos or Midea on the way. The concentration of military strength and population in this part of the Argolid was remarkable.

Tiryns, the most castle-like of Mycenaean citadels. Exterior view of the walls.

"Tiryns of the great walls" as Homer called it has overwhelmingly impressed some one hundred and thirty generations of men by the amazing strength and bulk of its fortifications. Although it was but one citadel within the Argive kingdom, probably always dominated by Mycenae and later subject to Argos, it had the physical might and the imaginative inspiration to attract myths and tales to itself. It enjoyed a mythical relationship with the goddess Hera and was recognized as the home of Herakles; it was the scene of the good hero Bellerophon's encounter with the amorous and unscrupulous Anteia.

If Pausanias was inclined to compare Tiryns with the Pyramids, today all European visitors must be struck by its castle-like appearance. The towering walls enclosing the narrow hill, and the inner fortifications of the royal hall, are far more suggestive of a medieval castle than anything else to be seen in the Mycenaean kingdoms. Especially is this so as one enters by the main East Gate. It lacks the architectural dignity of the Lion Gate, but the colossal blocks of the entry, and the narrow passageway inside the wall along which attackers would have had to pass under a rain of missiles before they could reach even the first of two great gates barring the way to the inner citadel and the hall, are not only imposing, but also ingenious in military design. This defensive skill is shown also in the famous corbelled galleries (plate 34) built into the thirty-three-foot thickness of the outer wall both here to the east and on the south side. These galleries give on to strong store chambers with embrasures designed to allow the defenders to fire down on the enemy outside the walls.

The citadel and hall were concentrated on this southern end of the hill, while the lower, northern end, a narrow oval area enclosed within curtain walls, was probably added mainly as a refuge for local farmers and their livestock. The East Gate was the original main entrance into the Tiryns citadel, but later another entrance was made on the south-western, seaward side – protected by a bastion and tower. Some have seen this as an addition made in the days of stress at the end of the thirteenth century, but others think it was intended for the convenience of men and merchandise passing between Tiryns and the sea. Before the building of the Lion Gate, the main entry into Mycenae may also have been from the inland side – perhaps from the north by the Perseia Spring. Such an innovation, from the Land Gate to the Sea Gate, would make a telling symbol of the change of outlook that came to the Achaeans when with their fleet and their overseas trade and settlement they had entered upon their imperial age.

Although dwarfed by their greater neighbours, Mycenae and Tiryns, remains of Mycenaean fortifications can be seen also at Asine and Midea. In mainland Greece north of the Peloponnese the finest are at Gla. Iolkos in Thessaly (the region in which Achilles's small kingdom lay) has been obliterated by modern Volos, but the

MACEDONIA

CHALCIDICE

Thasos

Haliakmon

EPIRUS

THESSALY

Mt Olympus •

Aegean Se

Dodona •

Peneus

• Karditsa   Sesklo •   Iolkos

Sporades

Skyros

Akheloos

AETOLIA

Mt Parnassus

Delphi •   Orchomenos •
                BOEOTIA
                • Gla
                • Thebes

EUBOEA

Ithaca

Cephalonia

Gulf of Corinth

ACHAEA

Marathon
Eleusis • •
ATTICA
Ephyra • • Athens
Corinth *Salamis*

Zakynthos (Zante)

ELIS

Olympia •

ARCADIA

Aegina

Mycenae •
ARGOLIS
Argos • Tiryns • • Lavrion
Lerna • • Asine

CORINTHIA

PELOPONNESE

• Kakovatos

• Malthi

MESSENIA

LACONIA
Sparta •

Vaphio •

Kampos •

Pylos • • Routsi
Koryphasion •

Melos

0   20   40   60   80 Miles
0   20 40 60 80 100 120 Kilometres

Kythera

possessions of the Bronze Age inhabitants often come to light there. Ancient Thebes, too, underlies modern Thebes, and is only occasionally accessible below its buildings. However, on one recent occasion the building of a new store made it possible to open a small part of the Mycenaean palace, and a discovery of quite extraordinary interest resulted.

The legendary founder of Thebes was Cadmus the Phoenician – whose sister was none other than Europa. The citadel built for him by the surviving progeny of the dragon's teeth was known as the Cadmeia, and in later stories Cadmus became a culture hero credited with the introduction of writing and other civilized arts. In the corner of the Cadmeia which the demolitions had exposed, probably store-rooms of the hall, the excavators found odds and ends of luxuries – a gold necklace, ivory combs, fragments of an ivory chair – and also some pieces of Linear B tablets. Such things were not surprising in a Mycenaean palace probably of the fourteenth century. Then something very different appeared – a collection of over thirty cylinders of lapis lazuli, many of them cut with beasts, divinities and cuneiform inscriptions. They were in fact Babylonian seals, and the owner of one of them was already known: a dignitary who had served under King Burraburias of Babylon in the first half of the fourteenth century.

It was one of those occasions when a story that has appeared to be a mixture of myth and legend seems to win some kind of historical confirmation. Cadmus came from the Levant, and was associated with writing. Here in the Cadmeia, and nowhere else in mainland Greece, were official seals brought from the Orient and charged with cuneiform characters.

Perhaps the presence of the seals in the Cadmeia has nothing whatever to do with the legend. Yet at least there is no doubt that anyone seeing them displayed in the Thebes museum must be startled into a new appreciation of the far-flung connections of the Achaean princes of this imperial age. Oriental influence is obvious in many features of Mycenaean culture, just as Mycenaean elements can be seen in the Orient, yet these little, dark blue cylinders carried over a thousand miles from the Land of the Two Rivers give the relationship a fresh and tangible reality.

Their strong and sometimes stark natural situations, and the scale of their fortifications, emphasize the military significance of Mycenae, Tiryns and other of these later Mycenaean citadels. But the royal residence was also the centre of a civil and religious life that was far from uncouth, and of a carefully organized administration.

To judge from those that have been uncovered, all the royal halls were very much alike. The plans were similar in essentials and so was the interior decoration; the domestic amenities and equipment did not differ greatly. In fact it is clear that although the Achaeans found it natural to live in many separate and sometimes hostile kingdoms, they were united by a common culture.

Mainland Greece.

Just as at Pylos, each residence was built round the great banqueting hall, and each hall had a circular hearth in the middle with a clerestory raised on four columns above it. All had painted plaster floors and frescoed walls. At Mycenae the subjects chosen included warriors and grooms preparing their horses for battle and part of a siege scene with a chariot and a man falling from a tower. At Tiryns there was a hunt with "a boar of flashing tusks" and a pack of spotted hounds all in full career. There were also two ladies in a chariot, decorously dressed in high-necked tunics, apparently about to drive off to the hunt.

All these were subjects of the kind that had appealed to the Achaean élite from the beginning. At Tiryns the continuance of the more purely Cretan taste, though by now frozen into timeless rigidity, is apparent in a frieze of elegant ladies, dressed in the usual full skirts and jackets, and with exceptionally full breasts and elaborate coiffures, walking in procession with offerings held out stiffly in front of them. In feeling and manner these motionless walkers are reminiscent of the women ministrants on the nearly contemporary Hagia Triada sarcophagus.

It is surprising to find that Achaean ladies of the thirteenth century were dressing almost exactly like their ancestors of over two centuries before, and like Cretan ladies long before that. Once wealthy aristocrats had accepted the idea of dressing stylishly it might have been expected that they would have gone in pursuit of changing fashions. But evidently this was not so; their view of dress must have been like that of the Chinese and Japanese. There was, however, some slight change of taste in jewellery – the barbarously handsome ear-rings and bracelets of earlier times giving way to lighter, more refined, ornaments.

Perhaps in fact Achaean ladies only appeared in the full glory of the old Minoan style on ceremonial occasions. The tunics worn by the supposed huntresses might well represent the common everyday dress – which would seem, incidentally, more compatible with the wearing of daggers. The men certainly favoured sleeved tunics, belting them tightly so that the lower part stood out above the hips.

While the halls inside the famous fortifications at Tiryns and Mycenae were at least as fine as any others (although Mycenae does not appear to have had the exceptionally splendid building that might have been expected), there is no longer much to be seen of them. Because the sites were reoccupied in later times and temples built upon them, the Mycenaean ruins and their contents were largely destroyed.

It was quite otherwise with the "Palace of Nestor" in Messenia. This building on the hill of Epano Englianos (pp. 199, 200), ten miles north of the little modern port of Pylos, has been left largely undisturbed, except for the usual stone robbing, since it was plundered and burnt in the late Bronze Age. While the Dorians, if they were indeed the destroyers, carried off the valuables, much of the building and its domestic furnishings remained hidden below the olive grove that flourished on the

Plate 27. Bull and stags and seven openings. Ritual vessel from a chamber tomb at Volimidia, near Pylos.

hill. Most important, the barbarians naturally took no notice of the piles of inscribed clay tablets, the accounts of the royal household, which the clerks had left behind when they fled or were massacred. The fire, by hardening them, assured the preservation of these, the most precious of all the finds from the "Palace of Nestor".

Can this place justifiably be identified with the home of the Homeric Nestor, king of Pylos? The site of his capital had already been forgotten in Classical times, and the variety of the speculations as to where it had been was something of a joke among the Greeks. "There is a Pylos before a Pylos, and there is another beside," an epigram began. Aristophanes, too, made a crack on the subject. Between that day and this, many were the sites chosen – from the Bay of Navarino almost to Olympia. But since the discovery (p. 15) at Epano Englianos of a hall built on as grand a scale as those of the Argolid, only a few scholars refuse to recognize this as the true "Palace of Nestor".

Nestor was a Messenian, and he had the power and wealth appropriate to so fine a building. According to the Catalogue of Ships in the *Iliad* he was able to furnish ninety vessels for the Trojan War – second only to Agamemnon himself, who provided one hundred. Conversely, there is no record of any other Messenian dynasty important enough to have lived in the style suggested by the establishment at Epano Englianos.

The hill commands lovely views southward to Navarino Bay and the island of Sphacteria and northward to the Mount Aigalion range. On this smooth hilltop, which may have been artificially levelled, the extent to which the architectural design centres on the main hall is more obvious than it can be in the rugged conditions of Tiryns and Mycenae. As the visitor approached the central block he was led across a stucco-paved court to a simple porchway with a single fluted wooden column on each face. Here there was a stand for a sentry who was probably responsible for guarding the main door, and also two rooms where the tax collector had his office. In the anteroom there stood an enormous jar where tax-payers poured their dues in oil. In the small inner room the tablets on which the administrative records were kept lay on shelves, or in boxes and baskets on a low bench.

If the visitor were no mere tax-payer, he would pass through the porchway into a court, open to the sky, where he was immediately confronted by the brightly decorated façade of the banqueting hall. If he had to wait for admission to the royal presence, the visitor would be ushered into a room to the left where there was a painted stucco bench and where servants would probably have offered him a cup of wine. If his appointment were immediate, then he would pass across the court, between the two columns of the open portico, through the two central doors of the vestibule, and find himself in the banqueting hall standing before the great hearth with the royal throne on his right hand.

Plate 28. Bull symbolism at Mycenae. Gold. From a chamber tomb.

Plate 29. Ornament for a princess. Gold. From the women's grave in the Upper Grave Circle, Mycenae, 16th century B.C.

"Some private houses were frescoed." Another type of demonic servitor (compare p. 154); Mycenae, 13th century B.C.

Thus there was an almost straight axis from the outer courtyard right through to the hearth, providing the balanced symmetry so characteristic of Mycenaean design and foreign to Minoan. Because the banqueting hall itself kept the ancient form of the megaron, with its single entrance, there was no possibility of the easy, often oblique, access from room to room achieved by the Minoan architects.

While the essential layout and living pattern of the hall was so unlike the Cretan

Minoan styles had a long life among Achaean women. Ivory. From a chamber tomb at Prosymna, near Mycenae.

palace, the construction was in some ways similar. Here at Pylos, as at Knossos, the main buildings had regular ashlar outside walls set in a stout framework of wooden beams. The more lightly built internal walls and floors were plastered and frescoed. The columns, too, were of wood on stone and plaster bases, but the fluting was new. The rooms were lit by stone-cut lamps that were very much like those used at Knossos.

While the banqueting hall (which was over forty feet long) probably rose to the full height of the building, and its clerestory above the main roof line, the residential quarters were certainly on two floors – the upper one reached by stone stairways from both ends of the vestibule. The women, who are not likely to have mingled with the men as freely as they did in Crete, had their apartments on this upper story. In one place where an upper room, burning at the time of the final destruction, had showered its contents on to the ground below, the excavators found a pitiful scatter of burnt fragments of the ladies' combs, brushes and toilet boxes. It will be remembered that at home in Ithaca, Penelope had her chamber on an upper floor.

The most important domestic quarters were in the north-east angle of the main building. Here there was quite a large room with a central hearth painted with flame symbols and running spirals like a smaller version of the one in the banqueting hall. It seems to have been decorated all round with life-size paintings of griffins, lions and other animals, but in smaller rooms adjoining stiffened and stylized renderings of the old Cretan motifs were preferred – octopuses, fish and dolphins. On the other side of the hearth room (usually assigned to the queen) was a narrow room furnished with one of the painted clay bathtubs that were very much more common in Crete than on the mainland. Near the bath two large jars set in a clay stand held the water – which seems to have been poured over the bather from stemmed cups of the kind more usually associated with drinking wine.

A series of small pantries ran along the west side of the banqueting hall, and the tremendous store of crockery they contained (p. 214) gives some idea of the drinking and feasting that went on in the hall itself. There were over six thousand vessels in as many as two dozen forms, but the commonest was the slender, high-footed goblet, like a champagne cup with a handle, from which the Achaeans liked to quaff their wine. One pantry, which had been fitted with wooden shelves, held nearly three thousand of these *kylikes*. The remains of vast numbers of broken ones were found in rubbish tips, and it looks as though on special occasions the royal and noble feasters smashed their cups after drinking – a custom which even now has not quite died out in Europe.

Other storerooms round the back and east side of the hall had been used for oil. There were numbers of big storage jars for the raw olive oil itself, and also the type of flask with a "U" handle and small, easily stoppered, neck or spout which

A lamp from the "Palace of Nestor" at Pylos. Stone, 13th century B.C.

Crockery of a royal household. From the pantries of the "Palace of Nestor", Pylos, 13th century B.C. Stemmed wine cups (upper right centre) were found in vast quantities.

For the collection of taxes: gigantic oil jar (approximately six feet high) from office annexe at entrance to "Palace of Nestor", Pylos.

archaeologists call stirrup jars (plate 38) and which were undoubtedly often used to contain scented unguents made on an oil base. The oil was heated and infused with aromatic herbs or spices such as coriander, safflower, cummin, sesame and many others. Tablets found in these actual stores, and frequently elsewhere, record the names of these herbs and also the fact that olive oil was known as *elawon*, essentially the same as in modern Greek – a word-life of over three thousand years. One of the tablets also records the names of Pylians engaged in the sweet oil business. It says "How Alxoitas gave to Thyestes the unguent-boiler spices for boiling in the unguent." Alxoitas was chief steward – an important official.

When, in the *Odyssey*, Telemachus spent a night as King Nestor's guest, having a "jointed bed" set up for him in the portico of the great hall, he was given a bath and anointing before he left for the long drive to the house of Menelaus in Sparta. "Meanwhile she bathed Telemachus, even fair Polycaste, the youngest daughter of Nestor, son of Neleus. After she had bathed him and anointed him with olive oil, and cast about him a goodly mantle and doublet, he came forth from the bath in fashion like the deathless gods." One could say (with due allowances) that Polycaste tended her father's guest in the bathroom near the queen's apartment, and that the unguent had been made on the premises, perhaps by a grandfather of Thyestes.

Pylos represents an extraordinary bringing together of new knowledge with old tradition. There is the hall itself with all its details from bath to hearth. There are the huge jars and the elegant painted flasks all seen much as they were left by the conflagration. There are the tablets hardened by the same fire, and read again after millennia of meaninglessness. From the tablets the citizens Alxoitas, Thyestes and many others win a sudden resurrection. From the tablets, too, comes a new under-standing of the importance of the oil trade and of the reasons why the painted flasks have been found throughout the Mediterranean world – including the new City of God of the Pharaoh Akhenaten. Then, preserved by very different means, for centuries existing only in the minds of men and therefore less reliable but more alive, there is the Homeric story with the young Telemachus sleeping near those fluted columns, rubbed with those unguents, before he climbed into the chariot with Nestor's son and they "flew towards the plain, leaving the steep citadel of Pylos".

In fact even the "goodly car" which Nestor (himself so often called "Lord of Chariots") had stocked with "corn and wine and dainties such as princes eat" for the journey can find its link with the Pylos tablets. In workshops near the main building of the hall, tablets dealt not only with the supply of bronze and leather and with repairs carried out with these materials, but also gave lists of chariot parts (the four-spoked wheels were easily detached from the car and seem usually to have been stored separately).

Plate 30. The Mycenaean love of gold. Necklace from the domed tomb of Dendra, *c.* 1400 B.C.

Overleaf Plate 31. Dragons in lapis lazuli, crystal and gold. Dagger hilt from the Upper Grave Circle, Mycenae, 16th century B.C. Plate 32. "Achaean women carried daggers". Inlaid bronze daggers. One (*centre*) from the Upper Grave Circle at Mycenae, 16th century B.C., and two from a woman's burial in the domed tomb at Routsi, near Pylos, *c.* 1500 B.C.

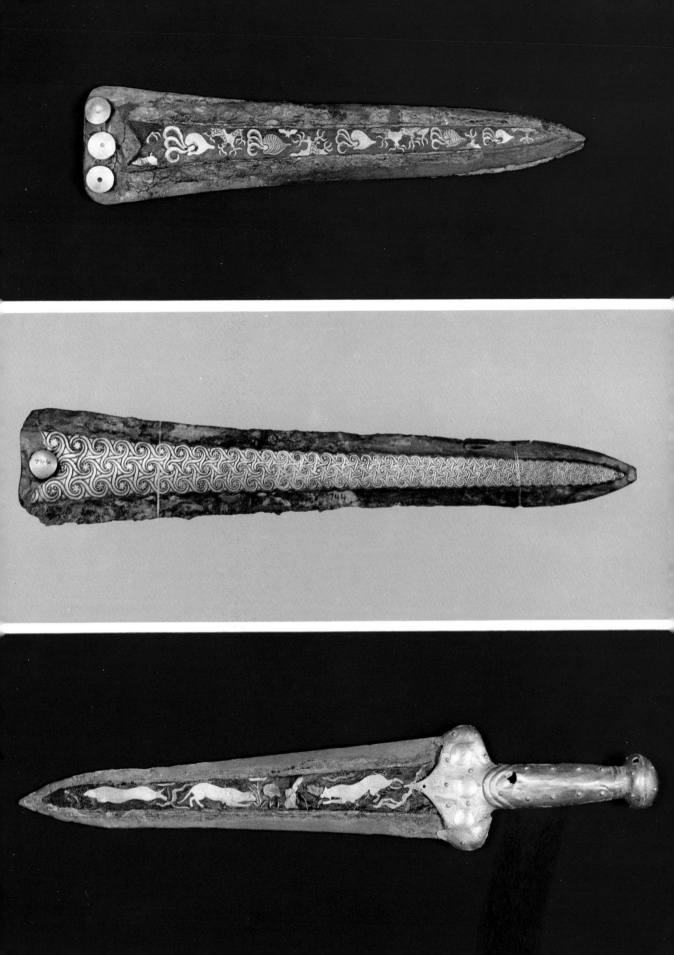

A set of thirteen tablets from the main archive room (the supposed tax collector's office at the entrance) proved to be an inventory of household goods in luxurious variety. Some interpreters believe that it was prepared for the induction by the king of an important official, and that it lists the furnishing of a reception room; others, reading just one word differently, believe that the occasion was the official's burial by the king, and that the objects were intended for the funeral feast and the furnishing of the tomb. The occasion, however, is of little importance, for whatever it was there is no doubt that the furnishing so conscientiously inventoried by the clerk belonged to the hall of Pylos.

The list begins with three jugs, almost certainly gold libation jugs, which are of interest because they at once represent two aspects of Mycenaean iconography. Two were decorated with the Mother Goddess (called The Queen) and bull heads; the third with "chariot scene and throng of soldiers".

Next follow quantities of bronze cooking gear and portable hearths – five out of the six tripod cauldrons clearly specified as of Cretan workmanship. One of these is described as having its legs burnt off – obviously from long exposure to the fire. That it should be kept in this useless condition suggests that the sacred associations of the tripod may have been too strong to allow it to be discarded.

There is nothing surprising in this equipment, for numbers of large and fine bronze vessels are already known. It is the sections of the inventory concerned with furniture that have come as a revelation. There are ten tables, five chairs and fourteen footstools, all of them of sumptuous materials.

Most of the tables were of stone, or stone and crystal, some of ebony and ivory and one of ivory with a marble shaft. Two were of humble yew wood. Many were splay-legged, and had six or nine feet. Their inlaid decorative motifs were relatively simple – mostly rosettes, spirals and shell and feather patterns.

The commonest material for the footstools was ebony, sometimes with golden struts, and again the inlaid designs, in ivory or gold, were usually such formal motifs as rosettes and spirals. Two were more ornate, one with ivory inlays of a man, a horse and an octopus, and the other with lion heads and flame patterns.

The chairs were the most elaborate of all. Ebony was the usual material, although one (if the reading is correct) was of crystal. The inlays in gold, ivory, cyanus paste and perhaps tin, represented such human subjects as a man with heifers and men with lions, and a variety of birds, bull heads, and perhaps stag heads. The full description of the crystal chair (with some uncertainties of reading) is: "One chair, of crystal, inlaid with cyanus, tin(?) and gold, the back(?) inlaid with golden human figures and a pair of stag(?) heads and golden bull heads and with golden palm trees(?) and with palm trees of cyanus."

Some fine words have been applied to the Mycenaean halls, and they were cer-

Plate 33. Rivalling the riches of Mycenae. Gold cups from a tomb at Peristeria, near Pylos, c. 1500 B.C.

tainly impressive and civilized places when compared with anything that had existed on the Greek mainland before. Yet by present expectations, and even in comparison with the Cretan palaces, they were small and lacking in architectural sophistication. The banqueting halls, by far the largest of the rooms, were smaller than the dining-rooms and drawing-rooms of very many English country houses. There was certainly nothing about these halls to encourage the idea that the princes habitually supported themselves on ebony and ivory, crystal and gold – in fact that Mycenaean kings were seated as richly as Pharaoh. Such grandeur must have been learnt in the Levant and Egypt, from where the valuable raw materials would themselves have been obtained. It is likely that some of this furniture was made in these countries and reached Greece as royal gifts.

Now that the existence of richly inlaid tables, chairs and stools is vouched for in writing, no doubt many inlays will be recognized. Indeed ivory fragments from Thebes have already been identified as coming from a chair, and probably many pretty pieces hitherto thought to have fallen from caskets will be seen instead to have embellished furniture. It remains puzzling why the remains of tables and chairs of stone or crystal have never come to light.

The importance of well-filled storerooms of the kind recognized at Pylos and more fully appreciated through the record of the tablets, is made very real by a famous passage from the *Odyssey*. Before he secretly leaves home in search of Odysseus, Telemachus goes to the royal stores to get provisions for the journey. ". . . he stepped down into his father's vaulted treasure-chamber, a spacious room where gold and bronze lay piled, and clothing in chests, and fragrant oil in plenty. And there stood jars of sweet wine, old and unmixed, ranged in order along the wall. . . . And the folding doors, close-fitted, were shut, and inside night and day a woman was in charge keeping guard over everything in the fullness of her wisdom." This account vividly recalls the lines of great jars along the walls behind the banqueting hall at Pylos – and those older ones in the much larger stores of Knossos. It is one of the passages in which Homer is most clearly describing wealthy Mycenaean conditions, and not those of his own day or any intervening century.

The sources of much of this royal wealth are made clearer and more precise by the tablets. They record a great abundance of those staple products wheat, barley, olive oil and wine. Complete cattle lists, a kind of Bronze Age Domesday Book, show that both at Pylos and Knossos the king owned enormous numbers of live-stock. Sheep and goats were the most important. The king of Pylos owned very many thousands of them, while the Achaean kings at Knossos possessed huge flocks scattered all over the island. They were tended by shepherds, each of whom normally had about a hundred animals assigned to him.

In addition to breeding flocks, which provided cheese as well as meat and wool, big flocks of wethers were kept – this is known from the Knossian tablets, but is likely to have been true also of the mainland. It can only mean that wool – of which wethers yield more than ewes – was of great value to the Mycenaean economy.

The large scale of the trade in "fragrant oil" has already been seen; now it appears that cargoes of wool and woollen cloth may also have gone from Mycenaean ports. Indeed the two trades were probably inter-related, for perfumes like those used for the unguents were also appreciated to sweeten woollen clothes. Just outside the citadel of Mycenae there is a building known as "The House of the Oil Merchant" which in fact was probably an annexe to the royal workshops. The business carried on there (as recorded in a small number of tablets) seems to have involved both perfumes and the manufacture of cloth.

Pigs were kept in some numbers, but, according to the tablets, a surprisingly small number of bulls, oxen and cows. It seems that they must have been kept largely as draught animals, for religious offerings, and perhaps for bull games. (The Achaeans presumably took over bull sports from the Cretans together with so much else. But there is nothing to suggest that they were anything like as important a part of their lives – they preferred hunting. Indeed, it is possible that the more subtle forms of bull-leaping were never practised on the mainland.)

There may have been herds of semi-wild cattle that never figured in the book-keeping, but which were hunted and occasionally captured in the manner shown on the Vaphio cups. Certainly the few domesticated beasts were regarded with individual affection – as cattle always have been until the days of industrialized farming. At Knossos the palace clerks recorded pet names of a touchingly familiar kind: they knew Blondie, Dapple, Darkie, Whitefoot, Chatterbox and Ginger.

Part of the wealth and comfort of the kings and their households depended on the large numbers of skilled workers, some free and some slaves, whose services they commanded. The craftsmen were highly specialized, including carpenters, masons, potters, shipwrights, bronze- and goldsmiths, bowmakers – and the unguent boilers who have already been encountered. In the cloth trade there were fullers, and (at Knossos) men and women shared in the weaving – the men working in pairs probably on vertical looms like those used in Egypt. Children seem to have helped their mothers in their spinning and weaving. In the preparation of bread, the women had the monotonous work of grinding the flour while men did the baking.

At the other end of the professional scale, the Pylos tablets mention a physician who was a land-holder. Some of the bronze-smiths were favoured by special tax concessions.

While the deciphering of the Linear B tablets has made valuable and sometimes startling additions to knowledge even in the field of material culture where archaeology is most capable, it has yielded entirely fresh information about social organization. More unexpectedly, considering that all the tablets are simple administrative documents, by good luck they also give some hints on religious questions – particularly about the names of the gods and goddesses and the relative esteem in which they were held.

The organization of Mycenaean society is obviously of the greatest significance for any understanding of what the Achaeans learnt from the Cretans and what they handed on to the later Greeks. Involved in this is, of course, the disputed question as to how far Mycenaean life was accurately represented in the Homeric epics.

It is difficult to compare the information provided by clerks and accountants with life itself. One would not want to depend upon the grocer's bills when trying to imagine a banquet at Buckingham Palace. It is still more difficult to relate such domestic accounts with the vision of the bard and poet. Yet it is fair to say that what has been made known through the reading of the Linear B tablets is not out of keeping with the Homeric scene. While the success of the Mycenaeanists cannot be as complete and simple as it was in the matter of the armour (p. 195), the balance of judgment falls on their side. The society that emerges is one of a warrior aristocracy centred on a king such as would seem appropriate to Achaean tradition. Foreign influence had perhaps heightened the divinity of the kingship, but it remained a feudal type of leadership based mainly on land and service.

The tablets with their gift of words have made it known that the man who sat on the throne in the banqueting hall was called the *Wanax*. His queen, who may have come down to join the company after the meal (as did Arete, Helen and Penelope), was the *Wanassa*. Both these titles might also be given to a god or goddess – a clear mark of the divine element in Mycenaean kingship.

The *Wanax* owned much land in his kingdom, some of which was in turn held from him by his *telestai*, who owed him service in exchange. The *Wanax*, however, also had his own estate, or *temenos*, which was situated near the chief shrine of the Goddess, and was just three times as large as the holdings of the *telestai*. Next to the king himself in dignity came the *Lawagetas* – the Leader of the War Host. He was the only other individual whose estate was called a *temenos* – a word which in later times was used only for a sacred enclosure. It seems that the War Leader's *temenos* was also situated near a shrine, in his case appropriately the shrine of a horse god, Hippos.

A further military grouping round the king, appropriate to an heroic society, was provided by the *equeta*, or Companions. They seem to have been close to his person, and perhaps to have represented him in the field. Undoubtedly they were of noble standing, and may have had their own large estates. In the tablets these Companions are sometimes given patronymics with a fine Homeric ring – such as Alectryon, son of Eteocles. They apparently had chariots at their disposal and were given an important part to play in the last, desperate attempt to defend Pylos from the barbarians (p. 236).

If the king and his service men and Companions, his War Leader and other officials, owned or held wide stretches of land, the gods and goddesses also had their estates. Among the wealthiest in this sense was the Goddess herself – usually referred to as Potnia, Our Lady. Poseidon, too, was of the highest standing (p. 234). Gold, grain, oil, wine, honey – offerings of many kinds poured into their stores, and they had large numbers of people, including slaves, in their employ.

Although the evidence of the tablets has helped to prove the economic importance of the religious establishments in Mycenaean Greece, this in no way contradicts the Homeric picture of society, nor identifies it with an Oriental style of temple economy. Homer, indeed, made it plain that land and even cities were dedicated to the gods, and that their priests grew to be rich men. One such, it will be remembered, gave Odysseus seven talents of gold and a silver bowl as well as the strong, sweet wine with which he was to befuddle Cyclops.

The existence of another class of landowners must finally defeat any attempt to liken Mycenaean society to an Oriental despotism. This was the *damos*, the commune or organization of the common people who may even have been the largest land-owners of all. The *damos* sometimes leased holdings to the *telestai* or to priestly groups, but they were vigorous and independent defenders of their rights. It is an exciting thing for the modern student of the tablets to discover not only that the people acting collectively took action against a priestess on behalf of a holder of common land, but also that their case was duly recorded by the royal clerks.

Long before the decipherment of Linear B, the existence of common land of this kind had been deduced from scattered hints in the Homeric texts. It is true that in the *Iliad* common men were treated with no respect at all by their noble lords, but they were, after all, on a military campaign far away from their land and the back-ing of their commune – moreover, this is an heroic tale where ordinary folk and their rights could hardly be allowed to exist.

Not only does the idea of common land fit in with Homeric assumptions, but there is a clue to link it with a wider historic background. A very plausible translation of the name given to this land by the tablet scribes has the meaning share-land – and this is a term which is found in many European languages – including Old English. And it is known that the principle of share-land was of great importance among the institutions of the early societies of western Europe. So it looks as though the tablets, far from revealing an Oriental type of society, may show how tenaciously the Achaeans had kept to social forms that were a part of their Indo-European inheritance.

Those who insist that the world of the tablets was dominated by borrowed

Oriental ideas, and therefore remote from the world of Homer, have one other argument. They say that the very existence of the tablets and the bureaucratic system they imply is in total opposition to the heroic spirit. Homer knew nothing of bureaucrats, and his heroes never exchanged the sword for the pen – or any other kind of writing equipment.

It has been seen that the Linear B script was adapted from the older Minoan Linear A for the purpose of writing Achaean Greek. Presumably methods of record-keeping may have been another part of the cultural debt which the Achaeans owed to the Cretans. The Achaeans also had their own direct contacts with the ancient centres of civilization, and the fact that they appear to have used a Meso-potamian system of measurement may mean that their bureaucrats took some lessons directly from the Orient.

It is also true that the Mycenaean kingdoms evidently had a well-devised and centralized administrative structure. Pylos was divided into two provinces each with a governor and deputy, and the provinces in turn were divided into a number of districts each with an official and his assistant. At the centre of this organization the clerks at the hall were thorough and meticulous.

Yet since the decipherment of Linear B, too great claims have been made for the overwhelming importance of this bureaucratic machine. Without any guidance from the tablets, it was already obvious that the royal establishments, with their need to gather taxes and look after manufacture and trade, military garrisons and fleets, must have had a degree of central control and regional organization. There is still nothing to prove that Mycenaean society was fully literate, or that it was dominated by an Oriental-style palace and temple bureaucracy.

All present evidence points to the fact that the clerks who kept the records were a specialized fraternity working almost exclusively in the royal halls. There is no certainty that such men as the district officers were literate. If only a small number of people could write, and they were mainly employed by the kings, then it is easy to understand how the art of writing could have been lost with the disappearance of the royal halls.

Mycenaean kings may have exchanged letters, and may even have taken part in the kind of international correspondence maintained by Oriental rulers. If the Hittite king did in fact address a letter to an Achaean contemporary (p. 166) he must have thought a correspondence to be possible. Homer, in his one mention of writing, makes Bellerophon carry a pair of tablets to the Lycian king. Yet against these hints, it remains a fact that no Mycenaean letters have come to light in the Egyptian or Hittite archives or in Greece itself. One explanation is that letters could have been written on papyrus or some other perishable stuff – but this has never been satisfactorily proved.

One other thing suggests that the Mycenaean clerks were not a large or important body. They never mention their own calling on the Linear B tablets where so many occupations are named. This is very unlike Oriental scribes – who were given to boasting about the dignity of their profession.

As for the kings and the nobility, there is nothing to show that they were much interested in literacy. If they were, it would seem incredible that they never had their names inscribed on personal seals or on their buildings. The great royal tombs, in particular, call out for inscriptions to commemorate the kings and queens for whose glory they were built. The contrast with Egypt and the other Eastern civilizations is striking. It seems likely that most of the ruling élite, like the heroes in Homer, could only "make their mark".

Were laws or literary works ever written down? This must be the most important question in judging the degree of literacy in Mycenaean society. No trace of either has been discovered as yet, and it becomes increasingly improbable that they ever will be. Both Pylos and Knossos were exhaustively excavated and yielded nothing but accounts and inventories.

Julius Caesar observed that among the Celts their Druid priests might use Greek writing for the conduct of practical affairs, but invariably learnt and taught by voice and memory. He thought that they did this to keep their knowledge secret. Another reason would have been that the written word had no traditional sanction. The oral transmission of epic and other forms of lore and literature was widespread among Indo-European-speaking peoples, and had its own ritual values. The method has been kept alive into modern times in the Brahminical schools of India.

It will be recalled that a lyre-playing bard was painted on the wall of the banqueting hall at Pylos. He wears his hair flowing in the Cretan style and his long, caped robe may be priestly dress. The dove winging in front of his face appears to be spellbound. Perhaps this "Orpheus" was a legendary figure, and yet he must have represented the inspiration of the bards who entertained the royal household. There is absolutely no evidence (at present) to make it appear that either they or their aristocratic listeners would have given a thought to the clerks who might be painstakingly at work with clay and stilos in the little office across the courtyard.

If, then, the bards were already reciting tales that were to be woven into the stuff of Homer, clerical affairs were no more likely to find a place in them than were the doings of the unguent boilers or most of the other humble folk whose unheroic activities were recorded on the tablets. The principle of writing was understood by Homer – that is clear from the Bellerophon story. It is all that is needed.

In turning from the social order of the Achaean kingdom to consider Mycenaean religion, it can be said at once that the revelations of the tablets can only cause rejoicing among historians. They do not contradict the accumulated archaeological evidence concerning the Mycenaean divinities and their worship, yet at the same time they add to it in a way which makes it easier to reconcile with what was to emerge in Homeric literature and in Classical Greece. Some scholars, never expecting their paths to run smoothly, have even cried "too good to be true".

The most striking thing about the material remains of Mycenaean religion – the scenes and figures shown in works of art, the ritual vessels, the symbols, the buildings – is that they are almost indistinguishable from their Cretan counterparts. Except for the glorification of their royal dead in enormous tombs and the different

Minoan elements in Mycenaean religion. (*a*) The Goddess in Minoan dress. Gold. From the Upper Grave Circle, Mycenae, 16th century B.C. (*b*) Naked Goddess with doves. Gold. From the Upper Grave Circle, Mycenae, 16th century B.C.

estimate of the significance of the afterlife that this may have represented, archaeology would suggest that the Achaeans took over Minoan religion in its entirety and
added very little of their own. So much was this the case that it has been usual to
refer to a Minoan-Mycenaean religion and not to attempt to disentangle them.

While in the reflections of life in secular art there is just the change of emphasis
one would expect from the feminine to the masculine, from the Minoan love of
nature, women, dancing and games to the Mycenaean love of battle and hunting,
the religious art shows the Goddess and her cult of fertility continuing undisturbed.

The Goddess maintains her absolute ascendancy over the young god; she is

(*c*) Double axe and bull's head symbols. Thin sheet gold. From the Upper Grave Circle, Mycenae,
16th century B.C. (*d*) The figure-of-eight shield symbol. Gold. From domed tomb at Epano
Englianos, Pylos; $1\frac{5}{8}''$; 15th century B.C.

The double axe often appears on pottery. From a tomb near Pylos, 15th century B.C.

Cattle in miniature. Stylized models of animals, usually cattle, became popular at the same time as the Goddess figurines (p. 232), and were probably used for cult purposes. Pottery. From chamber tombs near Nauplion, 13th century B.C.

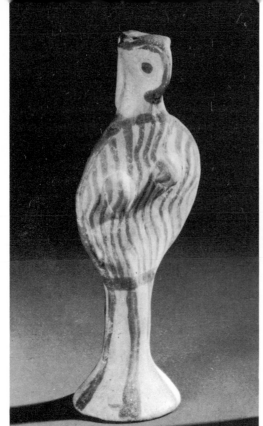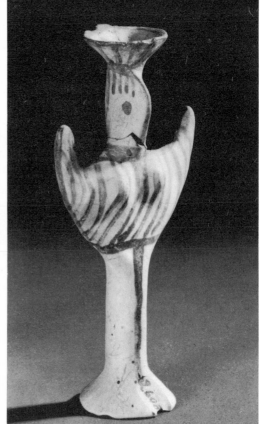

The Goddess mass-produced. These figures were extremely common in late Mycenaean times. Clay. From chamber tombs near Nauplion, 13th century B.C.

shown with women attendants dancing and taking part in vegetation rites in an identical manner. The familiar Cretan symbols, the figure-of-eight shield, the double axe, the pillar and tree, the dove and the horns of consecration, are all still there. Indeed, the pillar, so important in Crete, achieves a new monumental distinction in its proud display on the Lion Gate.

There were some slight distinctions in the mainland practices. The cult of snakes associated with the household aspect of the Goddess is less in evidence. Also, a new way of representing the divinity became popular during the thirteenth century. Thousands of little painted clay figures were set up in both tombs and houses. In some the Goddess was stylized towards a disc form, and in others towards a crescent. It is tempting, though probably wrong, to identify these shapes with phases of the moon. In a few of these attractively painted figures the Goddess holds an infant in her arms (plate 45).

The same similarity with no more than minor differences is found also in places of worship. With few exceptions, the Minoan avoidance of temples and large cult figures was maintained. The miniature gold cut-outs of tripartite shrines from the upper grave circle at Mycenae are identical with the Cretan originals. No actual remains of shrines of precisely this type have been identified in Greece, and perhaps they would not easily have fitted into the architectural plan of the halls. But small shrines to the Goddess existed in the halls just as they did in the palaces. On the other hand, cave and peak sanctuaries had not the same importance on the mainland as they had in Crete.

All in all, the picture of Mycenaean religion presented by archaeology would be harmful to the tenor of this book if it had to be accepted as the whole truth. It would seem against all probability that the Achaeans, who kept so much of the traditions of a warrior society, should have surrendered every vestige of the patriarchal religion that had been a part of them. It is true that a migrating people can keep and even strengthen their social organization while they leave their sacred places behind them. Yet the total surrender of the masculine conception of supreme deity to the feminine would seem to be unacceptable.

The words suddenly uttered by the tablets from Knossos and Pylos make it known that it need not be accepted. Although there is no theology in them, these lists of men, women, animals, precious vessels, sweet oils, honey, wine and other offerings made to the divinities and their shrines not only preserve the names of a medley of gods and goddesses, but give an idea of their hierarchical order and the relative honour in which they were held.

The divine society that emerges is just what would be anticipated from the historical situation. The Goddess of the Cretans is represented in various aspects, and is evidently still powerful. At the same time male gods who are far more than her inferior consort are being worshipped and richly endowed.

The other fact revealed by the tablets, to the profound satisfaction of all those who believe in the continuity of Mycenaean and later Greek culture, is that the names of the divinities worshipped in Mycenaean Knossos and Pylos compose the Olympian pantheon of Homer and his successors. Among the great Olympian figures only Apollo is missing, and that may be due to the chances of discovery. Those whose names are mentioned include Poseidon, Zeus, Hera, Athena, Artemis, Demeter, Eileithyia, Ares, Hermes, Dionysus – and Paieon who was later to be merged with Apollo. There is also a Dove Goddess.

The Knossos tablets refer to Our Lady (*Potnia*) of Athana. The strictest scholars say that this refers to a place-name and not directly to a goddess – and that the same is true of Our Lady of Labyrinthos. It is, however, quite irresistible to equate them with Athena herself and with the Lady of the Labyrinth – perhaps Ariadne. Indeed, it is no wonder that the Knossian tablets, in particular, seem "too good to be true" for the manner in which they link what was known of Minoan Crete with Homeric and Classical Greece. As well as Athena and the Lady of the Labyrinth, there is the assignment of a jar of honey to Eileithyia of Amnisos – beyond all reasonable doubt it must have gone to that cave of the goddess of childbirth named by Odysseus and discovered by archaeologists (p. 134). Then from another piece of clay, as it happens almost the first tablet to be unearthed at Knossos, come the words "To Diktaean Zeus OIL", and "To the Daedaleion OIL". Here already, in fact, is the Achaean Zeus identified with the young divinity of the Cretan Goddess (p. 133), and a totally unexpected proof that Daedalus, who by Homer's time had become a mortal, though an extraordinary one, had been a Cretan deity with his own shrine at Knossos.

In Pylos the fact that the king, or *Wanax*, had his estate beside the chief shrine of the Goddess is the clearest possible indication both of the king's religious function and of the continuing importance of the Goddess within the Mycenaean kingdoms. That it was a general and remembered arrangement is shown by a few casual words in the *Odyssey* – when Nausicaa says that the *temenos* of her father, King Alcinous, is close to "a lovely poplar grove of Athena". It was the exact counterpart to the Goddess having her shrine within the king's hall. The human king was fulfilling the rôle of divine son and consort to the Goddess. The Goddess herself is sometimes called *Wanassa*, or queen.

Further words deciphered from the clay tablets of Pylos throw light on the fine work of art excavated from the citadel at Mycenae (p. 197). The exquisite ivory of the two women watching over the little boy (which, significantly, was found with the remains of a Mycenaean shrine below the Classical Greek temple probably dedicated to Athena) is at once recalled by a dedication of perfumed oil to "The Two Queens and Poseidon", and another to "The King and Two Queens". Just which divinities are portrayed in the ivory is, of course, uncertain. Some identify them with Demeter and Persephone and the young god involved in the Mysteries of Eleusis, others with the two nurses and the infant Dionysus. The important thing is that here in yet another form is proof of the continued vitality of the Goddess through the Mycenaean Age and far beyond.

Yet by the end of the thirteenth century, when the Pylos tablets were written, the masculine gods proper to Achaean religious tradition must already have been coming into their own. The importance of the Diktaean Zeus in Crete was evidently already considerable – although he was far from being the Father of gods and men that the Olympic Zeus had become for Homer.

In Pylos, and indeed in the whole of the Peloponnese, the most important of the Mycenaean gods was not Zeus, but his brother Poseidon. This had already been suspected because cults surviving into Classical times in Laconia and Arcadia showed Poseidon to have received far more attention than his brother, and a Greek historian of the fourth century observed, "The Peloponnese in olden days seems to have been the dwelling place of Poseidon, and the land was considered sacred to him."

As for Pylos itself, there was a hint from the fact that when, in the *Odyssey*, Telemachus arrived there by sea, he found King Nestor on the shore with his followers sacrificing nine times nine bulls to Poseidon. It was therefore a satisfaction to scholars when one of the most interesting of the Pylos tablets confirmed this pre-eminence. It is a list of valuable offerings to shrines in the town of Pylos. The shrine of Poseidon heads the list with a gift of two women and an ornamental gold cup, while that associated with Zeus and Hera comes last of all and receives inferior offerings.

Poseidon appears in many other tablets, so that there seems no doubt his status in the Pylian kingdom was as high as in Laconia and Arcadia. Whether this was true in the more northerly parts of the Mycenaean world is not yet known, but with the supremacy of the Peloponnese within that world it looks as though Zeus did not win the universal crown from his brother until after its collapse.

After the accession of Zeus as Sky Father, Poseidon was given his familiar inferior rôle as ruler of the oceans. But in Mycenaean days he seems to have been worshipped as a lord of the earth – or Earth Shaker. Poseidon was also often worshipped in the form of a horse, and it may have been this aspect of the god that belonged to the ancient Indo-European tradition of the Achaeans. If so, it was represented by the shrine to Hippos on the estate of the War Leader (p. 224).

Looked at as a whole, the religious life of late Mycenaean Pylos shows a well-balanced marriage between the Cretan and Achaean divinities. If the Goddess was particularly involved with the king, that is to be expected, as it was, of course, in the civilized life of the royal household that the Minoan influence had always been strongest. Nothing is known of the role played by the queen, and it has been given too little consideration.

How far a Mycenaean king was regarded as divine in his lifetime it is hard to say. Indeed, the divinity of kingship is always shifting and elusive. Even in the twentieth century a queen may have an aura of it when she is being crowned and anointed which vanishes when she is at a horse race. There is a general reluctance, probably well founded, to allow an Achaean *Wanax* with his warrior tradition to have moved in the mystical atmosphere appropriate in Minoan Crete.

If the Goddess prevailed in the hall at Pylos, down in the town Poseidon was given first place. There, it would seem, when he was linked with the Goddess in one of her guises, it was he who was the dominant partner. The fighting men under their War Leader probably paid special honour to the ancient Hippos, who may have been worshipped among them since the days when they entered Greece with their horse-drawn wagons.

The gods and goddesses whose names were familiar at Pylos were a mixed assembly. They came from the north, from the Aegean, Anatolia and the Orient –

and from the unconscious minds of all men. What is most wonderful and significant about them is that they did not die with the royal houses and their civilization. In shrines and houses throughout the country their names were to be revered until they could re-emerge into history – as the immortals of Homer.

The Linear B tablets of Pylos, some twelve hundred pieces of baked clay, have been made to yield an astounding amount of information about the social and religious life of the kingdom in the days of its prosperity. Yet many of them were drawn up during the last days of peace as part of a vain effort to avert catastrophe.

Perhaps through his own agents or traders, the *Wanax* had received advance warning that he was to be attacked. Although it is not certain, the simplest inter-pretation will be accepted here – that the threat came from Dorians still living in the north in the region now known as Epirus. This was only about 120 miles beyond the northern frontier of the Pylian kingdom, yet these warrior tribesmen belonged to a different world. They had allowed the mountains to cut them off from the eastern Mediterranean and all the lures of civilization. Yet, like most peoples so situated, they were ready to descend upon the civilized and despoil them.

The kingdom of Pylos had been relatively secure against internecine Achaean wars or incursions from the east. Now it was most vulnerable to attack down the west coast by either land or sea, and may well have been the first of all the great Mycenaean strongholds to fall to the Dorians. There was a long coastline to defend, and even the hall was unfortified. It seems that there was a grave shortage of weapons.

The emergency was faced without panic. The clerks remained at their benches patiently recording all that was done – or needed to be done. They were concerned both with civilians and with fighting levees.

Women and children were evacuated – probably from villages most exposed to attack – and given jobs to do, such as the baking of bread. The main military effort seems to have been concentrated on manning a fleet stationed round about Cape Akritas. For this purpose dispositions of "rowers" were made, each group number-ing about forty and probably forming the crew of a warship. To equip the fighting men about a ton of bronze was collected, and nearly two hundred bronze-smiths brought together. It is a moving testimony to the crisis of turning from peace to war that bronze belonging to sanctuaries of the Goddess was requisitioned for the casting of spears and arrowheads.

The protection of coasts on either side of the Cape was assigned to units of men apparently serving under local commanders. "How watchers are guarding the coastal regions" is the tablet heading. *Equeta*, the king's Companions, were attached to some of these units, perhaps to provide liaison with the main command. One can imagine them galloping their chariots to Pylos, where the *Wanax* himself was

Plate 34. Within the thickness of Cyclopean walls. The East Gallery at Tiryns, with corbelled vault.

Overleaf Plates 35 and 36. Boars' tusks and bronze: armour for an Achaean hero. From the chamber tomb at Dendra, 15th century B.C.

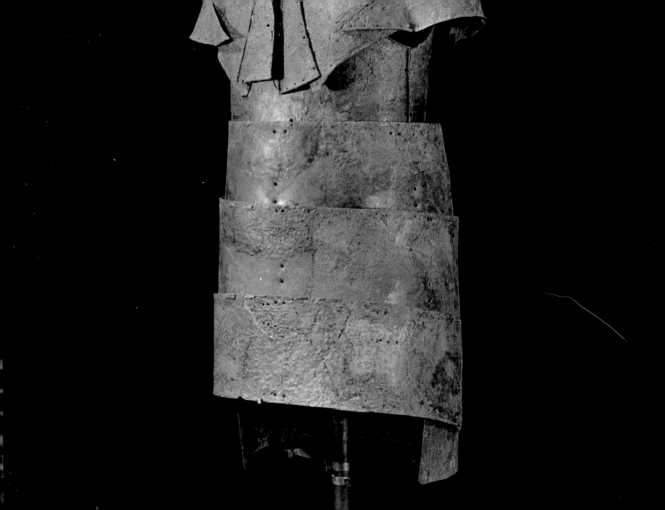

probably based, or to the headquarters of the War Leader, which seem to have been not very far from Leuktron on the Messenian Gulf – probably the capital of the southern province.

Masons were sent to Pylos, Leuktron and a few other key places, presumably to build fortifications. If this was the purpose, the decision was taken too late. There is no sign that the much-needed walls ever went up at Pylos.

Indeed, it was all too late. From the tablets that record the effort to save the kingdom, one must turn to the fabric of the royal hall to discover that it failed.

The barbarian warriors broke in. They must have been astonished by the painted rooms and the treasure they contained – perhaps augmented by precious vessels sent up from the shrines for safe keeping. When they had finished looting they cared nothing for the building with its unwarlike foreign embellishments. They set fire to it and it burned furiously – as a building laced with big timbers and stocked with oil was certain to burn. The heat was so great that some of the pottery vessels in the pantries melted into vitreous lumps, while stone was reduced to lime. A massive ashlar wall near one side of the banqueting hall, its timber frame consumed, fell outward in one piece as though thrown by the Earth Shaker himself. In the storerooms and the tax office by the entrance the abandoned tablets were fired to a hardness that was to preserve them for all time.

These tablets and the ruins where they lay have provided a unique record of how one great Mycenaean kingdom fell. Probably the story was everywhere much the same, as Mycenae, Tiryns and all the other royal strongholds except Athens were engulfed by the barbarian tide. Dorians in time took all the Peloponnese except Arcadia and went on to dominate Crete, Rhodes and the adjacent islands. The most venerable of all the royal houses, Knossos, may have been among the last to fall.

The descendants of Neleus and Nestor had failed at Pylos, but with a dramatic form that might have been devised by a great tragedian, they redeemed themselves in their places of refuge (p. 253). The story tells that when the Athenians decisively defeated the Dorians in the valley of the Ilissos, it was one King Codrus who secured the victory with the heroic sacrifice of his life. This Codrus was not an Athenian, but the son of a prince of the royal house of Pylos who had come as a refugee to Attica.

It has been suggested, though it is no more than a pleasing guess, that Athena's owl may have been brought to her from this royal house. Two golden owls have been found in and near Pylos (p. 242), and as this bird is otherwise rare among the symbolic creatures of Mycenaean art, it is possible that it was an emblem of the Pylian princes. If so, it might well have flown to the household goddess of their adopted kingdom.

Plate 37. Excellence in a domestic utensil. Bronze. From a chamber tomb at Mycenae, c. 1300 B.C.

Athena's owl at home in Pylos? Gold. From the domed tomb at Epano Englianos, Pylos, 15th century B.C.

The Athenians, and Ionian Greeks generally, continued to take pride in their inheritance from the house of Nestor. It was said that there were Pylians among the ancestors of Pericles. It was Neileos, too, a son of King Codros, who led Greek colonists across the Aegean to Miletus – the Ionian city where the Greek intellectual revolution was to begin. Other Pylian refugees had gone directly to Ionia and founded the city of Colophon – or so its seventh-century poet, Mimnermus, declares. "When from the lofty city of Neleian Pylos we came on shipboard to the pleasant land of Asia."

So it was that although the Dorians and the wider upheavals of the time returned Greece and the islands to the simple life, something of the Mycenaean tradition endured in Attica and in the trans-Aegean colonies – the lands that were to form Ionian Greece. In the changed social climate of this time, great royal houses and centralized governments could not exist. But on the Athenian acropolis the Goddess lived on, waiting for her brilliant revival, and the bards went from house to house telling their tales of the Mycenaean heroes. Homer, himself an Ionian from "the pleasant land of Asia", was to give to this oral literature the tremendous poetic force that inspired the Greeks, and, through them, the western world.

Chapter Six

Greek Revival

The fall of Pylos in about 1200 B.C. has been chosen as the event which most clearly announces the end of the Mycenaean Age. It is true that for another century its civilization struggled on in a decadent and impoverished style. Mycenae itself was re-occupied, and others of the old kingdoms held together for a while. In Euboea and islands of the west Aegean the twelfth century was still prosperous. But in general it was a period, like the present, when everyone must have felt "Things fall apart, the centre cannot hold". It would no longer have been remotely possible for a High King of Mycenae to have summoned forces from all the Achaean kingdoms and led a united army on an undertaking such as the Trojan War.

If the fighting men with their round shields painted on the Warrior Vase represent the kind of soldiers who tried to repel the invading barbarians, the comically clumsy way in which they are portrayed represents the rapid artistic decline that went with political disintegration (pp. 244, 245). Poor local styles marked the break-up of the old uniformity of cultural life. Craftsmanship, too, was disappearing; there were no more skilled goldsmiths or ivory carvers. As far as is known even the art of writing was lost – though this is now being questioned.

At the end of the twelfth century there seem to have been further barbarian incursions, iron began to replace bronze, and the flight to settle overseas which had begun with the fall of the palaces continued apace (p. 250). What had been left of divine kingship and the life of the royal halls disappeared for ever.

This was, in fact, the beginning of what used to be called the Dark Age of Greece, from which the Hellenic Greeks of Classical times were held to emerge an almost completely different people. The first celebration of the Olympic Games, from which the Greeks were to date their era, was in 776 B.C. This same eighth century saw the quickening of contacts with the Orient, and the all-important adoption of the simple Phoenician alphabet. Before its end the *Iliad* had been composed, and "the Greek miracle" was almost in sight.

Was this Dark Age really so dark, and how deep was the gulf separating the Mycenaean from the Hellenic Greeks? It is the purpose of this chapter to insist neither very dark nor very deep, and as it is bound to contain more argument than information, the writer intends to appear in the first person.

Marching against the barbarians? Soldiers such as these probably fought the Dorians. From the "Warrior Vase", Mycenae, 12th century B.C.

The woman laments their going. Detail from the "Warrior Vase".

Above The hound runs with the chariot. A lively kind of decadence. Pottery fragment from Tiryns, 13th century B.C. *Below* From the civilized to the naive. Simple rendering of an Oriental motif, the lion and horned beast. Compare p. 173. Clay. From Asine, 12th century B.C.

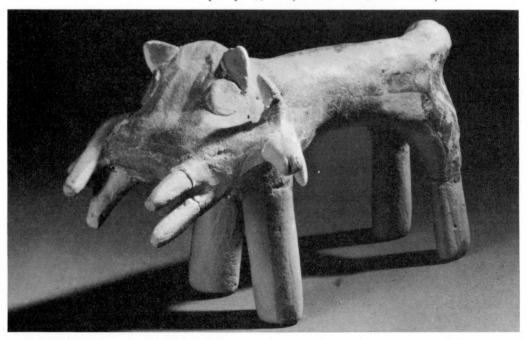

Right "The Lord of Asine." Late Mycenaean plastic art. Clay. From Asine, 12th century B.C.

A curious fish-head vessel from Nauplion, 13th–12th century B.C.

Ever since Schliemann proved the existence of an historical Troy, evidence of all kinds has been accumulating to enable us to link the two ages and their worlds and to recognize that the historical obscurity hid no real hiatus. In addition to what we have discovered, illumination has come from what we have experienced. Anyone who has watched the naturalistic, representational ideals of nineteenth-century art give way within a generation to abstractionism and a chaos of other non-representational forms, has learnt that a total artistic revolution can take place in the mind with no help from foreign invaders or violent social upheaval. Indeed, in many ways we have been forced into deeper understanding of ages of internal breakdown and transition.

A considerable change of outlook has, of course, been recognized, and the term Dark Ages is no longer used as freely as it used to be. But it seems to me that the degree of continuity between Mycenaean and Classical Greece, and the importance of the Bronze Age heritage, have even now never been stated with sufficient force. There has also been the counter-attack by the minority of scholars who have used their interpretation of the tablets to build up a picture of an Oriental-style palace bureaucracy, and in this way to create a gulf between the Mycenaean Age and Homer. If in the last chapter I argued against this interpretation too vehemently, it is because I am convinced of its perversity.

The further argument that has to be developed depends first of all on acceptance of the view that Mycenaean civilization was the product of a union between an Achaean society which in essentials never lost its northern-derived, Indo-European social structure and values, and a Minoan culture which, while it owed much to Oriental origins, had developed unique qualities in the fortunate haven of Crete. This blending carried with it the implication of a significant blending of masculine with feminine qualities.

It remains to show through the various forms of witness now available, that much that was vital and significant in that blended civilization must have persisted in what might best be called the culturally humble centuries between Mycenaean and Classical times. If this can be successfully done, the stirrings of the eighth century B.C. may be seen as in some part a *revival* – although a revival that was bound to lead to rapid growth and change.

Before going on to more rational discussion, I want to make use of an historical fact which can also serve as a symbol. It comes from a completely different historical context. The steep chalk slopes of southern England with their covering of fine green turf have encouraged a peculiar form of art – the blocking or outlining of figures by cutting away the turf to expose the pure white chalk below. Many have been cut in the last two centuries, but these were inspired by two or three which are ancient. The White Horse of Uffington was probably cut by Celts well before the

Roman Conquest; the Cerne Abbas Giant, a fertility figure, has probably exposed himself to the people of Dorset since Roman times.

Now I am perfectly certain that any archaeologist painfully recording all the cultural breaks that had occurred since the Celtic Iron Age, observing the vast number of abandoned sites and the complete change in the whole pattern of settlement, would have said that the maintenance of hill figures through all these upheavals was quite out of the question. I am equally certain that any historian thinking of the many invasions of Britain, the changes of religion, the replacement of one language by another, the rise and fall of feudalism and many other disturbances, would have been even more positive that nothing so perishable as a hill figure could possibly have survived. Yet they have. Through two thousand years the local people have kept the cuts in the turf open, holding regular festivals with appropriate rites and games as a part of the scouring ceremonies. Now, with another adjustment in our society, the figures are being maintained by a government department.

The hill figures of England can serve as a warning to all archaeologists and historians who think too much of change and too little of the underlying continuities. The truth is that good land is seldom seriously depopulated, and that whatever happens parents are always bringing up new generations of children, telling them stories about the past and showing them what is the customary thing to do. Whatever happens in history, much cultural traffic can float down on this stream.

Returning to the history of the centuries between latest Mycenaean and the dawn of Hellenic times, it has to be said that the greatest difficulty lies in the reconstruction of actual events. Archaeology has amassed a welter of information, but it remains even more confused than the times themselves. In general it confirms the picture of provincial societies, each with its own version of decadent Mycenaean culture, reacting equally variously to the effect of the incursions and resulting pressures coming mostly from the north.

Archaeology offers some evidence (always to be taken with caution) of severe depopulation in much of the Peloponnese, and also confirms the migrations across the Aegean beginning in the eleventh century and continuing for a long time. It puts no obstacle in the way of accepting the threefold nature of this migration, which is supported by tradition and by the pattern of Greek dialects. It seems that while in time the Dorians spread across the south Aegean (p. 251), the Ionian branch of the Greek people, those of Attica and the extreme north of the Peloponnese, formed the centre of the movement into Anatolia, where Miletus was to be one of their most interesting cities. In the north the migration is identified with the Aeolian branch of the Greeks, largely drawn from Boeotia and Thessaly.

What it is, unhappily, almost impossible for the archaeological evidence to prove is how far, if at all, these colonists on the coasts and islands of the eastern Aegean met with pockets of Cretan or Mycenaean settlers who had colonized, or at least established trading posts, in more prosperous times. Because of the brilliant future that lay ahead of it, Miletus is of particular interest here. The original Minoan settlement came under Mycenaean influence and then was violently destroyed, probably in the late twelfth century. But it was soon re-occupied by Ionians of Attic and Pylian background, and it is very hard to doubt that the newcomers, whose settlement marks the beginning of a new era, did not meet with and absorb survivors from the old. A temple of Athena stood in the heart of the area where occupation was most nearly continuous.

On the island of Samos, the famous temple of Hera may have been the centre of a continuous settlement, and it is easy to imagine that in a number of places among the islands and on the Anatolian coast, shrines and later temples to various aspects of the Goddess may have enjoyed an unbroken history of worship – whatever the political sovereignty.

Further overseas archaeology confirms the arrival of Achaean refugees in Cilicia and Cyprus. It also suggests a strong Achaean element among the Philistines, who settled in Palestine during the twelfth century. This is a further indication that there were indeed Achaean contingents among the mysterious People of the Sea who convulsed the eastern Mediterranean, destroyed Ugarit, and were finally checked by the Pharaoh Rameses III in about 1190. The chief interest of these distant movements for the present argument is that with Achaeans sailing the old sea route (albeit for different purposes) and settling down with conservative prosperity in the old Mycenaean depot of Cyprus, it is inconceivable that communications between Greece and the Orient were ever completely severed.

It remains uncertain how far these dispersals, and also the earlier destruction of Pylos and other cities, were due to the Dorians. Greek tradition made much of their conquests in a period beginning some three generations after the Trojan war. Tradition is supported by the later pattern of Greek dialects. The areas of Doric dialect accord with the idea that these northern barbarians spread over the Peloponnese (leaving a pocket of Achaeans among the Arcadian mountains) and extended eastward to Crete, the Dodecanese, and beyond.

Unfortunately, archaeology fails to find any sign of newcomers settling in Greece during the twelfth century of Mycenaean decadence. That is why there is now a tendency to blame the disaster of 1200 on unknown aggressors involved with the wider upheavals of the time (p. 168) and to delay the coming of the Dorians until later.

Yet so long as no historical identity can be given to such unnamed aggressors, this is a wasteful hypothesis. To explain the lack of recognizable Dorian remains for

the time after 1200 it can be said either that Dorian shepherds were wholly dominated by Mycenaean culture, or, more convincingly, that a phase of destructive
raiding preceded their actual settlement. I have thought it wiser, then, to adhere to
the old tradition of Dorian conquests.

What is here of the most vital significance about the Dorian take-over of southern
Greece is that it began the division of the Hellenic world into two opposing camps:
the Dorian and the Ionian. This division went beyond all political enmities. It was
to continue and grow in bitterness, until by causing the Peloponnesian War it broke
the highest promise of Hellenic Greece. It has always been symbolized for posterity
by the contrasting values of the two principal cities: Dorian Sparta and Ionian
Athens. For this book, Sparta and the Dorians must stand for the Indo-European
tradition unredeemed by the feminine influence of Crete, while Athens and the
Ionians enjoyed a direct inheritance from Mycenaean civilization that had long
tempered that tradition and helped them to create ideals of grace and harmony.
When Sophocles wrote of the Athenians as descendants of Athena's King
Erechtheus, he was not afraid to expose the power of the feminine principle.

> From old the sons of Erechtheus knew felicity;
> The children of blessed gods,
> Born from a land holy and undespoiled,
> They pasture on glorious Wisdom,
> Ever walking gracefully through the brightest of skies,
> Where once, men tell, the Holy Nine,
> The Pierian Muses,
> Created golden-haired harmony.
> On the fair-flowing waters of Cephisus
> They say that Aphrodite fills her pitcher
> And breathes over the land . . .
> She sends her loves to be throned at Wisdom's side
> And with her to work all manner of excellence.

The central position of "undespoiled" Athens in this book has already been
proclaimed in an evocative manner in the opening chapter. Soon the impregnability
of this position will have to be justified by a greater parade of fact. But no writing
concerned with filling the gap of the obscure centuries can go any further without
discussing the phenomenon of Homer. For it was the Homeric epics that linked the
Greeks with their Bronze Age past in a way known to no other people. It is also,
but quite distinctly, the actual fact of the transmission of the Homeric tradition that
offers one of the strongest proofs (a little after the fashion of the hill figures) that
there was a vigorous continuity of social and cultural life through the "Dark Ages".

Not that turning towards Homer means turning right away from Athens. For Athens with Attica played her part in the events preparing the ground for the composition of the Homeric epics in the Ionian colonies across the Aegean. We have already seen how, "undespoiled" by the Dorians, the city became a rallying place for refugees from those less fortunate Mycenaean kingdoms being over-run by the barbarous tribesmen. Most influential among them were members of the royal house from Pylos. Indeed, it was Codros, of the second generation of Pylians, who was honoured as a saviour of Athens (p. 241).

The city became overcrowded, and that is one reason why her citizens and people from the countryside, together with descendants of those to whom she had given shelter, began the great migration to trans-Aegean Ionia. Among the mixed crowds setting out to start a new life, there must have been bards whose stocks of songs were drawn from many Mycenaean kingdoms. Their cosmopolitan audiences would have favoured inter-kingdom Mycenaean stories such as those that went into the *Iliad* and *Odyssey*. In this mixed tradition of Mycenaean literature from which Homer was to draw his material and his inspiration, the Athenian-Pylian ingredient was probably the most important. Homer never knew of the lyre player of the great hall at Pylos, and yet he may have heard words that were sung there. An authority has declared: "I believe that for these two centuries (*c.* 1100–900 B.C.) the rôle of Athens, the unsacked city, to which refugees came, and from which immigrants went, may have been as important in literature as it was in art."

The debate as to how far the Homeric epics were the work of an individual poet, or poets, of genius appears to be endless. At the present time the weight of opinion favours the idea that a great poet (born in Smyrna or Chios) composed the *Iliad* as a coherent poem, and that the composition took place towards the end of the eighth century B.C. Some authorities believe that the same poet could also have created the *Odyssey*, but others find good reason to believe that this epic is a slightly later work, possibly the work of a son or disciple of the poet of the *Iliad*. There is, however, no doubt that additions and modifications continued to be made to both even after the seventh century.

These uncertainties are of no significance for the present argument, and, as is customary, the name of Homer has been, and will be, used to stand for the authorship of both epics. What is significant is that Homer built his great works out of myths and tales which had been handed on from generation to generation, and deliberately portrayed an heroic Bronze Age world in many ways quite different from his own.

No one could doubt that there would be changes to this stream of oral tradition as the young bards learnt from their elders and then adapted what they had learnt to the spirit of their time and to suit particular occasions and individual patrons.

It is difficult now to judge the relative importance of memorizing and improvising in the handing on of oral literature. Religious litanies of many kinds would have had to be memorized exactly, and this must have helped to maintain the life of myths. While, at any rate in later centuries, there were hack reciters, true bards improvised each performance, hardly knowing as they took up their lyres just what words would come. Yet learning by heart was an important part of their preparation – and their listeners would have expected to hear the traditional stories of gods and men. These stories, which the bards continually drew upon and added to, were first devised for such occasions as eulogies at the funerals of great men, religious festivals, and for entertainment in the banqueting hall.

On the lips of the bards the stories were altered and re-combined, but they remained recognizable, and carried with them many descriptions of things and scenes and social relationships that no longer existed after the fall of the Mycenaean kingdoms. At the same time, to help themselves along in their improvising, the bards used stock phrases of the kind that form so large and familiar an element in Homer – the wine-dark sea, rosy-fingered dawn, the well-greaved Achaeans, Hector of the shining helm, and scores of others.

The whole process can be likened to a slow winter river where the ice is repeatedly broken and stirred, but blocks large and small, though sometimes melted at the edges, sometimes added to, tend to remain in being and to recombine with each successive frost. The work of the frosts in this metaphor represents, obviously, the cohering power of individual bards or bardic schools. The genius of Homer, when it came, gave a much greater coherence and smoothness of surface, but the old blocks and splinters were still there.

So it is that the heroic age that is shown in such powerful colours in the epics does record at least something of Mycenaean history, and very much more of the Mycenaean scene. Fragments from different periods became compacted, intangibles such as social and spiritual values were always liable to change with the times, but very much else survived.

An enormous amount has been written about the Mycenaean elements in Homer, and it would be foolish here to attempt to do more than mention the most important. I hope that some idea of the relevance of many Homeric descriptions to the remains of the Bronze Age world discovered by archaeology has already become apparent in the course of this book. I have also touched on particular finds, such as the Dendra armour, which show how, since the days of Schliemann, archaeology has often proved that material things described in Homer were in fact in use in the Mycenaean kingdoms. It is not too much to claim that over the last century the sceptical anti-Mycenaeanists have fought a losing battle against the discoveries of the spade.

First of all there is the undoubted Bronze Age character of the whole of the

Hunters with figure-of-eight and tower shields. Inlaid bronze from Upper Grave Circle, Mycenae, 16th century B.C.

poems' setting. An eighth-century Homer living in Ionia would have known nothing of a confederation of rich kingdoms dominated by Mycenae. In his time Agamemnon's city was a modest place subject to Argos, while great Pylos, second only to Mycenae in the number of ships it sent to Troy, had long been overgrown. Homer could never have sung to high kings of such wealth and power, or who would so readily have been referred to as godlike, or as being treated like the immortals. Nor could he have known anything to approach the great halls that he describes so often, with their pillars by the hearth, their bronze-covered doors and store rooms filled with wine, rich clothes and golden vessels.

In the equipment of the heroes, both Achaeans and Trojans, there is a very great deal that belongs only to the Mycenaean Age. Homer has deliberately set them in a bronze-using world – iron is seldom mentioned. Indeed some of their weapons go back to centuries well before the Trojan war, and could not conceivably be known to Homer by any way except through the tradition of oral poetry. The boars'-tusk helmet (p. 197) was obsolete by the twelfth century. The shield of Ajax which he carries "like a tower", which is made "of seven oxhides" and can be slung by a strap over the left shoulder, must be one of the semi-cylindrical kind carried by the lion hunters on one of the inlaid daggers from the Upper Grave Circle at Mycenae. Hector's shield thumps against his neck and ankles, while that of Periphetes is described by the epithet "reaching to the feet", and proves, indeed, to be long enough to cause him to trip over the rim. These two shields must either have been of the tower type or of the figure-of-eight, bulging, oxhide variety already so familiar from Cretan art, and also shown on the lion-hunt dagger. Both these forms of body shield were going out of use by 1400 B.C. By the time of the Trojan War they had been displaced by small circular shields often with bronze bosses and handgrips – probably of Oriental origin. Agamemnon's shield appears to have been a glorified version of this circular type.

War chariots were another item of equipment which Homer allowed his heroes but which had gone out of use by his own day. It is often said that in the fighting outside Troy they only served to bring warriors to the field, as though the bard had forgotten how chariots were deployed in battle. Yet in Nestor's account of campaigns of his youth the use of massed chariots is implied. Thus both shield and chariot references make good examples of the gradual accumulation of material in the epics, of older fragments coalescing with less ancient.

There are a number of ways in which the language of the *Iliad* and *Odyssey* reveals how the poetry went from lip to lip through the generations. Some are grammatical – there are for instance details of an archaic syntax linking the epic with forms found in the Linear B texts. Among verbal survivals one of the most interesting concerns the *Wanax* himself. In the Pylos tablets the king appears as *Wanax* and the term *Basileus* is reserved for minor dignitaries. In the eighth century, when the *Wanax* and his glory had departed, Homer still sometimes used the title for his royal heroes, but he also employs *Basileus* as though it had the same meaning. In Classical Greek *Basileus* had become the standard word for king, and *Wanax* was reserved for divinities.

The most telling of all the linguistic arguments concerns the Arcadian elements that can be recognized underlying the later Ionian dialect of Homer. The tablets have now confirmed what was already suspected – that Arcadian comes very close to the Mycenaean dialect. The same ancient speech that survived in the mountain refuge of Arcadia survived also on the tongues of the bards.

There are also, of course, ways in which Homer had diverged from the Mycenaean past. Patroclus, for example, was cremated after Iron Age custom, whereas inhumation had been almost universal in the Bronze Age. Modifications of this kind are to be expected, but it is more surprising that there is absolutely no mention in Homer of the great royal corbelled tombs that had been such a conspicuous feature of the Mycenaean scene and must have played so significant a part in royal ritual.

Homeric religion is now more firmly linked with Mycenaean belief than it used to be before the reading of the tablets. At the time when we depended entirely on the archaeological evidence, the change from the apparently total supremacy of the Goddess in Mycenaean Greece to the paternalistic world of Zeus and his Olympians in Homer seemed a revolutionary change. Now that the tablets have shown that by the end of Mycenaean times all or nearly all the Olympians already had their seats of worship, and that although the Goddess was still very highly honoured and close to the throne, masculine divinities were already apparently equal to her, the transition can be seen to have been a gradual one.

Plate 38. For scented oil. A small stirrup jar from a tomb at Makresia, near Olympia, 14th century B.C.

Overleaf Plate 39. The Minoan spirit is still strong. Two young men. Fresco, from Pylos, 13th century B.C. Plate 40. Some foretaste of the Hellenic spirit? Goddess or priestess. Fresco. From Pylos, 13th century B.C.

Moreover, in spite of the rule of Zeus, Homer not only allows his goddesses very great power, but gives their affairs control of his central plot. Towards the end of the *Iliad* Homer gives the reason why Troy was doomed to fall and the Trojans to suffer. It was the Judgment of Paris. Hera and Athena had not forgiven Priam's son for turning them down in favour of Aphrodite when she "brought him deadly lustfulness". In the rivalry of these three goddesses, two willing the destruction of Troy, the third fighting to save it, is there not some memory left of the goddess who lived in the Mycenaean king's house and shared his enmities?

Two memories connected with the goddess of the royal household are certain. One is in the passage in the *Odyssey* where Athena, having led Odysseus to the hall of King Alcinous of Phaecia, left him and the island and "came to wide-wayed Athens, and entered the good house of Erechtheus". Here, quite plainly, Athena is thought of as returning to her city and to her own shrine in the royal dwelling on the Acropolis. The second, which has added interest because it could only be recognized after the decipherment of the tablets, has already been mentioned (p. 234). It is when, a little earlier in the story of Odysseus in Phaeacia, Nausicaa casually says to him that her father, King Alcinous, has his estate by the "poplar grove of Athena". This is one of the most telling of all the smaller Mycenaean memories in Homer, for it occurs in the flow of the narrative and is not involved with the stock phrases where ancient material is to be expected. It suggests that stories must sometimes have been extensively memorized. As it happens, this particular story of Odysseus's stay in Phaeacia appears to be set in a strongly Mycenaean atmosphere. The famous hall of King Alcinous with its mass of gold and silver ornaments and vessels, and its inlaid chairs, is right in idea if fanciful in detail. So are the fifty hand-maids grinding flour and weaving fine linen, and the minstrel leaning against the tall column among the feasters. Moreover, there is surely something of the Minoan tradition in Alcinous's queen, Arete, whom he honours "as no other woman is honoured. . . . Thus she hath, and hath ever had, all worship from her dear children and from her lord Alcinous and from all the folk, who look on her as a goddess . . . when she goes about the town". Again, there is a picture of the royal pair surely as evocative of the Bronze Age world as any in Homer. Nausicaa describes it to Odysseus: "When thou art within the shadow of the halls and the court, pass quickly through the great chamber, till thou comest to my mother, who sits at the hearth in the light of the fire, weaving yarn of sea-purple stain, a wonder to behold. Her chair is leaned against a pillar, and her maidens sit behind her. And there my father's throne leans close to hers, wherein he sits and drinks his wine like an immortal." Here is a scene that could be perfectly staged in the great hall on Epano Englianos.

It seems to me that scenes such as this not only recall the Mycenaean age, but

Plate 41. Stylization of natural forms: ivy leaf and rosette. Jug from a chamber tomb at Mycenae, 15th century B.C.

also bring out its essentially Achaean spirit. In this case Arete, who is looked on as a goddess, provides just the feminine ingredient in the Mycenaean blend that one would look for. If this is true, and if the reading of the Linear B tablets does on the whole reveal traditional Achaean forms in such fundamental matters as social structure and land tenure, it is puzzling that there has been so strong a tendency among recent students of Mycenaean life and literature to look always to the Orient for parallels while neglecting those that could be sought among other Indo-European peoples. This has gone so far that there appears to be a revival of the *mirage oriental*. Perhaps it is partly due to an honourable but excessive reaction against pernicious racialist myths of "Aryan" superiority.

The greater the Mycenaean element which can be proved to survive in Homer, the stronger the proof of the continuity of society through the obscure centuries. When the bards had lost their usual stage and their wealthiest patrons with the destruction of the royal halls and the scatterings of their households, how in fact did they keep themselves and their poetry alive until they found their apotheosis in the genius of Homer? Some may have been able to stay with princes who came to terms with the invaders, a few could have picked up a hard living in Arcadia, others may have gone overseas, but as we have seen many must have fled to Athens. Those who accompanied the royal refugees from Pylos when they took over the Athenian throne would probably have been fortunate, being able to perform in the "good house of Erechtheus" on the Acropolis. Their fellows from other kingdoms are likely to have been less well placed, and one can imagine them sharing humble lodgings in the city with their impoverished lords. Perhaps, though, they would not have had a bad time, for an international refugee society is always fond of drinking and of celebrating the golden days of the past.

This would have been the first stage of the long transition. But even unconquered Athens could not maintain the Mycenaean way of life against the forces of social change. Codros, who was killed in about 1100 B.C. (p. 241), was probably the last king who could possibly be regarded as *Wanax* in the full power and dignity of the Mycenaean title. In spite of the victory, it was at about this time that the hall on the Acropolis was abandoned and the site handed over to Athena.

The sons of Codros struggled for the succession, and at this time what was left of royal power began to be shared with an archon or chief magistrate of the city. The great king was diminished to the archon basileus, a priestly figure. Society was changing very rapidly from monarchy to aristocracy, just as the centre of city life was shifting from the royal citadel to the *Agora*.

The bards who stayed in Athens equally with those who went to the Ionian colonies (p. 253) must have adjusted themselves to the new order. It was in the houses of the nobles and of the petty kings, mostly proud of their lineage and eager to trace it back toward the heroic age, that they found their livelihood and their listeners.

For generations their conditions may have been hard. No longer would they have played on finely inlaid instruments or received elegant gifts. They would not have known what it was like to be praised and honoured by great men in a splendid court – like Demodocus in the hall of Alcinous. Yet they were probably always held to be divinely inspired, and whatever the conditions they were never so harsh or so disturbed as to prevent the bards from passing on the precious heritage of words and memories. It is amazing, as amazing as the defence of the White Horse against the encroaching grass, that this fragile chain of poetry was never broken. There must have been bad times, surely, when a few deaths would have ended it.

If the houses of the nobility and small rulers were stable enough to maintain an unwritten literature of great scope and complexity, there is no doubt that all kinds of lesser traditions survived as well. There would have been the little stories that mothers told to their children, cradle songs, children's games and dances. There would have been the endless gossip of women, always expressing assumptions and values not too easily changed, and old wives' tales of every kind that were even more tenacious. Most significant of all, of course, was the continuity of religious belief and practice. I shall return to that presently.

When prosperity began to increase again, religious festivals became more important and drew greater numbers. One of the greatest was the Panionia celebrated on the slopes of Mount Mykale; another the festival in honour of Artemis held every four years on the island of Delos. At this ancient shrine of Artemis there may have been a revered relic which would have helped the bards to evoke the Mycenaean age. This was an ivory throne carved with figures of warriors, and with battling lions, griffins and other well-known Mycenaean motifs. It is believed to have been made in the fourteenth century and to have survived until it was buried as a votive offering when the shrine was rebuilt in the eighth century B.C.

Great religious festivals were also, of course, developing in Greece itself, but these in Ionia are more significant in the Homeric story. They appear to offer exactly the right conditions for the recitation of epic verse. The nobles' houses would do for short performances, but the festival offered conditions where audiences could be held by relays of performers hour after hour, day after day. Homer himself may first have composed his epics for recitations at Mykale. The *Iliad* would have taken two or three days. In comparison with these, the audiences of communist orators or Japanese Noh plays might appear short-winded.

Homer may or may not have sung at Mykale. He may or may not have written down his own poetry in the new script that was now available to him. It may not have been set down until an agreed version was recorded in sixth-century Athens.

What is certain is that Homer soon assumed an extraordinary ascendancy over Greek life. Everywhere cults of the heroes were instituted and the ancient families liked to trace their ancestry back to them. The great poet himself was recognized as the "educator" of Hellenic Greece. Herodotus and Pindar were among his devoted followers; Aeschylus said that his own plays were "slices from the great banquet of Homer"; Sophocles was his "closest disciple"; Alexander the Great carried a copy of the *Iliad* with him into Asia and saw his campaigns there as a fulfilment of the Trojan War. Even those who, like Plato, deplored his influence, admitted its overwhelming effect. Xenophanes, who was among them, declared: "All men's thoughts have been shaped by Homer from the beginning."

This idea of Homer as educator was correct enough from the point of view of the individual Hellenic Greek. On the other hand it should not be forgotten that it was because his poetry embodied the myths and other unconscious expressions of the Greek people "from the beginning" that it had such a tremendous grip of the Hellenic mind. The epics undoubtedly strengthened the Achaean, masculine, side of the Greek inheritance.

There are various ways of looking at Homer, yet he must always appear as a gigantic figure standing between the Mycenaean Bronze Age and Classical Greece, handing on the traditions of one to the other, and in this way bringing about a living relationship between the two. There are, of course, partial analogies among other peoples. Yet the epics are distinguished by their length, the force of their literary genius, and above all by their essentially secular nature. The Homeric phenomenon is unique in the history of mankind.

The history of Homeric literature is relevant to the present argument not only for the sake of the Mycenaean heirlooms which the *Iliad* and *Odyssey* preserved for posterity, but still more for the very fact of their preservation. That they could be handed down in the Greek family for so long is in itself adamantine proof of social continuity.

Having once traversed the obscure centuries with Homer, I shall have to make the journey twice more. First I must follow the kind of continuities that archaeology can detect. Then I will return to pursue the course of religious conservatism, to see how the gods and the service of the gods persisted tenaciously in the minds and customs of men.

If Athens made a vital contribution to the traditions of oral literature (p. 253), her place in a history of the continuity of material culture and the visual arts is absolutely dominant. Indeed, it cannot be too often insisted that Athens is at the centre of the argument: Athens endured and Athens was the fount of Hellas.

Unfortunately so much has been destroyed or built over that it is not possible to follow the development of the city as a whole. We cannot see the Mycenaean town scattered round the royal citadel evolving into the *agora*-centred Greek *polis*. There is probably only one place in Greece where this kind of reconstruction might prove possible. On the site of ancient Iolkos in Thessaly there is an accumulated city mound like the famous *tells* of Asia. The buildings of modern Volos still overlie it, but enough digging has been done to prove that it was inhabited from early in the Bronze Age right down to the third century B.C. There are the remains of a burnt late-Mycenaean city sandwiched in the mound. Some day, perhaps, they will yield tablets as well as links with later history. The mere existence of such a *tell* is already significant for the theme of continuity – and it is striking that it should lie in the north where it might be expected that barbarian incursions would be at their most disruptive.

In "undespoiled Athens" itself the evidence has to be pieced together from scattered sites and tombs. Much of it comes from pottery – but this might be restated as "from the visual arts". It is in fact another sign of enduring traditions that from Minoan times onwards potting and vase-painting were taken seriously as fine arts – a recognition hardly allowed anywhere else except in South-east Asia and some parts of pre-Columban America.

To understand this evidence it is necessary, I think, to imagine how life must have looked to the Athenians. The Mycenaean city had not been outstandingly rich or powerful, but it had shared fully in the civilized life of the time. The women had charming possessions – fine carved ivory toilet articles, plenty of gold ornaments, the finest painted pottery for their unguents and general domestic use. That they were already a people of character with intelligent and determined leadership is proved by the prompt and effective steps they took to defeat one and then a second Dorian attack. Presumably just as at Pylos (p. 225) there was an independent *damos* of the common people.

The enemy was repulsed and the royal hall still crowned the citadel, but the Athenians were very well aware of what was happening elsewhere. The refugees brought descriptions of the hall of Pylos going up in flames and other stories of barbarous destruction. Probably, too, much of west Attica itself was ravaged. The supply of precious raw materials was cut off, and the hall could no longer afford to maintain its craftsmen. But in spite of this impoverishment, the Athenians themselves, and the Pylians and others seeking shelter with them, were men and women who had been brought up in civilized ways – and, as time went by, their children and grandchildren would still have had education and breeding – their mothers, if no one else, would have seen to that.

At first this society tried to keep going in the old way. When a Pylian king took over the throne, he seems to have done so peacefully. He lived in the hall, and such potters and weavers and other artisans as there were tried to maintain a Mycenaean

An appeal to the ancient virtues? A pre-Mycenaean style revived in post-Mycenaean times: jar from Olympia, 17th century B.C. (*above*), and amphora from Athens, *c.* 1000 B.C. (*right*).

style. But it is reasonably sure that the hall had grown shabby, and the backward-looking style was deplorable. Then came another attack, and the shock of the death of Codros. Immediately after this there occurred the conspicuous change in the ceramic art that is accepted as marking the beginning of a new era, with the spirit of Classical Greece already foreshadowed. It was also at this time that iron, the "democratic" metal, was brought into full use, and there was the great political change to the archonship.

What happened to the ceramic art must, it seems to me, give a clear sign of what took place in society. The shapes of vessels, which had become sloppy, were tautened and purified, and this was accompanied by a great improvement in the

technique of manufacture. The potters had not lost the art of preparing the fine, lustrous black paint dear to their Mycenaean predecessors, but, as with the shapes, the decoration needed to be tautened and made correct. Any last vestiges of plant or other kinds of naturalism were dropped, and the simpler late Mycenaean patterns such as concentric circles and semicircles, where the freehand vitality had degenerated into weakness, were now drawn with compasses, and most firmly and skilfully placed on the pot. Some of the motifs, and the panelled layout of the decoration as a whole, seem to imitate the old-fashioned designs in favour among the Achaeans of long ago – before the Minoan influence brought about the rise of Mycenaean civilization. This is not as impossible as it might seem, as traditional designs are very likely to have been kept going by the countryfolk in their weaving, basketry and woodwork.

The ceramic art itself suggests that in spite of the change in spirit, there was no break in the life of the craftsmen, or of the society for which they worked. This is proved in other ways. For example, a family with a rock-cut tomb to the north of the Agora continued to bury their dead there from prosperous Mycenaean times until after the adoption of the new style. Again, citizens used a large cemetery in the ancient Potters' Quarter of Athens for five centuries, and at the time of the transition mourners might furnish their dead indiscriminately with some vessels in the old style, some in the new.

It seems that by far the best way to read this material evidence in terms of human life is to see the changes that took place in the middle of the eleventh century as the fruits of a deliberate and successful social and spiritual reform. After the death of Codros and the final destruction of Mycenae itself, there was obviously no hope of a Mycenaean revival; all thoughts of "a return to normalcy", all admiration for attempts to "carry on as before" were recognized as worse than futile. There had to be renunciation and reform. As has so often happened in societies recovering after misfortune (Marshal Pétain and Vichy France being the last and most foolish example), there was an appeal to the ancient and simple virtues, and for greater discipline. This spirit is perfectly expressed in the pottery. There is the higher standard of workmanship, the disciplined design, the purification of form – and the appeal to the virtuous past and traditional country ways. At the same time a simpler, probably more classless, form of dress was adopted, and expensive ornament was no longer worn. It is a likely guess that there was a movement in favour of a stricter morality.

The reform would have been aristocratic – just as the institution of the archonship was aristocratic. Yet the new thought might have led to an improved attitude towards ordinary citizens. With the sharply reduced power and sanctity of the king, and with blacksmiths putting tools and weapons within the reach of others besides the élite, there may well have been some slight advance for the *damos* – a small step in the direction of Athenian democracy.

The eleventh century was the crucial transition period between the Mycenaean and Hellenic ages. Whether or not I have given a true picture of the nature of the events that took place, the important thing is that there was no social or cultural hiatus. The ceramic art alone is enough to prove that. The change of style was the result of reform and not of breakdown or alien intrusions. People who consciously alter their mode of expression do not feel themselves to be, and are not, a fundamentally changed people. When, towards the end of the eighteenth century, Europeans began to make all their possessions with straight lines instead of curves,

Plate 42. The octopus still full of vigour. Jug from Berbati, Argolis, 14th century B.C.

they did not feel less themselves. Even the total revolution in style of the present century has not made the British less British or the French less French. It has not cut us off from our pasts. It was the same with eleventh-century Greece. Afterwards the people of Athens looked back with pride to the time when they held out against the Dorians. They saw themselves as always having been Athenians.

Scholars have loved to draw subtle analogies between the geometrical composi-tions of the ceramic artists of the eleventh century and after and the poetic art of Homer. Such thinking tends to become obsessive and esoteric. Yet it is true enough that different arts usually follow the same trend, and it can be assumed that, like the potters, the bards were formalizing and making sharper constructions in their work. At least it is good to be reminded that spinners of words and of clay shared the same patrons, and that both were handling what had come down to them from a common Mycenaean inheritance.

The reforms of the eleventh century were immensely successful. The new styles spread in Greece and the Aegean and even beyond. More important still, everyone knows how from that time onwards the emergence of Hellenic civilization followed a well-marked track.

By about 800 B.C. the potters were producing some of the most monumental and nobly-proportioned vessels ever made. On the glossy, curving sides of these giant funerary vases, animal and human figures were reappearing (p. 272). At first, how-ever, they were kept locked up in compartments and their bodily parts forced into stiff, geometrical shapes (pp. 272, 273). Then came the burgeoning century of the first Olympics and of Homer, and Oriental ideas, little changed from those the Mycenaean artists had used so well, came back into their own. Lions, griffins and other creatures reappeared, human bodies regained their curves, human scenes their movement, and the Greeks were headed for the Hellenic humanism of the sixth cen-tury. Some city states, especially Corinth, gave an uninhibited welcome to Oriental modes, but Athens kept them firmly under the control of her own long tradition.

It is usual to emphasize the difference between Mycenaean and Hellenic art, and to insist that an entirely new cycle began with the austerities of the obscure centuries. Is this altogether true? Hellenic pictorial art had little in common with Minoan, except a fondness for the human figure and a recognition of its grace. It had no deep involvement with nature; no desire to catch the fleeting moment. Yet is it so remote from the art which the Achaeans created during the last centuries of the Mycenaean Age? Has the vase painting of sixth- and fifth-century Athens nothing to do with the fresco painting at Thebes, Tiryns and Pylos? It is more individual – the intensify-ing of individuality was the greatest thing to have been achieved in the interval – and it is therefore less purely decorative. Yet those rather remote, pensive-looking ladies with their slightly hung heads that appear in the frescoes, their hair and dress

Plate 43. The octopus as pattern. Stirrup jar from Asine, 12th century B.C.

Bodies in geometric shapes. Scene from the shoulder of a huge funerary vase from Argos, 8th century B.C.

"Animal and human figures were reappearing." Funeral scene on huge footed bowl from Athens, c. 750 B.C.

carefully exploited for decorative effect, surely find significant echoes in Classical painting. Or, to change to another medium, have not the battling warriors on the gold seal from Mycenae a much more than superficial likeness with many Classical illustrations of Homeric combat?

There are many differences, certainly. Yet if, knowing nothing, one was shown a range of art dating from the thirteenth century B.C. and asked to select that which was most likely to be in some sense ancestral to that of Classical Greece, would one not reject the Hittite and the Assyrian out of hand, the Egyptian on reflection – and turn with something like confidence to the Mycenaean? I believe that one would.

At this point it may appear that I have been forgetting that part of my theme which is concerned with the fruitful blending of masculine with feminine cultural personalities. If so, this is because both Homeric history and the early stages of the reformed visual arts are inimical to it. With all the prejudice in the world, it would hardly be possible to deny that Homeric poetry expressed an exaggeratedly masculine spirit. This may well also be true of the ceramic art and the cultural revolution it represents. If the eleventh-century reform was of the kind I have suggested, then probably for a time women suffered from it. All such reactions in

Battling warriors on a gold seal from the Lower Grave Circle, Mycenae, 16th century B.C.

The dove goddess again. From Karphi, Crete, 11th century B.C.

favour of the ancient virtues run against the feminine principle, and involve putting women back to a hempen bed to bear noble and virtuous sons.

It was in religion, the third of the planks with which I am bridging the obscure centuries, that the feminine principle was still able to find full expression, and in which many women must themselves have found fulfilment. It was certainly here that the Cretan contribution to the Greek inheritance remained at its purest and was to prove most stimulating in its meeting with the opposite Achaean element.

In pursuing the survival of Minoan divinities and cults into later times, it will be necessary to return, very briefly, to Crete itself. Enough has already been said about the continued life of the Great Goddess in the various female divinities of the Classical world. In particular Athena has been observed walking firmly through the whole story, bearing her attributes with her, turning perhaps from a Cretan goddess who could *be* a bird or a snake, to an Hellenic goddess who could be *represented* by a bird or a snake, but still remaining very much herself.

Enough has also been said about some of the cult places, such as the caves of Eileithyia at Amnisos, the Psychro cave on Mount Dikte and the shrine of the Cretan Zeus at Palaikastro, where worshippers went through the ages – from Minoan to Late Classical times – to honour the Goddess and her young god.

It remains only to look a little more closely at some other places in the island where the worship of the Goddess was maintained after the Dorians had invaded the island. Karphi, four thousand feet up in the Dikte range, was a little town of refuge that may well have been founded by Mycenaeanized Cretans escaping from Knossos itself. They were poor in material goods, and probably eked out what they got from their own cattle by raiding the lowlands in the spirit of "freedom fighters". The people of Karphi maintained a town sanctuary, and in it they set up large, rather crude statuettes of the Goddess, wearing a bell skirt and with her arms raised in the traditional attitude. On her head they placed emblems – including the full and crescent moon, doves, and the familiar horns of consecration (p. 275). On a very similar but earlier cult figure from a sanctuary to the west of Knossos, the Goddess is crowned with three opium poppy seedheads (p. 127).

Here at Karphi, then, at just about the time of the reform in Athens, Cretans who had lost their wealth and courtly refinement were still serving the old Minoan divinity with emblems representing her ancient aspects. She must also have remained in undisputed power in the mountainous district of east Crete, where the population continued to speak the old Minoan language into Late Classical times.

Indeed, of course, the insidious Lady was soon regaining much of her pre-eminence throughout the island. Exquisite jewellery showing heads of the Goddess, birds, snakes and other emblems probably belonged to a priestess. It was found in a tomb near Knossos dating from about the ninth century B.C. (pp. 278, 279).

Later again, and now clearly as Artemis, the Goddess is portrayed at the little temple of Prinias in central Crete. She is sculptured in stone, enthroned above lions and stags. By this time Crete was again exerting considerable influence on the mainland.

Returning now to that mainland, it has already been seen how, in spite of the force of the borrowed Cretan religion, most of the Olympian deities were already being worshipped in late Mycenaean times. This was confirmed by the reading of the tablets, but had been suspected ever since it was observed that nearly all the greatest Classical myths and mythical figures were associated with the centres of Mycenaean life. This most striking fact is in itself a sufficient proof of the predominantly Mycenaean origins of Greek religion. And to it can be added the further fact that the four greatest sanctuaries of the Greeks – Delphi, Olympia, Eleusis and Delos – are now all known to have been sacred places in Mycenaean times.

It was to be one of the most important achievements of the later bards and of Homer himself to set the assortment of Bronze Age divinities into the coherent order of Olympus, to assign them their fields of responsibility – and to turn them into the likeness of immortal human beings. This was, of course, a masculine, rationalizing process, an exercise of the conscious mind that developed what is known as the Apollonian aspect of Greek religion.

Goddesses were involved in this process equally with gods. Athena, Artemis, Hera, Aphrodite and Demeter were admitted to Olympus, but with greater honour than they would have enjoyed among the Achaeans if it had not been for the force of the Cretan Goddess who still lived within them. In many more places besides the famous royal shrines at Athens, Tiryns and Mycenae (p. 234) temples dedicated to the Olympian goddesses were built on sites sacred to the Minoan-Mycenaean divinity.

The Goddess in her various forms had joined the divine "Establishment" of the Greeks. No doubt women were devoted to these respectable ladies and sought their help over love affairs, marriage, child-bearing and other domestic matters. They found comfort in doing so and in the knowledge that, under Zeus, their female deities were powerful protectors. Yet Greek women, probably often the same individuals, turned also to the other side of the ancient Goddess and her worship – to the deity of the wild woods and the mountains, the dark earth and the unconscious mind.

We have seen that, as far as can be judged from the art, these cults with their ecstatic dances, plucking of sacred boughs, grappling with animals, were as popular on the Mycenaean mainland as they had long been in Crete. Later these uninhibited cults were more strongly associated with the Divine Child, usually Dionysus, than with the Mother – but the Goddess could never lose her important rôle in the

Gold pendant with birds and heads of the Goddess. From Teké, near Knossos, 9th century B.C.

Half moon and snakes on gold jewellery from Teké, near Knossos, 9th century B.C.

The divine doves. Clay. From Palaikastro.

A primitive Zeus confronts the Earth Goddess. He stands before the oracular
tripod; she appears below. Pottery shield from a burial at Knossos, c. 900 B.C.

enactments of death and rebirth. It was formerly thought that the worship of Dionysus first swept into Greece from Anatolia in time for its rise to popularity in the sixth century B.C. Now that his name has been read on the Pylos tablets it seems likely that he was already playing his part in Minoan Crete.

Certainly the association of Dionysus with bulls, snakes, wine and women, meant a continuance of Minoan religious cults – and, at the same time, the satisfaction of one of the eternal needs of the human psyche. Just as the Romantic Movement in Europe was a reaction of the unconscious forces against classical discipline, so the victory of Dionysus in sixth-century Greece was a reaction against Apollonian order and light. The Olympian divinities would appear as beautiful human statues to be worshipped from without. Dionysus stood for human salvation through total participation in the divine life.

The rites of this wild communion could be savage enough. In some forms they meant sexual abandon, intoxication, the tearing up and devouring of goats and other animals (a surrogate for the death of Dionysus). Women took part in these doings with full enthusiasm, finding in them exaltation and relief from excessive restraint. For us, familiar with the sight of girls "sent" by music and sexual excitement, the routs of the young god are more understandable than they were for our grandparents. Dionysus was often represented as "a youth of rather effeminate appearance with luxuriant hair. . . ."

Dionysus had his place in the myths and rituals of the two greatest Greek religious centres – Delphi and Eleusis. At both these places Cretan inspiration was traditionally accepted, and at both there were plentiful Mycenaean remains to prove the importance of the sanctuaries already in the Bronze Age. At Delphi, that place of natural holiness where the rufous crags of Parnassus tower above and the marvellous grey ocean of the olive groves stretches far below, the earth goddess Ge had her ancient shrine. It is not certain when Dionysus arrived on the scene, but probably he was there with Ge from the beginning – and one story says that he sailed from Crete. Then came the challenge from the Olympians. Apollo slew the Serpent of Earth and took possession of the shrine. Yet the old ones were not so easily banished. Dionysus was given one of the peaks of Parnassus, a tomb in the sanctuary, and was said to rule in Apollo's absence during the three winter months. As for the Goddess – Apollo's oracle uttered entranced words from a fissure in the ground – and her name was the Pythoness.

Archaeology almost miraculously illustrated the ancient Cretan element at Delphi. Below the very temple of Apollo lay a fragment of lion's-head rhyton almost identical with a noble specimen from Knossos.

The second great religious institution deeply rooted in the Minoan-Mycenaean past was that of the Mysteries celebrated at Eleusis – a few miles from Athens.

Athens maintained many ancient festivals connected with the agricultural year. The women had one of their own when they fasted for the Mother, for Demeter, at the time of the autumn sowing. But by far the most important of the autumn festivals were those of Eleusis.

The Cretans themselves claimed that they taught the Mysteries to the Greeks and that the initiation ceremonies held in close secrecy at Eleusis and elsewhere they had enacted quite openly at Knossos. There was probably truth in this, although no doubt in time the Greeks spiritualized the rituals and made them a more conscious means to personal salvation.

The secrets of Eleusis were so well kept that the exact nature of the final rites will never be known. Certainly they were centred on Demeter, Persephone, and the Divine Child, Dionysus, and promised the worshippers rebirth to a blessed and eternal life. The initiates could be men or women, slave or free. The celebrations were spread over many days, and involved the carrying of the sacred objects of Demeter (presumably fertility symbols) from Eleusis to Athens and back. The final rites were held in a darkened hall. They may have begun by a Death represented by the solemn reaping of an ear of corn. Then there was the Sacred Marriage, celebrated by the priest and priestess, followed by the Birth. At last the neophyte was allowed to see the Goddess herself and "was changed into the same image from Glory to Glory".

While at both Delphi and Eleusis Apollonian religion can be seen ordering and spiritualizing some aspects of the wild Dionysian communion, it was the teachings of Orpheus and the Orphic mysteries that went furthest in this direction. The Orphics extended Dionysian participation in the wholeness of divine life to include the intellect and imagination. Theirs was an austere, even ascetic sect. Yet the Orphics still worshipped Dionysus, and might even still share in his ecstasies. Euripides causes an Orphic priest to invoke the god as divine lord of Crete, and admit to having been one of his initiates:

> I have endured his thunder cry
> Fulfilled his red and bleeding feasts;
> Held the Great Mother's mountain flame . . .

If the Orphics were reformers of Dionysian religion, Pythagoras was a reformer of Orphism, and it was through him that mysticism entered Greek philosophy. Indeed Pythagoras himself is said to have gone to Crete and to have been initiated as a Daktyl in the sacred cave on Mount Ida (p. 149). This is of extreme interest here as one of the Dionysian elements adopted by Pythagoras was a strong feminism. He found in women a natural gift of piety, and for that reason enrolled them in his

School to seek after truth on equal terms with men. This successful innovation was followed also in Plato's Academy. It was the feminism that Plato learnt from the Pythagoreans that led him to advocate complete educational and political equality for women in his ideal Republic.

So it is not fanciful to claim that the lively independence won by the women of Minoan Crete in their service of the Goddess and the Young God came down by devious ways to exhilarate the life of Greek women of the Classical age.

One last ingredient in Greek life that helps to bridge the obscure centuries remains to be mentioned. The Olympic Games of 776 B.C. were chosen by the Greeks to mark the start of their era, and yet in fact many of these semi-religious athletic contests must have been played all over the countryside ever since the carving of the Hagia Triada rhyton (p. 117). The forms of boxing and of wrestling shown on that Minoan vessel are just the same as those practised by the Greeks. Even details of equipment remained unchanged. The boxing gloves so carefully represented by the Minoan sculptor are identical with the Classical *cestus*. Under Achaean influence Minoan bull games died out and chariot racing came to the fore: that could be taken for granted. But much went on – boxing, wrestling, javelin-throwing and running, as well as chariot racing, are all included in the funeral games of Patroclus described in the *Iliad*. It cannot be chance that both for the Cretans and for the Hellenic Greeks athletic contests had a profound meaning and played an extraordinarily important part in the national life.

Plank after plank bridges what was once seen as the gulf of the "Dark Ages". The visual arts, oral literature and the fondness for the lyre and pipes that went with it, athletics and the cult of the body, and the two great religious traditions, all these things evince the unbroken span uniting the Minoan and Mycenaean worlds with that of Hellenic Greece.

When Mycenaean society was decapitated with the destruction of the great royal houses, the continuity of existence was made more difficult to detect. But it was there, and proof of it can be found from the houses of the nobles where the bards never ceased their singing down to the life of the peasant communities where the Goddess was always at home. Of course the Dorian invasions caused impoverishment, suffering and disruption. But surely by now we ourselves have seen enough of such disasters to know that they are not final, that peoples recover and keep their inheritance?

I said that it could not be chance that for the Hellenes as for the Minoans athletic games and contests were of exceptional significance. Can it be chance that in so minute a corner of the earth's crust the unique quality of Minoan civilization should be succeeded by "the Greek miracle"? More particularly, can it be chance that it was throughout Ionian Greece where the Minoan-Mycenaean tradition had been longest established and least disturbed that the miracle began? Or, more particularly still, can it be mere coincidence that Hellenic genius was at its most brilliant at Athens and at Miletus, two cities with histories stretching back almost or quite unbroken into the Bronze Age, and where, moreover, Minoan influence had been strong? I am aware that questions such as these are not "scientific", but I believe them to be telling.

The tremendous vitality generated by Minoan and Achaean traditions – first evident in Mycenaean civilization, then further stimulated by the revival of the Dionysian religion and the development of its Mysteries – has already become obvious in many ways, and readers will be familiar with others. It is well known that Attic drama, both tragedy and comedy, began in festivals of Dionysus with country people singing hymns at his altars. Again, when Olympian reason and detachment enabled the first Ionian philosopher-scientists to look at the world without its gods, they could see it in the terms of the pre-Olympian dynamism which the mystics celebrated and which the first objective thinkers of the western world could recognize as *Physis* – Nature. There is a sense in which the Golden Mean of the Greeks really meant a balance of opposites.

It is useless to say more about the significance of the union of masculine and feminine in Hellenic civilization; in this book the pictures of things made by the peoples concerned out of their total experience of life are more revealing than any words can be. I will, however, try to forestall one obvious criticism of this interpretation. It will be said that Greek society was in fact conspicuously masculine; that in Athens in particular men loved men, and women were kept in the background.

There are two answers to this. First, I have already admitted, quoting the Japanese, that women do not necessarily have a high social status in cultures where the feminine principle is dominant. Nobody could deny that Hellenic civilization showed the highest respect to the feminine principle itself. Zeus might be the Lord and Father of All, but the Great Mother and the other aspects of the Goddess were in practice equally powerful. They probably received far more devotion and worship – even as the Virgin Mother does in Catholic lands today. Over the city state Athena presided; in the Mysteries Demeter offered salvation. The finest things of life were personified as Graces and Muses, Justice, Wisdom, Peace – all, all feminine. No other people, I think, has paid a greater tribute to the feminine principle.

As for women themselves in the Greek world, and in Athens particularly, I believe those who say that their subservience has been greatly exaggerated through the bias of nineteenth-century scholarship.

Just as in Crete, women shared in the power of the Goddess both psychologically and socially. Priestesses were of high standing, and priestly associations of women were formed round temples and holy places. There was an influential one, for example, associated with the famous temple of Artemis at Ephesus. At this city, and indeed in Ionia generally, women and girls enjoyed much freedom. Sappho herself, the finest expression of the spirit of Ionian women, was the leader of a religious group devoted to the worship of Aphrodite and the Muses.

While women certainly won influence and responsibility by serving at the temples and great state festivals of the respectable goddesses, there was also the liberation of the ancient cults. "Respectable matrons and girls in large companies, would spend whole nights on the bare hills in dances which stimulated ecstasy, and in an intoxication perhaps partly alcoholic, but mainly mystical." Husbands disapproved, but, it is said, did not like to interfere in religious matters.

As for everyday life, any idea of an Oriental seclusion of women is utterly misleading. It is true that they were at a serious disadvantage educationally and at law, and in Athens, where their position was worst (or only most grumbled at?), women were very far from enjoying the equality that Plato devised for them. Yet much of their home-keeping seems to have been of the kind that must always be the result of monogamous family life. A married woman in the *Lysistrata* declares: ". . . it is difficult for a woman to get out, what with dancing attendance on one's husband, or getting the servant girl up, or putting the child to bed, or bathing the brat, or feeding it . . ." Between that lament and Sappho's exquisite poem to her daughter:

> I have a child; so fair
> As golden flowers is she,
> My Kleïs, all my care.
> I'd not give her away
> For Lydia's wide sway
> Nor lands men long to see.

– it seems that the full range of normal maternal feelings were experienced.

There was much athleticism among young women – a fact expressed in the popular legends of Atalanta. In Ionia they ran and wrestled, naked, with young men. Even at Olympia, although they were barred from the main festival, women celebrated their own Games, sacred to Hera, where they ran races in *chitons* well above the knee.

The feminism of Pythagoras and Plato must have been widely influential, and if the system of *hetairi*, and of sisterhoods such as that of the sacred prostitutes at Corinth, were not ideal, they offered respected careers open to all the talents. So

Plate 44. Goddess with papyrus head-dress? Pendant gold terminal on long silver pin. From women's grave in the Upper Grave Circle, Mycenae, 16th century B.C.

far from being confined, Athenian women went to the theatres, watching not only tragedy but the bawdiest of comedy. Aristophanes wrote three other plays besides the *Lysistrata* to express his feminist sympathies, and they are full of rich sexual humour. Women who were free and able to enjoy this kind of thing were in no dire state of frustration.

I am not being so foolish as to deny that in many ways Greek society was very masculine. It was conceded in the opening chapter that in the marriage of cultures the Achaean tradition tended to dominate – and this was more true in social patterns than in cultural life. It showed itself, alas, nowhere more plainly than in the Greeks' dedication to warfare. In this their natural instincts were greatly encouraged by their ancient educator, Homer. Greek fought Greek, and brought about the untimely downfall of their civilization. Yet, like the Divine Child himself, it has been, and will be, forever reborn.

Plate 45. An eternal symbol: mother goddess with child. Pottery figurine from a chamber tomb at Mycenae, 13th century B.C.

Bibliography

The following books range from the popular to the scholarly, but all have been chosen as being readable by anyone interested in Minoan and Mycenaean civilization. Because there have been such great changes in the interpretation of Aegean archaeology, especially since the decipherment of the Linear B tablets in 1952, very few books of earlier date have been included – other than the great classics of Schliemann and Evans.

ALSOP, JOSEPH. *From the Silent Earth: a report on the Greek Bronze Age.* New York, 1964; London, 1965.

ANDREWES, ANTONY. *The Greeks.* History of Human Society series. London and New York, 1967. Includes chapters on Mycenaean and Dark Age society.

CHADWICK, JOHN. *The Decipherment of Linear B.* Cambridge and New York, 1958.

DEMARGNE, PIERRE. *Aegean Art.* London and New York, 1964. A finely-illustrated survey from Stone Age to Classical times.

EVANS, SIR ARTHUR. *The Palace of Minos at Knossos.* Four volumes, London and New York, 1921-35. The excavator's splendid publication of his work.

FINLEY, M. I. *The World of Odysseus.* Rev. ed., London, 1956. The author is one of the minority of scholars who minimize the Mycenaean elements in Homer.

GLOTZ, G. *La civilisation égéene.* Rev. ed., Paris, 1952.

GRAHAM, J. W. *The Palaces of Crete.* London and Princeton N.J., 1962. A study of Minoan architecture.

HAWKES, JACQUETTA, and WOOLLEY, SIR LEONARD. UNESCO *History of Mankind,* Vol. I. Part 2 of Vol. I (by Sir Leonard Woolley) deals with Minoan and Mycenaean culture seen in their general setting.

HUTCHINSON, R. W. *Prehistoric Crete.* London and Boston, 1962.

KENNA, V. E. G. *Cretan Seals.* London, 1960.

LACEY, A. D. *Greek Pottery in the Bronze Age.* London, 1967.

LEVY, RACHEL. *The Gate of Horn.* London, 1948. Remains one of the most revealing interpretations of the cult of the Great Goddess.

LORIMER, H. L. *Homer and the Monuments.* London and New York, 1950. Miss Lorimer was unfortunate enough to publish her life work on archaeological aspects of Homer just before the Linear B decipherment.

MARINATOS, S. *Crete and Mycenae.* London and New York, 1960. An abundantly-illustrated summary.

MATZ, F. *Minoan Civilization: Maturity and Zenith.* Two volumes, Cambridge, 1962.

MYLONAS, G. E. *Mycenae and the Mycenaean Age.* London and Princeton, 1966. Includes an account of the Lower Grave Circle.

NILLSON, M. P. *The Minoan-Mycenaean Religion and its Survival in Greek Religion.* 2nd ed., Lund, 1950.

PAGE, DENYS L. *History and the Homeric Iliad.* London, and Berkeley, California, 1959.

PALMER, LEONARD R. *Mycenaeans and Minoans.* 2nd ed., London, 1965. A forceful exposition of the author's views on the later history of Knossos and his criticism of Evans's *Palace of Minos.*

PENDLEBURY, J. D. S. *The Archaeology of Crete*. London and New York, 1939. Out of date in some of its interpretations, but still a valuable monograph.

PIGGOTT, STUART (editor). *The Dawn of Civilization*. London, 1961. This pictorial history of the early civilizations includes a Minoan-Mycenaean chapter by Sinclair Hood.

POULSEN, F. *Delphi*. London, 1920. An account of the long history of the greatest of Greek sanctuaries.

SCHLIEMANN, HEINRICH. *Mycenae*. London, 1878.

SCHLIEMANN, HEINRICH. *Tiryns*. Leipzig, 1886.

TAYLOUR, LORD WILLIAM. *The Mycenaeans*. Ancient Peoples and Places series. London, 1964.

VAUGHAN, AGNES CARR. *The House of the Double Axe*. London, 1960. A popular account of the palace of Knossos.

VENTRIS, MICHAEL, and CHADWICK, JOHN. *Documents in Mycenaean Greek*. Cambridge, 1956. The first substantial account of the decipherment of Linear B and its results.

VERMEULE, EMILY. *Greece in the Bronze Age*. Chicago, 1964.

WEBSTER, T. B. L. *From Mycenae to Homer*. London, 1958; New York, 1964. Especially concerned with the roots of Homer in the oral literature of Mycenaean Greece.

Acknowledgments

All the colour plates are from photographs by Dimitrios Harissiadis. The black and white photographs are also by Dimitrios Harissiadis, except for the following, for which grateful acknowledgment is made: pp. 142-3, 145 – the Ashmolean Museum; p. 59 *bottom* – J. Allan Cash; p. 187 *right* – Peter Clayton; pp. 68, 162, 274 – Alison Frantz; pp. 101 *right*, 107 – Hirmer Verlag; pp. 29, 272 – Edwin Smith; p. 267 – Nick Stournaras; pp. 132 *right*, 175, 193, 255 – T.A.P. Service, National Archaeological Museum, Athens.

The objects photographed by Dimitrios Harissiadis are in the following museums in Greece and Crete:

Argos: pp. 169, 273.

Athens, National Archaeological Museum: plates 17, 18, 19, 22, 23, 24, 25, 26, 28, 29, 30, 31, 32, 37, 44, 45; pp. 47 *left*, 49, 100, 106 *left*, 122, 123, 132 *left*, 138, 139, 140, 150, 154, 170 *top right*, 170 *bottom*, 171, 172, 173, 174, 182, 192, 196, 197, 210, 211, 228, 229, 242, 244, 245, 246 *top*.

Chora: plates 27, 33, 39, 40; pp. 47 *right*, 213, 214, 215, 230.

Heraklion: plates 1-16; pp. 32, 43, 44, 46, 48, 50 *left*, 50 *right*, 88, 91, 92, 96, 97, 98, 99, 101 *left*, 103, 104, 107, 108, 109, 114, 115, 116, 118, 119, 120, 126, 127, 135, 136, 141, 144, 151, 152, 275, 278, 279, 280, 281.

Nauplion: plates 35, 36, 41, 42, 43; pp. 50 *top*, 170 *top left*, 231, 232, 246 *bottom*, 247, 248.

Olympia: plate 38; p. 266.

The maps were drawn by T. Stalker Miller. The index was made by Myra Clark.

Index

References in *italic type* indicate illustrations